The
Skeptical
Economist

The Skeptical Economist

Revealing the Ethics Inside Economics

JONATHAN ALDRED

publishing for a sustainable future

London • Sterling, VA

First published by Earthscan in the UK and USA in 2009
Reprinted 2009

Copyright © Dr Jonathan Aldred, 2009

ISBN: 978-1-84407-705-2

Typeset by FiSH Books
Cover design by Rob Watts

For a full list of publications please contact:

Earthscan
Dunstan House
14a St Cross St
London, EC1N 8XA, UK
Tel: +44 (0)20 7841 1930
Fax: +44 (0)20 7242 1474
Email: earthinfo@earthscan.co.uk
Web: **www.earthscan.co.uk**

22883 Quicksilver Drive, Sterling, VA 20166-2012, USA

Earthscan publishes in association with the International Institute for Environment and
Development

A catalogue record for this book is available from the British Library

Library of Congress Cataloging-in-Publication Data
Aldred, Jonathan,
    The skeptical economist: revealing the ethics inside economics/Jonathon Aldred
        p. cm.
    Includes bibliographical references and index.
    ISBN 978–1–84407–705–2 (hardback)
    1. Economics– Moral and ethical aspects, 2. Economics. I. Title.
    HB72.A345 2009
    174–dc22

                                                                            2008046911

At Earthscan we strive to minimize our environmental impacts and carbon footprint through
reducing waste, recycling and offsetting our CO_2 emissions, including those created through
publication of this book. For more details of our environmental policy, see www.earthscan.co.uk.

This book was printed in the UK by Cromwell Press Group.
The paper used is FSC certified and the inks are
vegetable based.

Mixed Sources
Product group from well-managed
forests and other controlled sources
www.fsc.org Cert no. TT-COC-2082
© 1996 Forest Stewardship Council

Contents

Acknowledgements

The ideas in this book span a wide range of academic disciplines and I have benefited greatly from working in a multidisciplinary environment: Emmanuel College has been the site of many stimulating conversations which have helped develop my thinking. The Department of Land Economy is another multidisciplinary institution from which I have learnt a lot. Students in both Emmanuel College and Land Economy have challenged and helped sharpen my ideas. It has been a privilege to teach them.

This book has been influenced by discussions and correspondence over the years with many friends and colleagues, from whom I have learnt a great deal. There are too many to name, but I should at least mention Paul Anand, Geoffrey Browne, Anthony Gristwood, Geoff Harcourt, David Howarth, Paul Lewis, John McCombie and Serena Olsaretti.

Others who have helped make this book possible include Philip Arestis, Ian Hodge, Robert Macfarlane, Nick White and Anna Wierzbicka.

I have been lucky with Tim Hardwick, who has been a calm, perceptive and patient editor, and many others at Earthscan.

I am especially grateful to all those who have commented on drafts of chapters, often in time-consuming detail: Mike Gross, Clive Hamilton, Martin Heath, Michael Howard, Brent Kiernan, Simon Jacques, Rob Langham, David Lowen, John O'Neill, Cristiano Ristuccia, Derrick Robinson and Tom Warke.

I owe a particular debt of gratitude to John O'Neill, whose combination of philosophical insight and political passion continues to inspire me.

Finally, none of this would have been possible without two people. Hilary, for her faith in me and unwavering belief that 'the book' was worth writing. And I dedicate this book to my mother, Shirley Aldred.

Chapter One

Introduction: Ethical Economics?

Morality, it could be argued, represents the way that people would like the world to work – whereas economics represents how it actually *does* work. Economics is above all a science of measurement. (Levitt and Dubner, *Freakonomics*)

Few of us associate economics with ethics. Economics is a hard-nosed, pragmatic, 'dismal science'; ethics is philosophical daydreaming. And the quote seems to confirm the view that economics and ethics are strangers to each other. *Freakonomics* is perhaps the best-selling economics book, ever.[1] But its authors are wrong. Economics is not what it appears to be. Economics is an odd kind of science (if it is a science at all) and it is not just about measurement.

This book is not a conventional introduction to economics, although it will try to give an insight into how economists think. But a major obstacle to gaining that insight is that many of those who call themselves economists peddle a narrow or simplistic view of economics to serve vested interests and political ends. These people are better described as *policy entrepreneurs*.[2] Alongside the policy entrepreneurs stand others who are more naively confused in their misrepresentation of economics, but equally dangerous. Between them, these groups do a good job of misunderstanding, misrepresenting and misusing economics, with consequences from which we all suffer.

Policy entrepreneurs preserve their special claim to expertise by encouraging the myth that economics is a mysterious science whose workings are unintelligible to the uninitiated. Economics emerges in public debate as though out of a black box: we are supposed to accept various statements about economics as scientific facts, but the reasoning behind them remains hidden. 'Trust me, I'm an economist' seems to be the slogan. The effect of this black box presentation of economics is that its assertions become unchallengeable to outsiders. Skepticism is ruled out. We just have to accept on trust the 'inescapable economic logic', or similar threatening phrase, which leads to a particular conclusion, however unpalatable. Black box economics is not just the creation of policy entrepreneurs. Serious economists who make a virtue of their political neutrality can also unintentionally reinforce the black box image, because of their astonishing arrogance. For instance, Diane Coyle, formerly of *The Independent,* concludes her book with 'ten rules of economic thinking', one of which is 'where common sense and economics conflict, common sense is wrong'.[3] This imperious tone does not encourage people to embrace the wisdom of economists. People feel they are being told what to think, rather than encouraged to understand. Besides, common sense is sometimes wiser than economics. Traditional economic analysis recommends paying doctors according to the number of procedures or tasks they perform, in order to 'incentivize' them to increase productivity. Common sense points out that doctors will then stop doing anything for which they do not receive a financial incentive, and start claiming additional payment for activities they previously undertook freely out of a sense of professional duty. And traditional economic analysis recommends deciding what to do about climate change by adding up the costs and benefits of reducing carbon emissions, all measured in terms of money. But common sense suggests that not all costs and benefits of climate change can be measured in monetary terms, especially those costs which concern the loss of human lives, and the dramatic upheaval and dislocation of others. It is hard to escape the conclusion that economic analysis in these cases depends as much on value judgements and political and psychological assumptions as it does on neutral science. I do not object to value judgements and political beliefs creeping into economic arguments: I think they are inevitable. But then I do not claim economics is a science.

A close cousin of black box economics is veto economics, where assertions about economics are used as a kind of veto to rule out new ideas and proposals without further discussion. The veto is absolute because the assertions emerge from the black box: they are presented in a way that makes it extremely hard for the non-economist to dispute them. In its most extreme form, veto economics rejects ideas and proposals with just one word, offering no further explanation. Favourite veto words include 'inefficient', 'irrational', and 'anti-competitive'. For readers of the more specialist economics and business press, rejecting proposals on the grounds that they are 'suboptimal', 'time-inconsistent', or lack 'incentive-compatibility', has also become fashionable. And as a last resort there is always the plain but vacuous condemnation 'uneconomic'.

Veto economics serves to protect the economic orthodoxy. In some ways the orthodoxy has served us, in rich economies, quite well. For a brief period after the fall of the Berlin Wall, some even talked of 'The End of History'. Our economic problems were solved, and something called 'The New Economy' had arrived, promising endless prosperity – or at least an endlessly rising stock market. Although these fantasies are now largely forgotten, a more humble but still confidently optimistic orthodoxy prevails. The orthodoxy says that the role of governments is to maximize economic growth by providing a stable economic environment of low inflation and generally moderate levels of unemployment. And whatever the problem, markets are almost always the solution. This orthodoxy is not directly discussed in what follows. But a recurring theme is that the orthodoxy leaves something crucial out. Economic growth is not an end in itself. We should focus instead on our quality of life, our well-being, or to rehabilitate an embarrassing word, our *happiness*.

In rich countries the experience of recent years has been that increased material wealth has not led to improvements in quality of life. On the contrary, people report being less happy than 40 years ago. We seem to suffer from a kind of 'affluenza', a condition in which people become preoccupied with acquiring money and possessions, and gaining social status from them. A large body of psychological research suggests that these preoccupations are associated with increased rates of mental illness, including depression, substance abuse, anxiety and personality disorder.[4] Less dramatically, and anecdotally, we can live in a prosperous economic environment, and still discover that modern life is rubbish. So how can a better understanding of economics help?

Talk of improving quality of life might provoke expectations that the following chapters include detailed discussions of integrated transport policies, pension reforms and endogenous growth theory. In other words, the kind of policy wonkery which few of us care passionately about. But we *do* care about the principles at stake – whether it is fair to tax the rich more highly, whether environmental damage can be boiled down to a sum of money, whether surveys can really measure our quality of life or happiness. This book is about these principles. Black box economics obscures them. It takes certain views about these principles for granted, rarely mentioning them explicitly. In the two examples mentioned briefly above we have already seen that black box economics assumes:

- Employees are essentially selfish, and should be managed accordingly.
- The value of life can be measured in monetary terms.

Other presumptions include:

- What we buy always makes us better off.
- People respond predictably to financial incentives.
- Taxation damages the economy, and is morally wrong.
- Economic growth increases happiness.

Together, these assertions and many others form a web of beliefs which constrain and shape our economics and politics, affecting us in ways that extend beyond our economic lives as consumers and workers. These assertions are the subject of this book. Some might wonder whether they are about economics at all. It is true that these issues lie on the boundary between economics and philosophy – ethical economics – but that boundary is much more fragile than it seems.

Consider that favourite veto word of economists, inefficient. Efficiency is a core economic idea, one that to many seems like *the* core economic idea. The efficiency or otherwise of some proposal or outcome is often presented as a fact. In very rough terms, we do something more efficiently if we obtain the same desirable outcome using fewer valuable inputs of time, effort or resources more generally. Or instead, we can obtain a bigger or better outcome using the same inputs. So efficiency seems unambiguously a good thing, and also a scientific concept, referring just to the measurable relationship between inputs and outputs.

Unfortunately for this perspective, economics affects people. The scientific purity attributed to the efficiency idea is disrupted by people, because people are affected by actions taken in the name of efficiency. For example, economists and policy entrepreneurs use efficiency to make claims such as:

Cutting the regulatory burden facing employers makes the labour market work more efficiently.

These regulations might concern working hours, overtime rules or minimum wages. The argument boils down to the idea that the same output can be produced using fewer workers, or produced by people who are paid less. Or perhaps instead, a greater output can be produced. Economists sometimes argue in support of reducing labour market regulations by pointing to the increased national output (economic growth) in countries which have adopted such policies. My aim here is neither to agree nor disagree with these policies. The crucial point is simply that, in almost all cases, there will be both winners and losers. If national output has risen then materially we are richer; conventional economics deduces that some consumers must be better off. And shareholders should benefit from firms making higher profits. But some workers may suffer from lower pay, or longer working hours, or an unpleasant increase in work intensity. Whether, on balance, the changes taken together represent an overall improvement depends on, among other things, ethical views about the relative priority we should give to impacts on the rich and poor, and ethical concepts of need, justice, entitlement and just deserts. So the 'efficiency gain' in this example is not an objective improvement; if it is regarded as an improvement, that is an ethical judgement. Efficiency is not an ethics-free concept.

Still, it seems there might be occasional exceptions to this rule. In the last paragraph I wrote that there will be both winners and losers *in almost all cases.* But what if everyone gains? Surely *that* would effectively count as an objective improvement – an unambiguous gain for everyone. Consider the common argument that free trade makes the economy more efficient. Some economists argue that, at least in the long run, *everyone* will be better off from freer global trade. Suppose this is true. A sympathetic reading of the evidence on recent trade liberalization suggests that, roughly, rich countries have gained moderately, recently industrialized countries such as China have gained the most, while very poor countries have gained the least. And within countries, the gains are very uneven too, with the poorest in India and China gaining much less than others in their countries. Even though 'everyone's a winner', it is clearly reasonable to regard this outcome as *not* representing an objective, unambiguous improvement, because inequality has increased. The poor may be literally better off, but not relative to the rest of us. Again, whether we view the 'efficiency gain' from freer trade as an overall improvement is an ethical judgement. Even if everyone wins, 'efficiency' still comes laden with ethical baggage.[5] So when veto economics invokes the word as though it were a neutral factual concept to which no one could reasonably object, we are misled.

It is worth stressing that the misrepresentation here is often unintentional. Few economists, if any, set out to deceive (even if the same cannot be said of policy entrepreneurs). Instead, many economists believe that economics can be ethics-free for the noblest of reasons – they are loathe to foist their own ethical views on other people. So they try to make their economic advice ethics-free. But as I have already indicated, ethics is unavoidable in economics. We should simply be open and explicit about it. Besides, these economists need not worry. They should follow the example set by their greatest forebears.

The great economists of the past saw economics and ethics as inextricably entwined; one example of this is their emphasis on the limits of economic prosperity in bringing about broader improvements in the human condition, and hence the relative insignificance they attached to economic prosperity alone. Adam Smith was dismissive of economic success as an end in itself: 'if the trappings of wealth are viewed philosophically, they will always appear in the highest degree contemptible and trifling'.[6] John Maynard Keynes, the most influential economist of the 20th century, shared similar concerns. In 'Economic possibilities for our grandchildren', Keynes described the 'love of money as a possession' as 'one of those semi-criminal, semi-pathological propensities which one hands over with a shudder to the specialists in mental disease'.[7] Keynes accurately predicted British average income per head in the early 21st century, and went on to anticipate the problems of affluenza, and the renewed importance of an ethical framework once society ceases to be focused solely on economic growth.[8] In all this, he was remarkably prescient: the essay was written in 1930.

Clearly, the early great economists would have rejected the belief that economics deals solely with material prosperity and financial wealth. But this belief, a contemporary variation on the illusion that 'economics and ethics don't mix', can be seen in action every day in the news media. Economics is discussed as if it were just concerned with the business and financial aspects of an issue, narrowly defined. If an airport expansion is being proposed, for example, the effects on the local economy and on the airline industry are included under the 'economic' heading, along with the construction cost, but all the other impacts are treated separately. Impacts such as carbon emissions, and the effect on quality of life for those living near the airport – and those able to go on holiday more easily and cheaply – are relegated to the 'non-economic' category. The same intellectual apartheid system continues in government.[9] 'Non-economic' impacts are all too easily regarded as less important, especially if they are not quantifiable in terms of money. If impacts cannot be measured in monetary terms, they are seen as soft, fuzzy, ephemeral… No wonder some economists begin to doubt if they are really there at all.

So those who believe that economics can be separated from ethics have forgotten its history. And quality of life impacts, such as those arising from a new airport, are just as much the subject of economics as inflation, unemployment and economic growth, even if they cannot be quantified in terms of money.

Many people, economists and non-economists alike, resist this conclusion because they fear it leads to an 'anything goes' dead end. In other words, they object to ethical economics because they believe that ethical debate is a waste of time. Some economists themselves have helped perpetuate this myth. Regarding disagreements about ethical values, Milton Friedman believed that 'men can ultimately only fight'.[10] Skepticism about ethical reflection has been popular throughout history and is likely to remain so, because it saves people from having to bother to defend their beliefs. But that does not mean it is right. Even if ethical judgements cannot be literally true or false, almost all of us regard some judgements as better than others. Although some ethical questions are plagued by doubt and disagreement, others suggest ethical agreement is possible. There is widespread condemnation of slavery or torture, and most of us will willingly defend our objections to these practices against those people who disagree. We do not regard this kind of ethical debate as pointless or meaningless. Finally, some people worry that it is intolerant or illiberal to advocate a particular set of ethical values, particularly when these values have implications for the conduct of others. But this worry is not compatible with the idea that ethical reflection is futile: tolerance and liberalism are themselves ethical values, requiring an ethical argument to justify them.

As well as avoiding undue pessimism about the usefulness of ethical reflection, we should, on the other hand, avoid undue optimism about what economics can tell us. As the joke goes:

> Economists don't answer questions because they know what the answer is. They answer because they are asked.

Once we recognize that economics does not fit our picture of a typical science, we must be more modest in what we expect of it. This does not mean that anything goes, that all the constraints of veto economics can be swept away with a single liberating stroke. But this book will suggest that the truth is often more complex than the policy entrepreneurs would have us believe. Often the truth is that economists don't know. Not knowing whether there is a constraint – whether, for instance, a lower rate of economic growth must lead to increases in unemployment – is not the same as knowing there is no constraint, but it cannot act as a veto on new policies either. This kind of modesty is not what many of us want to hear. We yearn for the comfort and security of definite answers. But an honest economic analysis can typically hope to do much less than that. At best, it will point out some inconsistencies in aims, methods or assumptions; it will rule out some options but leave several others open – and pass the decision back to whoever commissioned the analysis in the first place.

In case this sounds too pessimistic, let me sum up why you should read this book. You *can* read this book. As well as stripping out the mathematics, which often kills off public debate about economics, I have eliminated almost all the jargon too. As an economist, it is deeply satisfying to economize on economic jargon; for example, there is only one more passage in this book containing the word 'efficiency'. The concept of efficiency is elsewhere too, but not in a way which needs gratuitous labelling. In the following chapters, I discuss shopping and consuming, pay and taxation, economic growth and happiness. Then I look at the practice of putting prices on life and nature, and more generally the process of bringing money into new contexts: turning things and activities into commodities which can be bought and sold. The chapters are essentially free-standing and can be read in any order, although later chapters inevitably contain occasional references to earlier discussions. Throughout I show that economics draws on hidden ethical assumptions, both in its foundations and its practice. Whether we agree or disagree with these assumptions, we all need to know what they are. It is futile to try to rid economics of its ethical foundations, because all economic theories and policies must draw on particular views about how we ought to live, and what we value. We cannot avoid making choices between these views, so in what follows I set out to uncover them, with due skepticism about the associated economic arguments.

Chapter Two

The Sovereign Consumer

What is the basic principle of economics? As a wise elder once told me, 'People do what they get paid to do; what they don't get paid to do, they don't do.' People respond to incentives; all the rest is commentary. (William Easterly, former World Bank economist[1])

[When] self-interest and ethical values with wide verbal allegiance are in conflict, much of the time, most of the time in fact, self-interest-theory ... will win. (George Stigler, Nobel Laureate economist[2])

The average human being is about 95 per cent selfish in the narrow sense of the term. (Gordon Tullock, Virginia economist[3])

Why is economics called 'the dismal science'? One reason is that many economists are profoundly cynical about human behaviour and the motivation that underlies it. Morality, they seem to suggest, is for losers: real people are almost always selfish. This is the key assumption behind the lead actor in modern economics, the 'sovereign consumer'.

Consumers go shopping, and shopping is clearly central to the economy – it is the fuel powering the engine of economic growth. And shopping is equally central to understanding how economists think. Modern economics is built on theories of 'rational choice', and the textbook example of rational choice is supposed to be the kind of choice made by consumers when they shop. All other choices – those made by workers in firms, or their managers or shareholders; choices made by bureaucrats and politicians; even choices made by private individuals about whom to marry or which moral values to adopt – are analysed by economists in essentially the same way, as variations on the basic story of consumer choice. The sovereign consumer is the actor at the heart of this story, a person who is fully informed, knows what they want, and never makes mistakes in getting it. In economics, the sovereign consumer is very much in control of their life.

As I suggested in Chapter 1, our anecdotal experience of shopping and consuming today is much less optimistic. We suffer from 'affluenza'.[4] But economists respond to these anecdotes with an awkward question: if our present patterns of shopping and consuming create problems and do not make us happy, why do we continue? This chapter begins to answer this question, with more to follow in Chapters 3 and 5. Before that, it is worth emphasizing what is at stake here. It is not just a matter of whether economists have an accurate picture of consumer choice. The story of the sovereign consumer lies behind some basic and influential ideas:

- economic growth is always beneficial
- people should get what they want
- more choice is always better.

These are widely held ethical views, which often masquerade as economic facts. In this chapter I will question them. I go on to argue that economic advice based on the assumption that people are selfish often has disastrous effects. The main problem is easy to summarize: assuming people are selfish becomes a self-fulfilling prophecy, with the result that altruism, trust and cooperation are all undermined. And the assumption of selfishness can even act to excuse, or indirectly justify, immoral behaviour. As we shall see below, for some economists, behaviour such as committing crime, or racial discrimination, can be both 'rational' and 'efficient'.

So there are two reasons to look in detail at the story of the sovereign consumer. It has influence far beyond the world of shopping. And at every stage it involves ethical judgements as well as economic analysis. The result is ethical economics.

The economist goes shopping

The economic analysis of how we choose is remarkably simple. It starts from the common-sense notion of choice arising from the combination of beliefs and desires. I *desire* to wash my clothes, and I *believe* that 'Razzle Dazzle' washing powder will help me wash them, so I buy some. The next step is to describe why I buy Razzle Dazzle rather than some other brand. Essential to making choice is not just desire, but *preference*: a desire to have or do this rather than that. I buy Razzle Dazzle because I prefer it to other brands. Obviously price and my budget play a part here too. I may prefer Razzle Dazzle to Washes Whiter, but nevertheless buy Washes Whiter because it is cheaper. There is a trade-off between my preference for Razzle Dazzle and its higher price. Economists are fascinated by these trade-offs, and have developed the theory in sophisticated ways to analyse how demand for a product may change in response to a change in its price, or the consumer's income, or the price of a rival product. But these complications need not concern us. The key components of the theory are just the preferences of the consumer, and the options available, such as different brands of washing powder. Together these determine what will be chosen: given her budget, the consumer will choose the most preferred option from among those available. But which will this be? In general terms, nothing can be said, because the preferences of different consumers will clearly vary for all sorts of reasons. I may prefer Razzle Dazzle just because I like the name, while you prefer Washes Whiter because you believe it does. And the pure economic theory stops there, making no assumptions about the content of people's preferences. But in practice, economists need to go further in order to draw practical conclusions from their analysis. They want to sidestep the details of consumer psychology, so instead they make a general assumption which is innocuous and self-evident to many – that consumers are largely self-interested. The idea is that in making choices between the available options, I pursue my own interests first and foremost. This assumption rules out, for instance, buying Washes Whiter because I think that the retailer or manufacturer makes more profit from it, and I want to help boost their profits. Also, it probably rules out buying Washes Whiter solely because my aunt will disapprove if I buy Razzle Dazzle, or buying Washes Whiter because I believe it is less harmful to the environment. 'Probably' because the definition of self-interest is opaque; we will be returning to this later.

The rest of the economic theory behind the sovereign consumer seems obvious enough. Indeed the theory is *so* obvious that it is easy to forget it is there at all, and to overlook the assumptions that were implicitly made in the outline above. To begin with, the theory takes both the consumer's preferences and the available options as given. Taking preferences as given implicitly assumes that the consumer already knows what they want – that they have had the requisite time and information to form a carefully considered set of preferences. Taking the options as given implies that the available alternatives are somehow fixed objectively and beyond the influence of the consumer. In reality, the process of making a choice is often very different. Preferences are hazy and hesitant because we lack the time and information to determine them. The decision-making process also leads to the discovery of new options, or the revision of existing ones to improve them; we do not act as if the available options are fixed in stone. Next, once the preferences and options are determined, the story of the sovereign consumer takes its conclusion for granted: the consumer chooses the most preferred option from among those available, implying that the consumer is infallible and never makes mistakes.

With these assumptions spelt out, you may be starting to have doubts. You certainly should be. This seemingly common-sense story of how we choose is far removed from reality. When the psychologist goes shopping, the world looks rather different.

The psychologist goes shopping

There is a rich body of research by psychologists on how we choose, much of it suggesting a sharply different picture of choice from that found in economics. For example, the options between which we choose are not as clear-cut or objective as economic theory implies. Essentially the same set of options can be perceived very differently, leading to completely different choices, due to *framing effects*, so-called because they concern the context or frame through which a person perceives a decision. A box of Razzle Dazzle can be perceived as expensive (if we remember that it cost less a month ago) or cheap (if the retailer displays it as being on 'special offer'). You may feel confident that you are not fooled by such simple retailing ploys (you always ignore 'special offer' claims when assessing price) but framing effects are pervasive and not always so obvious.

Framing effects: Two examples

1 Merely because an option is framed as the default option – one that will be selected unless the chooser actively decides otherwise – it is much more likely to be 'chosen', even when the decision is important. One study of enrolment in organ donation programmes in seven European countries found that on average 97 per cent of people were enrolled when this was the default option, but only 18 per cent otherwise.[5]

2 Suppose you have decided to see a show at the theatre, for which tickets cost $40. You arrive at the theatre, and as you queue to buy a ticket, you discover that you have just lost $40 in cash. Would you still go in? Most people say 'yes'. Now imagine instead that you had already purchased the $40 ticket, but as you arrive, discover that you have lost the ticket. The ticket is non-refundable and non-replaceable. Would you buy another ticket and still go in? In this situation most people say 'no'. Both situations involve a choice between seeing the show and being $80 worse off, or not seeing it and being $40 worse off: they are effectively identical choices, but framed differently.[6] The sovereign consumer is supposed to see through the surface descriptive differences between the two situations, treating them as irrelevant, and should therefore make the same choice on both occasions. Since most people in reality choose differently according to the way the choice is framed, they are irrational according to standard economic theory.

Another reason that the options should be thought of as subjectively defined, rather than as objective facts about the choice situation, is that our perception of them is heavily influenced by what psychologists term *availability*. Availability concerns how readily some piece of information can be brought to mind – how available it is to us – and depends on how vivid, striking or distinctive the information is. Availability often distorts our judgement. Many of us overestimate dramatic, vivid causes of death (murder, plane crash, lightning strike) but underestimate the much more likely causes, such as common illnesses. And watching one vivid interview with, say, a lazy recipient of state welfare benefits, will influence someone's judgement much more than overwhelming statistical evidence that most benefit recipients are not lazy. The distortionary effect persists even if people are told in advance that the interviewee is atypical.[7] The implications for consumer choice are clear. We pay more attention to available options, and may ignore others. We attach more weight to information about these options merely because it is more available. Advertisers of SUVs ('sports utility vehicles') can rest assured that one dramatic advert, showing a vehicle surviving a high-impact crash largely unscathed, will have more influence than well-publicized scientific research suggesting that SUVs are no safer for their occupants. Even if consumers know that the advert is unrepresentative, or downright manipulative, it still seems to exert its subconscious influence on choice.

Advertising also exerts its subconscious influence, via the availability effect, using brand recognition. Branding ensures an otherwise identical product becomes more familiar, and so more available to be brought to mind. This familiarity alone has been shown to breed approval of the product, again subconsciously. In one study, people were played different snippets of music, different numbers of times. On average, they preferred the snippets that were played more frequently, although their conscious verbal explanation of their preferences made no reference to frequency.[8]

Even without the distractions of availability or advertising, our predictions of the satisfaction from future experiences are unreliable, and so we struggle to choose the best option.[9] In particular, our predictions are biased by our current emotional state. We all know the danger of buying more food than intended when shopping on an empty stomach, a danger confirmed by psychological evidence.[10] Similarly, catalogue shoppers ordering by telephone seem overly influenced by the current weather: warm clothes ordered on cold days are more likely to be returned later.[11] And many people join gyms and health clubs which they subsequently rarely use, because at the time of joining they focus on the health benefits, rather than how they will feel in the future when visiting the gym.[12] A form of framing effect also distorts our predictions of future satisfaction. Suppose you are trying to decide between two equally expensive pairs of stereo speakers. In the audio shop, you will probably put great weight on which sounds better, and purchase on that basis, even though the differences are likely to be small. Unfortunately, at home you realize that you care more about the speakers' appearance, because the marginally superior sound quality is undetectable in isolation.[13] The context of choice in the shop leads us to put too much weight on an attribute which we later find less important.

The psychological phenomena mentioned so far all affect the framing of the choice situation, the options we consider, and the way we assess them. But even if these troublesome influences did not arise, there is a more fundamental worry about the consumer sovereignty story. So far we have assumed that the consumer's goal is clear – their own self-interest – and choice is just about pursuing that goal effectively. However, this assumption is questionable, even if we set aside for now the more philosophical doubts about the meaning of self-interest. Consider instead a simple consumer choice: choosing the best holiday destination. You may have noticed that you can find a holiday rather mixed at the time, with both good and bad experiences, but a few months later, the whole holiday seems good when looking back on it. In fact, even a short time later our memory provides an inaccurate guide to how pleasurable or otherwise an experience was, because of a form of availability effect known as 'Peak-End evaluation'. We remember any experience in terms of the extreme moments (peaks and troughs) and the final, end moment of the experience. This was vividly demonstrated in a famous experiment conducted by psychologist Daniel Kahneman.[14]

Kahneman studied a group of patients undergoing a colonoscopy, an uncomfortable medical procedure. For half the patients, the colonoscope was deliberately left stationary inside them for an extra minute, causing them to experience mild discomfort for this period, but less pain than earlier in the procedure. That is, this second group experienced the same procedure as the other patients, but with an additional one minute of mild discomfort at the end. And this is how the second group described their experience at the time. Nevertheless, a short time later, they rated the whole experience as *less* unpleasant than the first group, because they focused on the end moment, which was less painful. These Peak-End evaluations determined later choices. Over a five-year period after the colonoscopy procedure, patients in the second group agreed to more follow-up colonoscopies than members of the first group, presumably because they remembered the procedure as less unpleasant.

This tale casts doubt on the idea that pursuing our self-interest is as straightforward as it often appears to be. I may have an apparently clear goal – minimizing the unpleasantness of a medical procedure – but fail to attain it because of Peak-End evaluation. I favour the medical procedure involving not just a colonoscopy, but further discomfort on top. The problem is not just that we sometimes make mistakes in pursuing our self-interest. The deeper difficulty is identifying my self-interest, even after careful reflection, once 'mistakes' are pointed out to me. Suppose I had a choice: should I minimize the pain experienced during the colonoscopy procedure itself, or should I choose the option which, although it involves additional discomfort at the time, will make me feel happier about the whole experience shortly afterwards, and less fearful of follow-up operations?

Self-interest is also far from clear in the theatre example discussed earlier. Economic theory prescribes that we should reach the same decision about whether to see the show, regardless of whether we discover outside that we have lost $40 cash or a $40 ticket. We are supposed to choose solely on the basis of the material benefits and costs involved, and not be influenced by framing effects, the context of the choice. Does our self-interest demand this type of 'consistency'? Context matters. Even if the net financial impacts in two situations are identical, most of us distinguish them. Losing $40 cash is seen as one of life's minor misfortunes that inevitably befall us, with no implications for whether we see the show. But having to buy a replacement for a lost $40 ticket means that it will effectively cost $80 to go in, a price that may deter us. This kind of reasoning seems as legitimate as it is widespread, despite economists' advice that it runs counter to our interests.

Perhaps the most direct evidence that self-interest may be ill-defined comes from situations where we seem incapable of deciding what will satisfy it – where we lack the self-control at the heart of consumer sovereignty. Self-control problems are ubiquitous.[15] Often we anticipate them and take successful evasive action. I move my alarm clock out of reach, so that I will not be able to switch it off without getting out of bed. I join a pension scheme to commit myself to saving enough for retirement. But sometimes we struggle to decide where our self-interest lies, that is, whether to exercise self-control at all. I vow before dinner in a restaurant to forgo pudding, but succumb when the moment arrives. However, I never buy fattening puddings to eat at home. I buy cigarettes, but give them away, then run out to buy more. These changes of mind are not due to new information or hurried decision making. Many smokers and heavy eaters know that they are very likely to suffer from poorer health later in life, but continue to smoke and eat heavily nonetheless. They look back on years of similar behaviour, and have no regrets. Nor can we assume that they would resist if they had 'more will-power'– just ask a veteran smoker such as the painter David Hockney.[16] In short, people repeatedly have preferences pulling in opposite directions. They cannot decide what will best serve their self-interest, no matter how hard they scrutinize their preferences.

Whether due to framing effects, self-control problems, Peak-End evaluations or other common features of how we think, our 'self-interest' may not be clearly defined, even with the benefit of hindsight. And the bulk of psychological research more generally provides powerful evidence that consumer sovereignty is a myth.[17] But, you may be beginning to ask, so what?

Consumer sovereignty: An influential myth

While it might be embarrassing to economists that their description of how we choose is very often false, does it matter to the rest of us? Absolutely, because consumer sovereignty is taken for granted in all sorts of unlikely but crucial places. Consider advertising: if government policy were made by psychologists, then certain forms of advertising would surely be banned, because they lead people to buy too much, or things they later regret. In contrast, starting from the story of the sovereign consumer, economists have developed an entirely different perspective on advertising, one which has been very influential in justifying it. This is surprising, because the ubiquitousness of advertising poses a challenge for consumer sovereignty. If consumers are sovereign, they will not be influenced by advertising, but if they are not influenced, why do manufacturers and retailers bother to advertise? It seems that either consumers are influenced by advertising, implying consumer sovereignty is an illusion; or they are not, in which case it has no effect, and advertising spending is irrational for companies and an inefficient waste of society's resources.

The simplistic reply to this conundrum emphasizes that advertising can be informative: it tells you what is available, where and at what price. It does not *change* your preferences, but provides information which can help construct them. Thus informative advertising can influence the things we buy, without undermining consumer sovereignty. The problem with this reply is that most advertising seems persuasive rather than informative: it wants you to change your preferences between products – to buy Razzle

Dazzle rather than Washes Whiter, or this brand of car rather than that one – often on grounds which seem to have nothing to do with the quality or function of the product itself. The sovereign consumer would not be manipulated into changing preferences in this way. But economics offers a more sophisticated response to the conundrum.[18]

The essential idea is that our underlying preferences – the ones which the consumer sovereignty story holds sacrosanct – do not directly concern *products* at all. Rather, they concern the underlying *characteristics* of products.[19] For example, our fundamental preferences do not concern cars but characteristics of cars, such as speed, comfort, reliability, economy and image. We seek cars with particular bundles of characteristics. I prefer cars which are speedy, fashionable and comfortable to those which are reliable, economical but dull, while you may prefer the opposite. With this framework in place, it is argued that advertising serves a useful function. It provides information about the bundles of characteristics embodied in the products it promotes, information which may lead people to change the products they buy, even though their underlying preferences over characteristics are unchanged. An advert involving interviews with people who have owned a particular make of car for 20 years may convince you that it is a reliable brand. So advertising may *appear* to change consumer preferences – hence overturning consumer sovereignty – when in fact it simply provides the information to enable consumers better to fulfil the preferences over characteristics they had all along. In essence, the two assumptions mentioned above, that preferences are predetermined, and consumers never make mistakes in acting upon them, have merely shifted one step back. Since consumer sovereignty is indefensible for preferences over products themselves, it is invoked for preferences over characteristics instead.

Whatever the other drawbacks of this story, one lesson is clear. It is crucial to any defence of advertising. For example, the defenders of 'junk food' advertising have sought to convince the UK Food Standards Agency with an argument along exactly these lines.[20] And conversely, if consumer sovereignty is a myth, then the case for restricting some forms of advertising becomes much stronger. It is ironic that while one theory of choice is used to justify the value of advertising to society at large, another altogether is used by companies deciding how much to spend on advertising: they do not think in the narrow terms of preferences-over-characteristics. They draw on insights from psychology and sociology to create vague but emotive brand images to persuade people to want new and different goods; they are not just providing facts about their products.

Justifying advertising is not the only surprising use of the consumer sovereignty doctrine. If consumers are sovereign, then the choices we observe them making should be a reliable guide to what they actually prefer – their preferences are revealed by their choices. Economists use this *revealed preference* assumption frequently, in arguments which many other people find bizarre. Economic theories of 'rational addiction' assume that drug addicts' choices always reflect what they truly prefer. The possibility that their choices could be irrational is ruled out by definition.[21] And in Chapter 6 we shall see the revealed preference trick pulled again. Here's a brief glimpse. Policies to tackle climate change may save lives in the future, but involve large economic costs now. What should we do? Economists answer this question by trying to value the lives saved in terms of money. The first step in the calculation is to put a money value on an increased risk of death. Economists do *that* by measuring how much extra people are paid in risky occupations. This extra pay is supposed to reflect how much employees care about the risks, how much extra they must be paid in order to tolerate them. But this conclusion is only valid if employees' choices reveal their true preferences. In reality, workers are often unaware of the true magnitude of the risks they face, and they may end up in jobs because there seemed to be no alternative, not because they have consciously chosen extra risk in return for extra pay. Real people do not choose jobs as sovereign consumers choose washing powder.

The revealed preference device and the preferences-over-characteristics account of the role of advertising show the broad influence of the consumer sovereignty story. But the most important use of the story in modern economies is in justifying economic growth. The argument brings together the key assumptions behind consumer sovereignty: specifically, that consumers have clear-cut predetermined preferences which reflect the pursuit of self-interest, and that they never make mistakes in identifying their self-interest, or choosing in accordance with it. Since consumers are self-interested, they only prefer things that they believe will make them better off than any other available alternative. And since they are never mistaken, their beliefs are always correct, so they only prefer things that in fact *will* make them better off. Once this crucial link between preference satisfaction and being better off is in place, the conclusion that economic growth is a good thing follows quite easily. This is how:

> Growth is good, because it leads to more consumption.
> Consumption is good, because it leads to more preference satisfaction.
> Preference satisfaction is good, because it makes people better off.

Although this is clearly a simplified outline, it captures the essentials of an argument for economic growth in developed economies that is so widely taken for granted that it goes unmentioned. But I am *not* suggesting that economic growth is a bad thing (see Chapter 3), simply that this common argument for it begins with a very dubious premise, built on the myth of consumer sovereignty. Once the myth is abandoned, we cannot conclude that more material consumption is good just because more preferences are fulfilled, more wants are met. But what *can* we conclude? It is time to return to the question posed at the start of this chapter: if consumption creates problems and doesn't make us happy, why do we continue?

Addictive and competitive consumption

> Want is a growing giant whom the coat of Have was never large enough to cover.[22]

> A house may be large or small; as long as the neighbouring houses are likewise small, it satisfies all social requirement for a residence. But let there arise next to the little house a palace, and the little house shrinks to a hut.[23]

'Addictive' is a strong word. Very few of us are *compulsive* shoppers, in the sense of suffering from a psychological pathology. But many people's attitude to shopping is nonetheless akin to addiction. There is powerful psychological evidence that just having material goods, things, stuff, gear, is not enough. The satisfaction they provide depends on having more and more of them.[24]

When I first buy something, be it new clothes, electronic gadgets or even a car, it typically brings pleasure at first. The problem is that I rapidly become accustomed to owning and using the item, so my mood, or general happiness, returns to what it was before I made the purchase. To experience the pleasure I had from that purchase again, I now need to buy more, bigger or better things. Just like an addiction to alcohol or nicotine, I must constantly increase the dose in order to gain the same satisfaction. I am on a happiness treadmill. The most famous application of the treadmill idea has been to the experience of lottery winners and paraplegics.[25] Although they tend to feel happier for a while after their win, lottery winners typically return to their previous happiness or life satisfaction levels within one year. Similarly, paraplegics often suffer from depression immediately after the accident that disabled them, but on average their happiness eventually returns to normal.

The happiness treadmill is part of a broader psychological theory of *adaptation*. Since lottery winners and paraplegics ultimately adapt, it is unsurprising that comprehensive adaptation to new material possessions occurs too. Although the influence of adaptation on our experience of shopping and consumption seems plausible, a skeptic would rightly ask two questions. First, if we rapidly adapt to material consumption so that its pleasure fades, surely we will foresee this. So why do we remain addicted to shopping? Second, surely we do not adapt equally to everything. Are we particularly prone to adapt swiftly to having more material things?

Regarding the first question, our failure to foresee adaptation to increased material consumption is to be expected – it is but one aspect of our inability to predict our satisfaction from future experiences. The general pattern is that we expect future experiences, good or bad, to affect our well-being much more than we report equivalent experiences in the past doing so.[26] We overestimate the impact of specific future experiences on our well-being, and ignore adaptation, because of our well-established psychological tendency to exaggerate the importance of any thought or subject we are focusing on, and underestimate the broader context. So when considering how much happier an increased income might make me, I focus on the income change, forgetting that I will become accustomed to it in the future. Our distorted thinking is summarized by the maxim: 'Nothing in life matters quite as much as you think it does while you are thinking about it.'[27]

Turning to the second question, research on the differing degrees to which we adapt to different things is growing, but still limited at present.[28] So it is not possible to compare adaptation to more material possessions against every other experience. However, there *is* extensive research on adaptation to increased income, which is a good proxy for increased material consumption. Perhaps the most telling evidence is the extent to which the income we say we 'need' or 'require' rises with our actual income.[29] We become accustomed to increased actual income, and this adaptation leads us to raise the amount of income we believe we need or require. This then forms a benchmark against which income gains in the future are judged. We are on the happiness treadmill again. In contrast, we adapt only slowly, if at all, to unpleasant noise and the stress of commuting; or to the satisfactions of food, sexual activity, time spent with friends, or time spent on physical exercise.[30] And we continue to value our close personal relationships highly, struggling for years to adapt if we suffer bereavement.

Some explanations for these patterns of differing adaptation are beginning to emerge. For deep-rooted evolutionary reasons, we adapt less to stimuli essential for survival (food or sexual activity), or stimuli which suggest a threat to survival (loud noise or extreme temperature). We adapt more to experiences involving certain, permanent change, and experiences shared by those around us.[31] Improvements in material living standards are prone to both these diluting influences. For most employees, salary increases are rightly regarded as permanent rises in income. We would adapt to them far less and 'live for the moment' if future income was highly uncertain and vulnerable to sudden decline. Even more reliably, income gains lead us to mix with wealthier people, because we shop in more exclusive places, take up more expensive hobbies, or move to a new neighbourhood. Or we simply boast to our friends about our new electronic gadget – only to be told they already own one. This brings us to the other key feature of the shopping experience: it is competitive as well as addictive.

Competitive consumption, red in tooth and claw, will be familiar if you have ever been shopping on the first day of the sales. And we all know people who are obsessed with accumulating – and usually displaying – more and better stuff than those around them. Conspicuous consumption and related forms of 'status anxiety' are widespread.[32] More generally, people increasingly shape their identity through their shopping choices and consumption patterns. 'You are what you own' comes to dominate thinking as other means of developing identity collapse. I cannot define myself by my occupation if that is fluid, rather than a job for life. Identity is no easier to establish within occupations either, as organizational hierarchies erode. And for most people, religion and various forms of deference now have little relevance as frameworks for structuring their sense of self.

Whether driven by a search for identity or pure conspicuous consumption, the effect is the same. Things we own that others do not are more valuable than things everyone has. Consumption is competitive in the sense that we compete for this exclusivity. We are rivals. When rivalry matters, if you buy something that I already own, then that purchase undermines my well-being. I must buy something new myself in order to maintain my identity and status.

Both adaptation and rivalry are powerful engines of acquisition. Adaptation entails that material consumption is unfulfilling, so we go back for more. Rivalry compounds the problem: my consumption spurs you to buy more, better, or just different, and vice-versa. We are trapped in a process of endless buying, unsatisfying consumption, and buying more again. It does not make us happy, but we still continue.

It is worth summing up the chapter so far. Economics offers a simple picture of how we choose, based on the consumer sovereignty story, and assuming we are self-interested. We have seen that consumer sovereignty is often a myth, but a highly influential one. In particular, it helps sustain the argument that economic growth is necessarily beneficial, because it leads to more material consumption. Not only is this argument flawed because of its reliance on consumer sovereignty, but there are two good reasons to believe that more material consumption does not make us happy: adaptation and rivalry. The focus up to now has been on doubts about consumer sovereignty, that is, on reasons why people may fail to pursue their own self-interest, even though they want to do so. We turn next to that last assumption – that people *do* want to pursue their own self-interest – but first it is worth asking how an economist might respond to the criticisms I have made.

This is not the place for a debate over every detail between economists and their critics.[33] However, it must be acknowledged that some of the criticisms are accepted by many economists, or attack views which they no longer hold. There has been a quiet revolution in the way economists understand how we choose, with the objections of Daniel Kahneman and others becoming widely accepted, so much so that Kahneman recently won the Nobel Prize in Economics – an especially significant award, since he is a psychologist. However, for several reasons, the objections made here should not be dismissed as merely criticizing a theory which no one accepts. To begin with, while the cutting-edge economists studying how we choose have adopted the psychological perspective of Kahneman and others, this adoption has not filtered down to economists working in other fields. This new perspective has been termed *behavioural economics* because it studies how people actually behave – in contrast to the approach taken in orthodox economics.[34] Whether studying the decisions of company managers, or the choices of employees in the labour market, economists almost always assume that the decision makers are self-interested and think like the sovereign consumer; and they advise governments and clients on that basis. Nor is there any sign of this default view changing in the near future, not least because behavioural economics has had little impact on core undergraduate economics texts, which make absolutely no mention of it.[35] Unsurprisingly therefore, it remains business as usual for the conventional wisdom on, say, advertising and economic growth.

Another reason why the objections I have outlined are not redundant is that they go much further than the widely accepted psychological criticisms. While many economists accept that their old picture of how we choose is mistaken, they still insist that it is a good guide to how we *ought* to choose. The sovereign consumer driven by self-interest shows how we ought to choose; anything else is irrational. So when people make a different choice because of framing effects, self-control problems, or Peak-End evaluations, economists regard their decision as mistaken or irrational. But we have seen that this verdict is often wrong, because people can offer good reasons for their allegedly 'irrational' choices. The fragile link between what we ought to do, and what economists *say* we ought to do, breaks completely when we finally confront the self-interest assumption.

Are we always selfish?

As we saw in the epigraphs at the head of this chapter, most economists believe that we are selfish most, if not all, of the time. As a leading management textbook states, individuals pursue their own 'self-interest unconstrained by morality'.[36] It is important to be clear about what is at stake here. So far we have mainly focused on the kinds of everyday shopping choices which are obviously at the heart of economics. Less obvious or well known is the extension of the same way of thinking into areas far from ordinary economic life. The Chicago economist Gary Becker analyses love. He argues that rich people avoid poor people in order to reduce the risk of falling in love with them. The idea is that once in love the rich will want to share their wealth with their partner. The rich can predict this in advance, so stay away from the poor in order to avoid the temptation. Becker has developed an economics of guilt as well as love. For example, parents try to nurture guilt in their children, because then the children are more likely to take care of their parents when they grow old.[37] Becker is not a lone eccentric. He won the Nobel Prize for this work, and it has been enormously influential as well as controversial. Its main impact has been that economics now commonly assumes a fully functional *Homo economicus,* an economic man or woman who acts as a sovereign consumer in pursuit of their self-interest, every day in every way, not just when they go to the shops. With such an enormously enlarged scope of operation, the self-interest assumption is scarcely believable. It is tempting to parody Becker's work, but as the economist and *Financial Times* commentator John Kay observes, 'no parody is required'.[38] Nor is it necessary to report evidence that people sometimes act unselfishly, sacrificing their own interests, in their personal lives with friends and family. Less obviously, the evidence of unselfish behaviour extends into our economic lives and our dealings with strangers too. People give substantial sums of money, often anonymously, to charities from which they cannot hope to benefit. In many European cities, it is easy to avoid paying for travel on public transport systems, with almost no risk of detection, but almost everyone pays. And striking evidence comes from an experiment that has been repeated several times in many countries. Researchers leave wallets containing cash, and sometimes the apparent owner's address, on city streets.[39] Although it involves time and effort to do so, on average more than half the wallets are returned to the enclosed address or a nearby police station. And yet the self-interest assumption persists in economics. Why?

The obvious answer might seem to be a hard-nosed, cynical view of human nature, sometimes associated with the political Right. But cynicism alone is not a good reason to believe anything. And many economists fervently embrace the self-interest assumption, without hailing from the Right. Besides, the Austrian economist Friedrich von Hayek, arguably the strongest intellectual influence on both British Thatcherism and American neoconservatism, did not assume self-interest; on the contrary, he was worried that people are too altruistic for market forces to operate successfully.[40] So there is no simple political explanation for the self-interest assumption. Instead, the answer lies in modern economists interpreting the assumption in a way which makes it hard to challenge. There are two strategies. The first strategy interprets acts which appear unselfish as in fact serving future or overall self-interest. I may seem to act unselfishly, but in fact my motive is my own hidden or future benefit. For example, when I give to charity it is not because of a feeling of duty or moral obligation to help others, but because of the self-satisfied 'warm glow' I will feel, or because I wish to avoid the guilt that will plague me if I do not donate. My concern is my own well-being, not that of others. Similarly, those who return lost wallets do so because otherwise they will feel guilty. This first strategy for defending the self-interest assumption boils down to a series of assertions about what motivates people. These are assertions about matters of fact: we should in principle be able to test them against reality, a task to which I turn below.

In contrast, the second strategy cannot be defeated with empirical evidence. It argues that people must inevitably pursue their self-interest if they are rational. The pursuit of self-interest is simply a logical consequence of being rational: assuming we are rational, it cannot be disproved. The argument runs as follows: choosing rationally means choosing what you want, what you prefer. It means choosing what *you* want, rather than what others might prefer. So it is self-interested. This kind of lazy thinking is bogus. Just because you want something does not imply it serves your interests. That is just a restatement of the self-interest assumption; assuming it in the process of trying to demonstrate it is circular reasoning. Whether people are self-interested depends on *what* they prefer, not merely that they seek to satisfy their own preferences.[41]

Although this second strategy fails, it is easy to see why it is tempting. Defining self-interest as 'choosing what you want' allows us to sidestep the crucial problem: when we observe behaviour in reality, it is often very hard to pin down the motivation behind it. A more promising recent attempt to resolve the problem has focused on observing behaviour in controlled laboratory conditions rather than the messy real world. If there is one piece of evidence which has begun to persuade economists that we sometimes act truly unselfishly, at immediate cost to ourselves even when there are no hidden or future benefits, it is a laboratory experiment, the ultimatum game.

The Ultimatum Game

There are two players, a proposer and a responder, who have to agree on how to share a fixed sum of money. The proposer makes a proposal to the responder on how the money should be split between them. The responder is only allowed to accept or refuse the proposal; he cannot make a counter-offer. If the responder accepts, the money is split as proposed, but if the responder refuses, then both players receive nothing.

There is no doubt what two *Homo economicus* players would do. The proposer would offer a tiny amount to the responder, who would accept, because it is better than nothing. But real people behave differently: the most common proposal is an equal split of the money, and if the proposer offers less than a quarter of the money to the responder, the offer is almost always refused. Most players refer to fairness in explaining their actions. These results are indisputable: they have been observed over hundreds of trials in various cultures, with large and small stakes of money, where the researcher cannot observe the players' choices, and most importantly, where the players are strangers who play the game just once and never meet.[42]

The existence of unselfish acts in laboratory experiments such as the Ultimatum Game has led many more economists to accept the possibility of unselfish behaviour in the outside world too. But it remains just a possibility, because they struggle to see how people's motives can be determined outside the laboratory. So the conventional wisdom remains the first strategy mentioned above, where every apparently unselfish act is argued to involve the pursuit of hidden or future benefits. Some questions arise: can this strategy provide a selfish rationale for all seemingly unselfish behaviour? And does it matter? That is, why does it matter to the rest of us how economists distinguish between selfish and unselfish behaviour? It turns out that the answers to these questions are closely connected.

Why the *Homo economicus* doctrine matters

The most important reason is easy to state: the predictions economists make and the advice they offer depend crucially on the assumption that people are fundamentally self-interested. Following their advice, we see the widespread use of explicit monetary incentives to encourage people to behave in particular ways. For example:

- performance-related pay
- paying people to donate blood
- fining parents who are late collecting their children from nursery
- legal systems to enforce tax compliance which assume and imply that people will evade tax whenever possible
- offering compensation to persuade citizens to accept unpopular government decisions, such as the nearby siting of a nuclear waste facility or a ban on forest logging.

But if people are regularly unselfish, then these policies will backfire, having the opposite effect to that intended, as we will see below. And there are many other examples of government policies which are inefficient: they lead to an unnecessary waste of resources because of the presumption that everyone is selfish. For example:

- setting income tax rates without allowing for intrinsic job satisfaction
- excessive enforcement of fare-paying on public transport
- heavy use of targets and audits in the management of schools, hospitals and universities.

With this much at stake, how can we convince the economists that we are not always selfish?

The story of the lost wallets seems a good place to start. Although it was a contrived experiment, it exactly mimics a familiar real-life situation. Can those who returned the wallets really be understood as acting out of self-interest? The wallet returners incurred a cost in terms of time, effort (and possibly postage); and they were unlikely to be especially concerned with the well-being of the people who had lost wallets, who were strangers to them. Therefore, to explain wallet returning in terms of overall self-interest, economists turn to motives such as guilt avoidance, or the desire for esteem (because you can tell your friends that you returned a stranger's wallet). But these attempts to squeeze complex emotions such as guilt into the simple world of *Homo economicus* are doomed. Emotions cannot be treated as psychic costs and benefits, to be weighed up just like material costs and benefits. Such a cost–benefit view of the emotions treats our conscience as if it were external to us, a kind of virtual ball and chain that stops us from doing what we want.[43] The cost–benefit view of emotions completely misunderstands their role, as shown in the following thought experiment.[44]

The guilt-prevention pill

Imagine that you could take a pill which would remove all feelings of guilt that would otherwise follow from a particular action. Suppose you find a wallet in the street. Now, if guilt is just a psychic cost, you would simply take a pill and keep the wallet (providing of course that the cost of the pill is more than covered by the money in the wallet).

Yet guilt does not work like this. Even if such a pill existed, many people would not take it, knowing that if they did, they would simply feel guilty about the act of taking the pill instead, because the pill does not alter the morality of the situation. Anyone capable of being deterred by guilt would not take the pill, while those willing to take it would not need to bother: they are willing to take a pill because their greed overwhelms their guilt. The general lesson is that attempts to manipulate our emotions by artificial means are usually futile or counter productive. Although the guilt-prevention pill is a thought experiment, the same lessons apply to messier real-world choices.

Israeli day-care centres and *Freakonomics*

Some day-care centres in Israel had a problem. Parents were arriving late to collect their children, forcing some staff to remain beyond closing time. For two economists advising the day-care centre, the solution seemed obvious: fine the late parents.[45] While this would have worked on *Homo economicus*, real parents behaved differently. The number arriving late increased after the introduction of the fine. So the economists switched their focus from financial self-interest to the broader version of self-interest outlined above; they saw the fine as akin to a guilt-prevention pill. The fine, they concluded, was like a price, the price you pay to buy off your guilt. You're paying the fine, so you're entitled to be late. But this interpretation could not predict what happened next. After 16 weeks, the fine was removed. Yet the number of late collections remained as high as it had become under the fines system.

While the economists struggled to reconcile this pattern of behaviour with orthodox economics, at least they recognized the problem.[46] Levitt and Dubner, the authors of *Freakonomics*, missed the point altogether. They announce that 'incentives are the cornerstone of modern life', and repeat this message throughout *Freakonomics*.[47] Many policy entrepreneurs and academic economists would probably agree. Levitt and Dubner add that 'Economists love incentives… The typical economist believes that the world has not yet invented a problem that he cannot fix if given a free hand to design the proper incentive scheme.'[48] Remarkably, Levitt and Dubner use the Israeli day-care centre as their first example – when it shows the exact opposite. The day-care centre tale, and similar accumulating evidence, demonstrates the great difficulty of using incentives to manipulate behaviour in practice. Economists frequently mispredict how people will respond to them. Levitt and Dubner seem determined not to see this, instead hinting that a much larger fine would have solved the problem, presumably because they believe that incentives come in 'three basic flavors … economic, social and moral'; so that more of one will counterbalance less of another.[49] But this is back to the cost–benefit view of emotions again.

For a deeper understanding of the day-care centre story, we must abandon the cost–benefit view. Not only are guilt-avoidance pills futile, but they can provoke resentment against those proffering them. A gift can trigger gratitude or resentment in the recipient, depending on how the recipient perceives the motives of the donor. Similarly, a fine can trigger resentment in parents if they feel manipulated like puppets, rather than consulted as affected parties capable of understanding the day-care centre's problem. In particular, if I feel I am being treated as though I am a selfish *Homo economicus,* prodded by financial carrots and sticks, then I will probably respond by withdrawing favours, cooperation and other forms of unselfish behaviour. In short, people live down to economists' pessimistic expectations of them. The parents continued to arrive late after the fine was abolished because their sense of moral obligation had already been eroded away by the fines system.

Sadly, this is far from the only example of policies based on the self-interest assumption causing people to become *more* self-interested than they were previously. Economists may feel reassured that the self-interest assumption is in this way self-fulfilling, but in reality the process can wreak havoc. In a famous study, *The Gift Relationship,* sociologist Richard Titmuss compared blood collection in Britain and the US.[50] He found there were more blood shortages in the US, arguing that this was due to the fact that not all blood in the US is donated – some is sold. Once blood has a market price, say $200 per transfusion, potential donors see themselves as giving the equivalent of $200, rather than the priceless 'gift of life'. In this way, commercializing blood collection largely destroys the value of the gift, and so less is donated.[51] Although debate continues over exactly *why* donations fall when blood collection is commercialized, the effect itself has been demonstrated repeatedly.[52] More generally, there is overwhelming evidence that introducing monetary incentives can be counterproductive: internal intrinsic motivations to do something for its own sake are eroded by the introduction of external explicit incentives.[53] In one Swiss village, support among residents for the local siting of an unwanted nuclear waste facility *fell* by more than 50 per cent once monetary compensation was offered.[54] And most managers believe that formal performance-related pay schemes undermine employee morale (the reasons are explored in Chapter 7).[55]

As well as the eroding effect of explicit incentives on unselfish intrinsic motivations, exposure to the *Homo economicus* worldview increases selfishness more directly. To begin with, it states that people always behave selfishly. But if I expect others to be selfish towards me, I am less likely to cooperate with them, trust them, or be altruistic, because I do not expect my generosity will be reciprocated. If I expect others to cheat on their taxes or welfare benefits, I will be more likely to cheat too. In sum, expecting selfishness in others, I become more selfish. More obviously, the *Homo economicus* doctrine actively *recommends* selfishness. As we have seen, pursuing self-interest is always seen as rational. Acting otherwise is not. But does anyone really believe this?

Well, economics students seem to – studying economics makes you more selfish. Survey evidence on charitable giving, and laboratory studies of behaviour in games such as the Ultimatum Game, both show economics students becoming more selfish over the duration of their courses.[56] If this kind of intensive exposure to the *Homo economicus* doctrine increases selfishness, there may well be a similar, albeit milder, effect on people with more limited exposure to the doctrine. Does reading *The Economist* or *Freakonomics* make you more selfish? Although exposure to the doctrine from just watching television news is much more limited, the effect may be exaggerated because by that stage the doctrine is caricatured, becoming simply 'Greed is Good'.[57] Unfortunately, in the absence of research studying the impact of the doctrine as presented in the mainstream media, these questions cannot be answered directly. But there is evidence on a related issue. Some constitutional frameworks and legal systems both presume and affirm that citizens can be trusted to act responsibly, cooperate and not always put their narrow self-interest above the common good. Other systems assume and imply the opposite, encouraging their citizens to adopt a *Homo economicus* view of the world. And citizens living in these more distrustful systems are more likely to act selfishly, evading taxation and breaking other laws whenever they expect the benefits to exceed the personal costs.[58]

Even if the *Homo economicus* doctrine does not directly affect how people behave, it affects the moral judgements they make. When the legendary American bank robber Willie Sutton was asked why he robbed banks, he replied, 'Because that's where the money is.'[59] Sutton misses the moral point in a way that is uncannily echoed by Gary Becker in his Nobel Lecture:

> I was puzzled by why theft is socially harmful, since it appears merely to redistribute resources, usually from richer to poorer individuals. I resolved the puzzle by pointing out that criminals spend on weapons and on the value of their time in planning and carrying out their crimes and that such spending is socially unproductive...[60]

When economists redescribe all behaviour as being driven by hidden or overall self-interest, the effects are not limited to poor predictions, bad policies and increased selfishness. The assertion that all behaviour is actually self-interested implies that critics of selfishness, who appeal to morality, delude themselves. So-called ethical behaviour is just as much a matter of personal taste as a taste for chocolate over strawberry ice-cream. Although this view of ethics is not unknown among philosophers,[61] it is rejected by most of them. But whatever its philosophical virtues, economists who adopt this view should be more aware of the implicit value judgements they make. If breaking the law serves the law breaker's self-interest, then it is by definition rational, according to the *Homo economicus* worldview. And it is but a short step from lawbreaking being rational in this technical sense to treating it as rational in the wider sense of being justified by legitimate reasons. The step is taken by those who rest content with a self-interested explanation for action, regardless of the moral reasons for behaving otherwise. Self-interested behaviour becomes understandable, legitimate, justified, even excused. This worldview is pervasive; for instance, it lies behind explanations for lawbreaking which focus solely on the absence of penalties – short jail sentences or inadequate law enforcement. It is as though blame for lawbreaking has been switched from the lawbreakers to the law makers. This conclusion might seem far-fetched, but many economists and policy entrepreneurs following Becker see a particular form of lawbreaking, tax evasion, in just this light. They regard voluntary tax compliance as a mystery. Tax evasion is seen as the norm, the default to be expected, and it is entirely the responsibility of governments, not taxpayers, to address the problem.

While this perspective on tax evasion remains a minority one among economists, many of them side with self-interest when the clash with morality is less stark. Suppose a company dumps toxic waste on a marsh, claiming it 'cannot afford' to dispose of the waste safely. Many economists regard this action as unfortunate, although predictable and understandable if safe disposal is so costly that the firm would go bankrupt (it could not sell its product at the price it would be forced to charge). But they should not be satisfied with this self-interested explanation for the action, because it leaves unanswered the crucial question of why profit, or avoiding bankruptcy, matters more to the company than dumping toxic waste on the marsh. The answer is not self-evident, as a comparison reveals: 'if a firm facing bankruptcy hired gangsters to kill the managers of a competitor, few economists would show the same attitude towards an explanation in terms of economic pressures'.[62] So hidden value judgements determine what counts as an acceptable explanation. Self-interest can trump moral scruples when it comes to dumping toxic waste, but not killing competitors. We may agree with this implicit moral scale – but it ought to be acknowledged. Economics here is not a science.

Finally, for many of us, acting morally is good in itself, and acting selfishly is bad; so an economic way of thinking which leads people to be more selfish is harmful, over and above any unwelcome effects that selfish behaviour may have on outcomes such as charitable giving, blood donation, tax evasion and so on.

I posed two questions a while back. Can the *Homo economicus* doctrine provide a selfish rationale for all seemingly unselfish behaviour? And does it matter how economists distinguish between selfish and unselfish behaviour? Let me now summarize the answers. Insisting on a self-interested story to explain all seemingly unselfish behaviour leads to empty explanations. When self-interest is stretched to include everything, it means nothing. It can explain away blood donation and the day-care centre tale *after* the event, but only by inventing arbitrary, question-begging rationalizations of unselfish internal motives and emotions. But before the event, the *Homo economicus* doctrine often fails to predict behaviour, leading to the wrong policies being adopted. Admittedly, the doctrine is partly self-fulfilling. Policies, organizations and legal systems which assume people are always self-interested tend to bring this behaviour about – but with harmful consequences. Altruism, trust and cooperation are reduced, making previously benign outcomes unachievable. Equally important, the self-interest assumption is not a neutral factual claim but a doctrine which subtly shapes our ethical judgements. I have focused on the way in which it can be used to justify or excuse immoral behaviour. It also supports an assertion mentioned much earlier in the chapter, the view that preference satisfaction makes you better off. This in turn leads to two further ethical judgements which are now very influential – people should get what they want, and more choice is always better. These ideas are increasingly seen as basic ground rules for a modern economy and society. Should we welcome them?

Getting what you want in a world of overwhelming choice

'People should get what they want'

Treating the idea that preference satisfaction makes you better off as a ground rule, an unquestionable fact, commits two fundamental errors. To begin with, it is not a fact but an ethical judgement, because what makes someone better off, what makes for a good life, is a matter of ethical debate. And insofar as it can be treated as a question of fact by setting the ethical disagreements aside, then it is false. We have seen this is so, for two broad reasons. First, I may make mistakes in trying to pursue my own self-interest, what makes me better off. Second, I might not even be trying; I may be intentionally pursuing different goals, moral commitments or the interests of others.

Admittedly, this conclusion clearly rests on some assumption about what counts as my self-interest, what makes me better off. So perhaps we can avoid the conclusion by somehow tying the meaning of 'being better off' to preference satisfaction. After all, preference satisfaction makes you better off on most occasions in practice. From the perspective of an economist advising a benevolent government on how to improve 'quality of life', your preferences are a reliable guide to what makes you better off – arguably the best guide available, without resorting to the kinds of paternalistic, philosophical pronouncements about how to live, which make economists queasy. From this perspective, we can respond to the two broad reasons given above. If the problem with using preference satisfaction as a guide to what makes you better off is that sometimes you have 'mistaken' preferences – such as wanting a cigarette when really you want to give up – then we should focus on the kinds of well-informed preferences that people have after careful consideration of their long-term interests. And these preferences would reflect everything that matters to us, including our moral concerns, and the interests of all other people we care about. There is no suggestion here that you must, to avoid being irrational, pursue your narrow material self-interest.

The upshot is that the so-called fact 'preference satisfaction makes you better off' is replaced with an ethical judgement: the satisfaction of *ideal* preferences makes you better off.[63] This judgement says nothing about whether, in reality, people have mistaken preferences, but it preserves the underlying idea that at least in principle – under ideal conditions – the best way to make people better off is to give them what they want. This idea might seem both trivial and self-evident but it is neither.

It is not trivial because there are intractable problems with adopting 'giving people what they ideally want' as the basic organizing principle for economy and society. To begin with, how do we ensure that the mistakes people make in forming and pursuing their preferences are ignored? In other words, how do we determine what someone's ideal preferences are? This label does not convey how demanding the standard is. 'Perfect preferences' – the preferences of a perfectly rational individual who is perfectly informed and perfectly predicts their future interests – might be a better name. As we have seen, even in the laboratory it is hard to establish which preferences are 'true' and which are erroneous (for example in the colonoscopy experiment), and trying to draw these distinctions outside the laboratory is harder still. Besides, I argued that these distinctions should be thought of as subjective value judgements about what preferences a rational person would have, not objective scientific attempts to uncover true preferences. So if one motive for 'giving people what they ideally want' is to avoid controversial value judgements, then it fails. The mantra is inescapably ethical.

Nor is it a self-evident ideal, because there is a near universal consensus that governments should prioritize satisfying some preferences over others, even if they are equally 'perfect'. For instance, governments should satisfy the preferences for food and shelter of the destitute before addressing other wants. And the consensus seems to go further: some perfect preferences are explicitly rejected; others simply ignored. Racist and sadistic preferences can arguably be expressed by a perfectly informed, perfectly rational individual, yet we rightly reject them. And we ignore preferences that we struggle to make sense of, although they may reflect a perfectly rational, careful consideration of all the consequences. An elderly person may appreciate extra heating in the winter, but she may have a stronger desire to spend a little more on extravagant food for her dog. Nevertheless most of us endorse policies which frustrate her preference, such as heating fuel subsidies rather than pension increases.[64]

Finally, there is a 'paradox of perfect preferences'. Even in principle, a perfectly informed, perfectly rational person would not have perfect preferences. They would *choose* to give up thinking about their interests and options long before they discovered what would be best to do. Up until now in this chapter, I have ignored the huge costs in time and effort that we incur in trying to decide for the best. A cyborg would not face this problem in constructing its preferences, but all humans do. Human preferences are inevitably imperfect, and it is perfectly rational that we abandon thinking about our choices long before we perfect our preferences. Many economists seem to believe this problem can be neatly resolved within the *Homo economicus* framework. Spend more time and effort on decision making, they argue, whenever the extra benefit to the ultimate decision of obtaining more information, thinking about all future consequences, and so on, exceeds the cost of these activities in terms of time and effort. Unfortunately this cost–benefit balancing exercise begets another: how to know *when* the benefits of say, extra information, outweigh the costs of obtaining it? *Homo economicus* would undertake a second cost–benefit exercise to answer this question, and a third to answer an analogous question provoked by the second... Such an infinite regress of decisions would take infinite time and effort to resolve. The idea of perfecting one's preferences leads to an infinite regress of endless decision making.[65] In this way, perfect preferences are not coherently defined even in theory – so it would be foolish to organize economy and society around the ideal of attempting to satisfy them.

'More choice is always better'

Once we recognize the time and effort involved in decision making, it seems clear that more choice is not always better. More choice – increasing the number of options available – adds significantly to the costs of making a decision, in terms of time, effort, money and stress. But advocates of increasing choice believe they have a knock-down argument in its favour: if you do not like more choice, why not just ignore it? People who feel overwhelmed by additional options can simply ignore them. They can choose just from the original range of options and so avoid any additional decision costs. In reality, though, people do not think in this way.[66] Psychologists have found strong evidence that adding extra options discourages people from choosing *any* of them.

The burden of choice

1 *Stereos in stereo.* Researchers asked people whether they would buy a stereo advertised at a bargain price in a shop window. Separately, they were asked whether they would buy either of two bargain stereos similarly advertised, one of them being the same stereo at the same price as in the first case. Adding the extra option, the second bargain stereo, reduced the number of people willing to buy either of them.[67]

2 *Medical excess.* In another study, doctors were presented with the case history of a man suffering from osteoarthritis and asked if they would prescribe a new medicine or refer him to a specialist. Other doctors could choose between *two* new medicines and referral. Only two-thirds as many doctors in the second group chose either medicine; that is, referrals to a specialist doubled.[68]

3 *The Communist party.* In regions of eastern Germany, formerly part of the Communist bloc, people regularly throw parties themed around the drab clothing, food and music of the Communist era. One explanation given by many participants is nostalgia for a simpler consumer society of limited choice. Although this is merely anecdotal 'evidence', these intriguing parties are too well-established social phenomena to be ignored.

Part of the explanation of these and many similar results is that the increased burden of decision making puts people off making a decision altogether. More choice also reduces the apparent attractiveness of whatever we might choose. Both before the moment of choice and afterwards, we keep thinking about the attractive features of the other rejected options, and this kind of brooding undermines the satisfaction associated with the chosen option. Complex choices in reality involve uncomfortable trade-offs, especially uncomfortable if the decision is important. A new job or house will rarely be better than the existing one in every respect; instead it is better in some ways and worse in others. As the number of job options increases, so too do the number of job options which are better than the job we chose in *some* respect, and each such job chips away at the satisfaction from the one we chose. More choice increases both the sense of missed opportunity associated with options not selected, and the chance of disappointment with whatever option we finally choose.

These adverse effects are greatly exacerbated by our feelings of responsibility for our choices: disappointment is bad enough, but regret is worse. Disappointment is what I feel after a bad meal in a restaurant which was selected by a friend. Regret is what I feel if I picked the restaurant. The full force of regret only becomes apparent in important decisions for which we feel painfully responsible. More choice forces this responsibility upon us. As one young person overwhelmed with major life decisions in their twenties put it, 'what happens when you have too many options is that you are responsible for what happens to you'.[69] And rightly, one might retort: personal responsibility should be encouraged. This belief is certainly widely held, and usually linked to a broader set of cultural, ethical and political values. Advertising and rising inequality combine to foster high expectations of achievable material living standards. The culture of individualism places people firmly in control of, and responsible for, their own lives. More choice is promoted as a political goal on the grounds that it brings more freedom. The message is that we now live in a world of unparalleled freedom of choice, which offers great autonomy and opportunity, if only we would embrace it. People who shun it are seen as old-fashioned, lacking self-confidence, lazy or incompetent. Defenders of this brave new world conclude by again pressing the rhetorical question posed earlier: if you do not like more choice, why not just ignore it?

We can now see that this perspective is naive: humans do not simply ignore the introduction of new options. And while we are in one sense free to choose, we are victims of psychological mechanisms such as brooding about missed opportunities, and feelings of disappointment and regret, all of which are exacerbated by increased choice. To this list can be added the manipulative influences of advertising discussed earlier in the chapter; it is the job of advertising and marketing to make new options hard to ignore. Beyond these insistent psychological pressures, there is the philosophy of the brave new worldview itself, which strongly encourages embracing wider choice for the sake of our own emancipation, not ignoring it. In a culture which sanctifies choice, it is unsurprising that people pay attention to new choices, even if they are aware of the added decision costs. In Britain, digital TV has seduced with promises of an exciting explosion of TV channel choice – even though we recognize the absurdity of spending so long scanning through the programme choices that, by the time we find what we want, it has finished.

While few people consciously endorse the sanctification of choice, many embrace a closely related idea – choice as the expression of identity. You are what you wear; you are what you eat. Once upon a time, before the growth of internet shopping, people living outside large cities were constrained in their shopping choices to the relatively limited selection available locally. But nowadays no one can hide behind the excuse of limited local choice. In a world of unlimited choice, our purchases reveal our tastes: we are responsible for constructing our consumer identity, whether we like it or not. The choice *not* to participate in the consumer identity game has effectively disappeared. Although the game is liberating for many, it is a burden for others, and for good reasons. Especially for those on low incomes, it can undermine self-respect, and reduce social mobility and participation in the community. And the rest of us may come to resent the time and effort devoted to our increasingly elaborate lives as consumers, at the expense of other activities.

I am not arguing that choice is harmful. But more choice is not always better. As well as making us miserable via the psychological mechanisms already mentioned, there are deeper problems. Although the research is still tentative, there is some evidence that the kind of freedom of choice offered by the new consumer culture is associated with intense feelings of regret and self-blame, and these feelings in turn are linked to the explosive rise in rates of clinical depression.[70] In case this sounds exaggerated, consider attitudes to body shape and weight. Cultures that promote thinness as an ideal for women have much higher rates of eating disorders, and relatively higher rates of depression among women.[71] Implicit in these cultures is the idea that thinness is a choice, despite evidence that, for some people, genes and early childhood experience mean it is highly unlikely they can ever become thin.[72] More choice turns out to be an illusion.

The same illusion arises in many everyday choices too. We see an additional option as a sign of expanding choice, but neglect to notice that the cumulative effect of a series of additional options may be the elimination of some other options entirely.[73] Digital TV certainly widens channel choice, but with viewers so widely dispersed, private TV channels can rarely afford to make very expensive programmes such as major drama series. In this respect, programme choice is reduced. Car owners can choose to go virtually wherever they want, whenever they want, but the car-based society precludes other choices: many people have little choice of shops and amenities within walking distance, even fewer can choose to live in a home free from traffic noise and pollution where children can play safely in the street outside. This example also shows how increased choice for some people, some of the time (motorists) is often accompanied by reduced choice for others (almost everyone else, including car owners when they are not driving). Similarly, the internet has widened choice for most of us but those with limited or no access (typically the poor and elderly) face reduced choice because some services and information are only available online.

Summing up, it is clear that economists and policy makers should be aware of the psychological limitations of human decision making, and its costs in terms of time and effort, before advocating policies which increase choice. There is no realistic default option of ignoring new choices, so more choice can leave us worse off. And sometimes the increase in choice is itself an illusion. But the crucial lesson is less obvious: more choice is not an ideal. The sanctification of choice as an end in itself increases the pressure to choose and the sense of failure when the selected option turns out to be less than perfect. This is ironic, because perfect choice is impossible. The paradox of perfect preferences shows that it is impossible to mimic *Homo economicus* without spending infinite time and effort on decision making. More choice is not an ideal, because perfect choice is self-contradictory.

Conclusion: Ethical economics

The sparseness and simplicity of the economists' theory of how we choose is both a strength and a weakness. It is a strength because, other things being equal, simple theories are better than complicated ones. And because the theory is so minimalist, it can be applied in almost any context. There is nothing in the theory which assumes or requires that the choices it analyses are those made by consumers while shopping for the things that consumers normally buy. So it can be generalized from the sovereign consumer to *Homo economicus*. But the context-free minimalism of the theory is also its greatest weakness. It tempts us into thinking that choices can be understood without reference to their context. Just because the theory *can* be pressed into service in almost any context does not imply that, alone, the theory will tell us much. So in practice economists must add extra assumptions, about how we choose, or how we should choose. This is where the value judgements enter. Throughout this chapter I have shown how these ethical assumptions repeatedly creep into the analysis. They are inevitable, given the subject matter of economics. We should not try to expunge them, but simply recognize when they arise and what they are. We will look at economics in a different way. Ethics and economics are inextricably interlinked. The ethical principles we adopt are both causes and effects of important economic outcomes. And these principles are themselves affected by how economists describe and judge them.

Of course I have made my own judgements in this chapter. *Homo economicus* is not just mistaken as a description of how we choose; it is not a model for how we ought to choose either. Encouraging people to emulate the model has harmful consequences. Altruism, trust and cooperation are undermined. Immoral behaviour is excused. And the facts of human psychology imply we will often be happier behaving less like *Homo economicus,* not more.[74] We need a much richer understanding of choice than *Homo economicus* provides, one which explicitly incorporates emotions as well as reasons. A vivid insight into life as *Homo economicus* is provided by the neuroscientist Antonio Damasio's studies of patients suffering from damage to the part of the brain responsible for the emotions. Damasio was trying to arrange the date of his next meeting with one such patient:

> The patient pulled out his appointment book and began consulting the calendar... For the better part of a half-hour, the patient enumerated reasons for and against each of the two dates: previous engagements, proximity to other engagements, possible meteorological conditions, virtually anything that one could reasonably think about concerning a simple date... [H]e was now walking us through a tiresome cost–benefit analysis, an endless outlining and fruitless comparison of options and possible consequence... [We] finally did tell him, quietly, that he should come on the second of the alternative dates. His response was equally calm and prompt. He simply said: 'That's fine.'[75]

Developing a better understanding of choice is the task of another book. In the rest of this one I will explore in more detail some of the themes raised so far: whether economic growth makes us better off (Chapter 3), ideas of entitlement and just deserts (Chapter 4), the meaning and measurement of happiness (Chapter 5), whether all options can be compared and ranked, especially in terms of money (Chapters 6 and 7), and the implications of assuming people are selfish (Chapter 7).

Chapter Three

Two Myths about Economic Growth

To what purpose is all the toil and bustle of this world? … It is our vanity which urges us on. (Adam Smith, *Theory of Moral Sentiments*)

Economists take for granted that higher output per capita means higher utility and increased happiness. (Olivier Blanchard, *Macroeconomics*)

The vast majority of European Union citizens do not make a connection between their quality of life and the economic situation in their country. It is therefore necessary to eliminate this discrepancy, otherwise it may eventually create a problem when it comes to explaining certain public policies. (European Commission, 'Eurobarometer' report)

Economic growth is the dominant aim of government policy. Although this states the obvious, its implications are grossly underestimated. The pursuit of economic growth is taken so much for granted that it often goes unnoticed. Yet it is the canvas on which policy is painted, and it colours almost everything a government does. The growth imperative demands a fast-flowing transport system, which in turn means that some deaths and accidents must be tolerated. It has led to irreversible changes to our environment, such as the loss of species and unique habitats, and fossil-fuel emissions which make substantial climate change now unavoidable. It encourages governments to narrow the focus of education from a broad preparation for life to the development of skills which have economic value in markets. It lies behind every news report on the advantages of globalization, the need for labour market flexibility, and the pros and cons of US and European 'economic models'. As these examples show, the pursuit of economic growth influences our everyday lives in countless ways, far beyond the intuitive idea that we all have a bit more cash to spare.

None of this is to suggest that a zero-growth economy would be desirable. A zero-growth economy would probably bring higher unemployment, which might persist even if radical changes to our working practices were implemented. The aim of this chapter is instead to debunk two myths about economic growth:

- it makes people happier
- it makes desirable tax-funded services such as health care and education more affordable.

The thinking behind the first myth will be familiar from the last chapter: more growth–more consumption–more satisfaction. Most economics textbooks make no mention of a link between growth and happiness; they simply assume one, as the above quotation from Olivier Blanchard suggests (Blanchard's textbook is a rare exception). Similarly, economists use the broad-sounding term 'standard of living' interchangeably with 'GDP per head', implying living standards are solely determined by economic growth. The second myth is more sophisticated and appeals to people who do not believe the first myth, but still seek to justify economic growth. The audience for this second myth may be smaller, but since it includes politicians and policy entrepreneurs, it may be more influential.

Happiness and economic growth

The first myth is essentially 'growth buys happiness'. For many people it is so obviously false that it begs the question: does anyone believe this? Do governments really seek economic growth on this basis? This is not the place to jump into an historical study of why governments have pursued growth, or a sociological analysis of what they really believe. But our past pursuit of growth and its adoption as a measure of progress need not be so mysterious. Economic growth *is* a good indicator of progress in increasing the consumption and production of the goods and services traded in markets. Until very recently, this kind of progress was essential to any hope of increased happiness. Adequate food and shelter for all would have been impossible without economic growth. So for most of our history, economic growth has meant progress, and greater happiness. The only problem with this explanation is that it suggests a better target for government policy all along – why not pursue that elusive happiness directly, or at least pursue some more obvious measure of quality of life directly, rather than hoping it will drop out of economic growth as a by-product? Economic growth leaves out so much, often arbitrarily. For example, unpaid housework is just as valuable to our standard of living as paid housework, but it is ignored by measures of growth. Surely there is *some* measure of quality of life that is a less misleading proxy than economic growth?

Until very recently, governments, advised by economists, have answered this question negatively. But despite the question's importance, a key reason for economists' skepticism is not widely known. It began with a relatively obscure philosophical principle, embraced by most economists around the time economic progress was first systematically measured. It is known as 'the impossibility of interpersonal utility comparisons'. Take any measure of overall quality of life you care to name – happiness, 'well-being', life satisfaction – and define it as you wish. (It does not matter which concept you choose, because economists have used 'utility' as a kind of generic label for them all.) Then the principle says that person A's progress, prosperity or success according to that measure cannot be compared with person B's. There is no means of measuring, say, my happiness in such a way as to make it comparable with yours. And without interpersonal comparability, we cannot add up the individual 'happiness scores' to obtain an overall measure of happiness for society as a whole.

The economists and philosophers who insist that interpersonal comparisons are impossible argue, in essence, that we cannot get inside another's head. As William Stanley Jevons, the economist first associated with this view, argued: 'Every mind is inscrutable to every other mind [so] no common denominator of feeling is possible.'[1] But if interpersonal comparisons of feelings and happiness levels require getting inside another's head, then so too does making sense of what people say. And yet we seem to manage to communicate satisfactorily with each other most of the time. As one blunt retort to Jevons put it: 'Nobody can prove that anybody besides himself exists, but, nevertheless, everybody is quite sure of it.'[2] For many years the possibility of interpersonal utility comparisons seemed lost beneath these murky philosophical waters, which might seem to explain why most economists were unwilling to admit the possibility. But then we would expect economists to be influenced by the emergence of something like a consensus among philosophers that interpersonal comparisons are possible.[3] In fact this near-consensus has had little impact. And most undergraduate textbooks, if they confront the issue at all, remain steadfastly on the fence, dismissing the entire question as a value judgement. This raises a more convincing explanation of economists' skepticism: interpersonal comparisons were regarded as dangerously unscientific, because they cannot be based on observation alone. If economists adhere to a naive vision of science, then they will be reluctant to modify their views on explicitly philosophical grounds.

It is against this background that the recent explosive development of 'happiness economics' is so significant. Happiness economics offers indirect evidence that interpersonal comparisons are possible, and points to the undoubtedly scientific discipline of neurophysiology to provide more direct support. This combination may finally persuade economists to take interpersonal comparisons seriously, and in turn lead them, when advising governments, to consider the impact of economic growth on happiness.

Together, the belief in the impossibility of interpersonal comparisons and the importance of basic material goods for quality of life go a long way towards explaining why economic growth has historically been given strong priority. But this priority now looks like a relic of the past: there is accumulating neuroscientific evidence that interpersonal comparisons are possible, and economic evidence that material progress is no longer bringing increased happiness. The neuroscience is discussed in Chapter 5; we begin here with the evidence that has recently had the most impact – the evidence from happiness economics. Three broad conclusions emerge:

Conclusion 1. Above a certain level of national income, people in richer countries are no happier than people in poorer countries.[4]

As the following diagram indicates, above about $10,000, there is little if any association between additional income and increased happiness. Countries as diverse as Colombia and the Philippines show similar happiness levels to far richer countries such as France and Canada, and their people appear happier than those in Portugal and the Czech Republic.

Income and happiness across countries

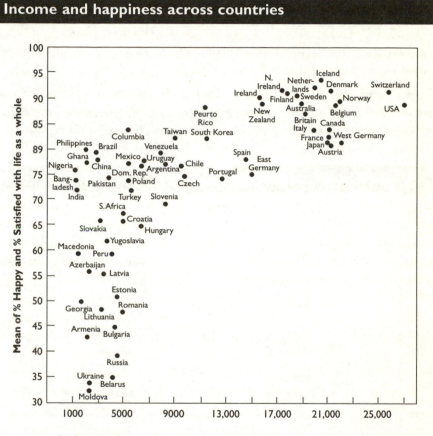

GNP/capita (World Bank purchasing power parity estimates, 1995 US$)

Source: Inglehart and Klingemann (2000), p168

There is an obvious explanation for these patterns: poverty causes unhappiness, because it is associated with poor food and water, inadequate education and health services, and shorter life spans. All these indicators of quality of life are lower in poor countries. However, once poverty is alleviated, further increases in income may not bring greater happiness;

any apparent association in the above diagram may be due to other factors correlated with income rather than income itself. For example, people in richer countries may be happier not merely because they are rich, but because richer countries are more likely to be democratic and respect human rights. These differences suggest it may be more useful to examine trends within a country.

Conclusion 2. Within each country, increases in income over time do not make people happier.

There is strong evidence to support this conclusion for the US, Britain and Japan.[5] Perhaps the most striking example is Japan, where life satisfaction remains unchanged despite a sixfold increase in income:

Income and life satisfaction in Japan

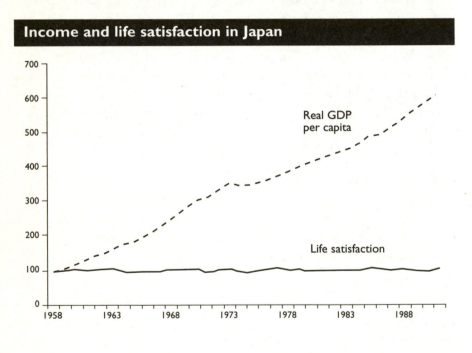

Source: Frey and Stutzer (2002), p9

In continental Europe the data have only been available since 1975; they show a slight rise in happiness since then, but one which is very small relative to the large increase in income over the period.[6] There is further evidence from studies of specific cohorts of people; they show that the average happiness of a generation of people remains largely unchanged over time, even though their income rises over the years, and then falls in retirement.[7]

The conclusion so far is clear: there is little or no evidence, across countries and over time, that the higher incomes arising from economic growth bring increased happiness. And if we look within a particular country at a particular time, then we might expect to find there is no relationship between income and happiness there either. So it is surprising to find that there is:

Conclusion 3. Within each country at a given time, richer people are happier than poorer ones.

Since it provides the first evidence of a link between income and happiness, and seems to conflict with the previous findings, this claim is crucial, but unfortunately it is also the one for which the evidence is least secure. The link between income and happiness fades for the rich: as incomes rise, a given increase in income is associated with progressively smaller increases in happiness.[8] And factors such as health and unemployment may explain the correlation at lower incomes: the poor may be less happy because they are on average less healthy, and more likely to be unemployed.[9] These doubts suggest a more cautious statement:

Conclusion 3 (revised). Within each country at a given time, rich people are slightly happier than those on middle incomes, and both groups are significantly happier than the poor; the link is weakened after allowing for other factors (particularly unemployment and health).

Before going any further, an explanation of what is meant here by 'happiness' is long overdue. Do not assume that the researchers – I shall call them 'happiness experts' – have spent much time grappling with this question. Their priority is empirical measurement, and 'happiness' simply means whatever respondents to survey questions take it to mean. All the evidence reported above is based on surveys of happiness or life satisfaction; the two questions most commonly asked are:

> Taken all together, how would you say things are these days – would you say that you are very happy, pretty happy, or not too happy?[10]

On the whole are you very satisfied, fairly satisfied, not very satisfied, or not at all satisfied with the life you lead?'[11]

It is easy to be dismissive about attempts to measure happiness (or life satisfaction) via these naive, prosaic questions. The survey approach of happiness economics will be assessed at length in Chapter 5, but in the meantime we can still reach the following limited conclusion: happiness economics offers the only method yet devised of measuring the relationship between income and happiness, and it provides very little support for the view that economic growth buys happiness. Conclusion 3 should not be understood to suggest otherwise: it suggests that what matters is *relative* income, and economic growth does not affect this, insofar as it leaves the distribution of income unchanged. If growth alters the distribution by increasing inequality – the experience of Britain and the US in recent years – then this will have a separate adverse effect on happiness.[12] The additional happiness gained by those who become relatively richer is outweighed by the fall in happiness of those who become poorer.[13]

These findings are also consistent with other indicators of happiness or its absence. For example, within a given country at a particular time, higher income is associated with increased life expectancy, echoing Conclusion 3.[14] And in most Western countries over the past few decades, despite higher incomes, the incidence of depression and mental illness has been rising steeply.[15] This is consistent with Conclusion 2. More controversially, it is arguable that recent economic growth has been associated with adverse effects on overall happiness, including longer working hours, damage to local environments, and erosion of local communities due to increased job mobility.[16] (Against this, growth increases happiness if it reduces unemployment. I return to this 'costs of economic growth' debate below.)

Although some economists have begun to dispute it,[17] the overall evidence that economic growth no longer brings increases in happiness is persuasive. But it would be more convincing if our three conclusions had an underlying explanation, and without one it is impossible to predict how economic growth will affect happiness in future.

The most plausible explanation begins with the powerful psychological evidence of Chapter 2, showing that money does not buy happiness. People become accustomed to any increases in their material living standards through a process of adaptation. And they constantly compare themselves with others, with rivalry preventing general increases in material prosperity from making anyone feel better off. What follows can be seen as a 'top-down' economics complement to that 'bottom-up' psychological analysis; taken together, the implications are very different from what the psychological story alone might suggest.

Adaptation

At first glance adaptation seems to provide a neat and complete answer to why money does not buy happiness. Like the lottery winners, we rapidly become accustomed to increased material affluence. We are on a happiness treadmill. Adaptation is clearly an important part of the story, especially in some instances – for example, in the case of the affluent individual struggling to understand why they do not feel happier now than 20 years ago when they were an impoverished student with few material possessions. But the economist's analysis operates at the level of society, not the individual, and it immediately raises the question: if adaptation has always been with us, why did growth deliver happiness in the past, but no longer? It is fair to say that the happiness experts' answer is less well developed here. The usual explanation is that in the past material progress made a real and lasting difference to our living standards, but now we have reached a point where further economic growth is superfluous. The rough idea seems to be that we did not adapt to past material gains – they were 'real and lasting' – but we do adapt to present and future gains. Yet this intuitive explanation simply passes the question about our break with the past one step back: *why* adaptation now, but not then? Since it is unlikely that there has been a shift in our basic psychological mechanisms, the explanation must be that the pattern of consumption has changed, *and* we adapt more readily to some things than others. As discussed in Chapter 2, there is mounting evidence that we become much more rapidly accustomed to gains and losses in material possessions than to changes to other things that matter to us, such as our work, family or personal relationships.

Consider Henrietta the high-flyer, who moves from a high-paid job to one offering still greater financial rewards, because she anticipates that she will be happier with more money. (Henrietta fails to notice that the pay increase provided by her last job did not make her happier.) Crucially, her pay increases are accompanied by sacrifices such as longer hours and increased commuting time. Henrietta might reply smartly: 'Well, if we rapidly get used to every change, then I will soon become accustomed to longer hours and more commuting. So why worry?' In fact, as the economist Robert Frank has emphasized, we adapt fully to the pain of a long commute through heavy traffic only slowly, if at all. There is rich evidence that long-distance commuters are more likely to suffer emotional problems upon arrival, higher blood pressure, suppressed immune function, various cancers, and a shorter life span.[18] The incidence of these effects rises with the length of commute, and is lower for those who commute by public transport, and lower still for non-commuters. Even city bus drivers, who have had great opportunity to adapt to the stress of driving in heavy traffic, suffer persistent long-term stress and are more likely to retire early due to ill health.[19] In contrast, Frank has also documented evidence that the positive effects on happiness and physical health of exercise for 45 minutes a day, or more social contact with friends, or longer holidays, or more autonomy in the workplace, all persist over time.[20] We do not simply adapt to them and return to our previous happiness levels. This kind of 'consumption', then, is much less prone to be whittled away by adaptation than the more usual consumption of material possessions.

To explain the long-term trends in growth and happiness, these differences in adaptation need to be combined with evidence on changing consumption patterns. And it does seem plausible that much of our historic material progress brought lasting increases in happiness through changes to which we did not readily adapt, if at all. Economic growth paid for lasting improvements in health and education, better working conditions, and a civilized society with relatively little crime. Partly because of this, in recent times opportunities for material improvement which is not vulnerable to rapid adaptation have declined, while those *adverse* effects of growth to which we do not readily adapt have spread. Examples include rises in crime, working hours, perceived job insecurity and traffic congestion; but falls in trust, quiet open space, long-term relationships, family stability and social life. For many of these negative developments, there is concrete evidence of slow adaptation, although such a broad argument inevitably involves some speculation.[21] But even if the task of explaining past trends is incomplete, some questions can nevertheless be answered. To begin with, it is clear that, contrary to some churlish doomsayers, further economic growth is not worthless. Precisely because adaptation is more pronounced for some things than others, there is the possibility of directing the fruits of future economic growth towards those goods, experiences and social states which are not as prone to adaptation. For example, resources could be directed towards improving public transport in order to cut commuting times, rather than tax cuts to facilitate across-the-board increases in consumption. The possibilities for redirecting the benefits of growth are much broader and more radical than this banal example suggests, and I outline some options below. But first we must understand why, if spending differently would make us happier, we have not already done it. The answer lies in the other underlying explanation of why growth does not buy happiness.

Rivalry

In Chapter 2, we saw how our lives as consumers are shaped by competition with others. So it is hardly surprising that there is very strong evidence that relative income has more effect on happiness than absolute income.[22] People compare themselves to others, and define what is a satisfactory level of income for now, or the one they aspire to for the future, in terms of the incomes of those in the comparison group. If my peers earn more than before, I will be less happy unless my income rises too. This is why so many employers encourage a culture where employees do not disclose their salary levels to each other. On a subject where some people might not be entirely truthful, many economists find the evidence based on peoples' behaviour, rather than surveys, more convincing. It shows that people mainly compare themselves with those with the same personal characteristics, particularly gender, education and occupation.[23] But there are comparisons closer to home too: the more your spouse earns, the less satisfied you are likely to be with your job.[24] And a woman is more likely to take paid employment if her sister's husband is earning more than her own husband.[25] One survey asked a group of Harvard students to choose between two possible worlds:[26]

A You earn $50,000 a year, and others earn on average $25,000.
B You earn $100,000 a year, and others earn on average $250,000.

It may come as no surprise that most chose the first scenario, but less obvious is the fact that relative position matters more for some goods than others. The students were also asked to choose between another pair of alternatives (assumed to be entirely independent of the choice above):

C You have 2 weeks' vacation, and others have 1 week.
D You have 4 weeks' vacation, and others have 8 weeks.

With holiday entitlements, it seems that relative position mattered much less, since only 20 per cent chose the first scenario.

Some early investigators of relative position assumed that *only* relative consumption levels matter for some goods while *only* absolute consumption matters for others. Of course life is more complex. The latest research confirms this: for almost all goods both relative and absolute levels of consumption matter, with relative consumption being the dominant influence for some goods, and absolute consumption for others.[27] But what makes relative position more important for some goods than others? Since concerns with relative position are a major factor in preventing growth bringing extra happiness, explaining why relative position matters brings us to the heart of understanding why growth does not buy happiness. And it raises the possibility of switching consumption towards goods where relative position matters less, so that growth can bring increases in happiness after all.

There are several interrelated explanations of why relative position matters more for some goods. One explanation is status-seeking and conspicuous consumption. This idea has become so prominent that many seem to think that 'concern with relative position or relative consumption' is just a long-winded version of 'status-seeking'. But despite its popularity among economists,[28] this explanation does not take us very far along. To begin with, there are many forms of status and many ways to achieve it beyond increasing relative consumption. The natural way to understand status-seeking in consumption is as part of the broader development of image and identity through the symbolic meanings of different goods.[29] But since almost all acts of consumption involve these symbols, they all involve some kind of concern with status too, and it is hard to pin down which consumption is more status-driven. Put another way, 'status-seeking' does not explain the evidence: relative income seems likely to be a matter of status, but why not relative vacation length too? *Why* do people not envy others' longer holidays, if they envy their higher income?

In some cases the answer is that people know how much others earn, but not their holiday entitlement. This brings us to one general explanation of why some goods are more 'positional' than others. Relative consumption of some goods is unimportant simply because it is unknown. I do not know whether I am consuming more or less of some goods than my peers, because I do not know how much they are consuming. It might be called a case of *inconspicuous* consumption.

But obviously this answer does not address the research mentioned above, where the question stated the holiday entitlements of others. If 'status-seeking' does not distinguish income from holiday entitlements, then something else must. It seems that an increase in your income may have an adverse effect on me in a way that an increase in your holiday entitlement does not. If some goods are absolutely scarce, then only those with the highest relative income will be able to afford them. A reduction in my relative income then implies a reduction in my opportunity to consume such goods. These are *positional goods*, since consumption is affected by relative position.

Sir Roy Harrod, friend of Keynes and originator of the theory of economic growth, was the first to note the existence of positional goods. But Harrod did not attach much importance to his small contribution, a two-page article for a US conference, confessing later that he wrote it mainly because the conference organizers heavily subsidized his air fare to the US...[30] So it was not until years later that the significance of positional goods was first appreciated, by Fred Hirsch. The essential feature of positional goods is some kind of inherent scarcity, so someone cannot ensure access to these goods simply by becoming wealthier. Hirsch was the first economist to realize that inherent scarcity comes in various guises, and suggested an explicit categorization of different scarcities (see Box on p60).[31]

Absolute physical scarcities generate the most obvious positional goods. There is no possibility of producing any more van Goghs, no matter how great the demand, so consumers must be willing to pay more than their rivals to obtain one: only relative income matters. The same is true of any good subject to absolute supply restrictions.

Sometimes the supply restriction is not physical but socially induced, because some things are only desired *if* they are sufficiently scarce.

Diverse scarcities: Diverse positional goods

I Physical scarcity: e.g. natural landscape, 'Old Master' paintings.
II Social scarcity:
    1 Direct. Satisfaction derives from scarcity itself – 'pure' positional
       goods, e.g. personalized car number plates, 'limited edition' products.
    2 Indirect. Satisfaction derives from the *combination* of intrinsic
       characteristics and scarcity to reduce congestion:
       a Physical congestion, e.g. sports cars (low car ownership reduces
          traffic congestion and hence increases satisfaction).
       b Social congestion, e.g. higher education (access to elite jobs
          increased if few others have equally high educational attainment).

Examples include personalized car number plates; 'limited edition' products (football shirts, Gucci handbags); and wine bought because of its cost or rarity, not its taste. These goods have a mainly symbolic function to signal the consumer's status, image or group identity. Arguably almost all the satisfaction they provide is due to their relative scarcity. They are positional in the purest sense, since they would have little value if made available to all who desired them regardless of relative position. The football shirt may be affordable for most people, but it would lose its symbolic value if it were available to anyone who wanted it. Demand must exceed supply, so relative income matters.

In these cases, scarcity is the *reason* why the item is desired. Something may be desired instead because of its intrinsic characteristics, yet scarcity emerges as a desirable by-product, since it enables much more satisfaction to be had from the item in use. A sports car is much more desirable if car ownership is low so there are open roads to roar along. A house in the outer suburbs is more attractive if there are few others in the area, so it is peaceful and the roads into the city are not congested. These are examples of scarcity driven by physical congestion, but congestion may also have social roots. Leadership is not comfortably shared. I might be interested in the post of vice-president at a bank because of its intrinsic attractions, but nevertheless, as Hirsch puts it, 'the first thing one wants to know … is how many others there are'.[32] Education is perhaps the best example of a positional good caused by social congestion. There are by definition few elite occupations, conferring status, power and privilege, and *relative* educational attainment controls access to them. Now that so many young people obtain a degree, someone in that age group must obtain a good class of degree or one from an elite university, or a postgraduate degree, in order to distinguish themselves from the crowd. A plain undergraduate degree may have intrinsic attractions, but its overall appeal would be greatly enhanced by its scarcity.

Of course the appeal of many positional goods cuts across these motivations; again education is a good example. Tom values his economics degree course largely because of his intrinsic interest in the subject (this is a fictitious example). Dick has no intrinsic interest, but wants to pursue a career in finance, and a good economics degree on his CV will greatly increase the chance of a job interview. Harry wants a first-class degree purely to show his peers that he is cleverer than them. For all three, education is a positional good, although much less so for Tom. Dick's positional concerns are a by-product of (social) congestion among applicants for financial occupations. Harry is a pure status-seeker; a first-class degree is valuable if and only if few obtain one.

This categorization of different forms of inherent scarcity, combined with the empirical evidence that relative consumption matters, leads to the conclusion that many goods have positional characteristics to some extent, but some are more positional than others. This will come as a shock to the average economist, who may be dimly aware of positional goods, but only dimly, because economists have been taught that they are perverse exceptions, not the norm. (Although the boundary between positional and non-positional goods is not a sharp one, for the sake of simplicity I will continue to write as if it were.)

It is time to sum up the discussion so far. The analysis of adaptation and rivalry from Chapter 2 has been developed in a number of ways. The causes of rivalry are much deeper and more diverse than 'status-seeking'. Whether 'economic growth buys happiness' depends not just on the psychological phenomena of adaptation and rivalry, but on the way in which these affect different forms of consumption differently. We adapt to some goods – and 'bads' – much more readily than to others; and analogously, rivalry is much more pervasive over some goods than others. The discussion of adaptation concluded by asking why, if spending differently would make us happier, we have not already done it. The same point can be made about rivalry, because by changing how we spend our money, we can affect the extent to which relative income matters. It would seem that, as individuals, we can sidestep the frustrating competition over relative position, which is bound to bring disappointment for most of us, by shifting consumption towards goods where rivalry is insignificant. So what is stopping us? The obstacle is that these proposals are mostly misunderstood. They are wrongly interpreted as focusing on individual action – encouraging people to change their consumption patterns through education and self-help. But that is only part of the solution.

Self-help is not enough

In recent years the psychological research on adaptation and rivalry has become increasingly well known, and a particular story of why growth does not bring more happiness is increasingly told. It is heavy with irony: we pursue growth because it supposedly brings a kind of psychological satisfaction (happiness), but we do not succeed precisely because of our own psychological flaws. Adaptation and rivalry mean we have only ourselves to blame for the disappointments of economic growth. The solution is better self-understanding, and there are plenty of self-help manuals on offer.

This story is very misleading. It suggests that only unilateral action by the individual can help – presumably with business as usual for political and economic policy. It is true that greater self-awareness of the extent to which we adapt to increases in income should be strongly encouraged. But even here, it is important to recognize that society should be organized in light of our psychological make-up – including our tendency to adapt – rather than some idealized notion of *Homo economicus*, who never tires of material abundance. So, adaptation alone has significant implications for government policy.

However, it is the implications of rivalry which have been most misunderstood. The portrayal of rivalry as status-seeking or envy fits in well with the story of humanity as a crooked timber. Concern to maintain relative status or relative position shows the individual must be duped by advertising, or driven by envy or some other foolish or morally reprehensible motive. There are two distinct errors in this description: first, that concern with relative position implies the individual is ultimately motivated by envy; second, even if this is not the case, attempts to *improve* relative position are irrational – a futile waste of time and effort. The first error arises from interpreting rivalry as motivated by pure status-seeking alone. Other categories of positional good are ignored. Even when someone does appear to be driven by envy, the true picture may be more benign. Buying a grand and fashionable house may be less about status-seeking than a desire to live in the catchment area of a good local school. The second error is less obvious. It confuses irrationality for the individual with irrationality for the group. Suppose I am at a sports match. I stand up to gain a better view. This is a rational act, even if almost simultaneously, everyone around me stands up too, so that now I can see no better, and I knew that would happen. Regardless of what others do, I am better off standing up. If they remain seated my gain is obvious. If they all stand, I must stand too, otherwise I will see nothing. Of course everyone follows this reasoning, so we all stand up. We are collectively worse off than if we all remain seated, but individually rational. The problem is that we cannot coordinate our actions. Exactly this coordination problem applies to positional goods. Each of us tries to get ahead in the race for positional goods. I try to signal my superior ability by securing an additional educational qualification; you attempt to buy a peaceful house in the suburbs. But others do the same, so the suburbs are no longer peaceful, and my educational attainment is no better than my contemporaries. As Hirsch put it, 'Consumers, taken together, get a product they did not order.'[33] In this process of chasing positional goods, there is much waste of time, effort and other resources. In extreme cases we would prefer the positional good to be literally unobtainable (or have never existed) so that the wasteful chase is avoided. And yet, failing that, it is still rational for each of us to join the chase. In very crowded cities, cars are increasingly this kind of positional good. We would all prefer an effective public transport system (even if cars are banned in the city centre), and yet in its absence we are forced to buy a car, fully aware that we will spend hours sitting in traffic jams with thousands of others.

Some economists offer a different interpretation of the 'people have only themselves to blame' theme, but one that again directs attention towards the individual and away from economic and political priorities. Confronted with the evidence of the costs of economic growth mentioned above (work–life imbalance, environmental damage, erosion of local communities etc.), the economist agrees that growth has costs, but it has material benefits too. There is a trade-off and in choosing, say, a lucrative job with long hours away from home, many people show they prefer material benefits to time at home or community involvement. If people did not want the benefits of growth, they would not pay the price and growth would be slower. The economist has a point: it is not enough merely to draw attention to the costs of economic growth in order to demonstrate that growth does not buy happiness. Some environmentalists have overlooked this essential point, and consequently appear genuinely mystified that growth continues to be pursued enthusiastically in the face of such obvious costs. The significance of the happiness research is that it claims to show that the *net* impact of growth on happiness is negligible (and possibly negative), even allowing for its material benefits. And adaptation and rivalry offer an overall explanation of this result, in a way that simply documenting impacts on communities, work–life balance and the environment does not. The economist's interpretation here does not represent people as irrational dupes – on the contrary, it swings too far the other way, into the world of consumer sovereignty and the revealed preference argument introduced in Chapter 2. Everyday choices do *not* reveal that people prefer the benefits of growth to its costs, because these choices are buffeted by external forces (the inherent scarcity of positional goods and the coordination problem) and involuntary internal psycho-logical mechanisms (relative income as a rule of thumb, underestimating adaptation).

So self-help is not enough: individuals acting alone cannot overcome adaptation, rivalry and the social limits to growth. New political and economic policies which move beyond the unquestioning pursuit of economic growth are just as important.

Making growth happier

Thus far, little has been said about the meaning of 'economic growth'. The textbook definition is that it is the growth rate of national product. There are various technical distinctions between the different definitions of national product, such as gross national product (GNP) and gross domestic product (GDP), but they need not concern us. However defined, national product can be measured by adding up all the money incomes derived from economic activity; dividing this total by population size, a figure for average income per head in that country is obtained. This is why, in a primitive definitional sense, economic growth must imply higher average incomes. But a much deeper understanding of growth is to be had by appreciating what causes it. Matters rapidly become complex and controversial if we attempt to trace the causal chain very far back, but the first step is revealing. Assuming a stable population, most growth in advanced economies is caused by productivity improvements. Again, we can gloss over the technical details; 'productivity improvements' simply refers to changes which enable resources to be used more efficiently. There is more output from the same inputs. Workers may have adopted more efficient working practices, or there may have been some technical innovation which allows material inputs to be used more productively. These are just two of many possibilities which in the real economy are deeply interrelated. Technical innovation can lead to changed working practices – consider the invention of the internet. But productivity improvements, whatever their cause, do not in themselves entail particular economic outcomes. They simply present a series of options, or 'growth paths'. The basic choice between these various growth paths can be stated simply.

Options for economic growth

Productivity improvements imply we can:

1 produce more of the same outputs, but using exactly the same inputs as before

   or

2 produce the same outputs as before, but work less and use fewer resource inputs

   or

3 use the same inputs, but switch part of production towards more desirable outputs which are input-intensive.

Of course there are other permutations too, and in reality economy-wide productivity improvements tend to lead to some combination of them all. Although all these options arise from the very productivity improvements which are essential to economic growth, and most economists would therefore call them all 'growth paths', only *some* of them yield the kind of growth that is conventionally measured. Option 2 would not involve any increase in national product as it is usually defined, even though shorter working hours are usually associated with improved living standards. In a sense there is symmetry: this kind of 'non-growth' *can* buy happiness, while growth generally does not. However, to think of option 2 as 'non-growth' is clearly a misleading artefact of measurement. All these options require productivity improvements; they do not involve the kind of backward-looking green utopia where scientific innovation and progress are deemed pointless or redundant, and hard work is unnecessary. Nevertheless, it is true that option 2, and some versions of option 3, will be ignored if the goal of economic policy is growth as currently defined. And yet they raise many possibilities for making us happier.

One possibility is a combination of options 2 and 3 which takes as its starting point the two key facts which have emerged in explaining the sorry contribution of our current growth path to increasing happiness: adaptation to some goods is easier than to others, and rivalry is stronger for some goods than others. Lasting increases in happiness (which are not cancelled out by the unhappiness of others) are more likely if we redirect our economy towards one in which the benefits of growth are less rivalrous, *and* we adapt only slowly to them. Adaptation and rivalry are independent psychological mechanisms, but crucially and fortunately, there are some changes we can make which simultaneously address both of them.

As already noted, the happiness from goods such as daily exercise, time spent with friends or longer holidays is not eroded over time by adaptation. Other goods subject to little if any adaptation include most forms of reduction in ill health, reduced traffic congestion, and environmental benefits such as more accessible green space, or better urban air quality. Strikingly, all these goods are also less prone to rivalry than conventional private material consumption. They are not positional goods, and the evidence – such as the relative holiday length survey reported above – confirms that people do not compete for status in terms of these goods.

There is no evidence, for example, that my satisfaction with better health or more time with friends is compromised by knowing that you experience these goods too. A move towards a society in which these goods were more common would combine options 2 and 3: changes which are relatively input-intensive (some forms of health care or public transport improvements), as well as reductions in some inputs (particularly shorter working hours).

These proposals are not fanciful. They arise solely from an attempt to take the phenomena of adaptation and rivalry seriously when orienting future growth paths for society. They do not presume any dramatic change in our political and moral philosophies, or radical views about economics, inequality or the environment. In this sense, the proposals are extremely modest and do not demand any abandonment of the widespread enthusiasm for economic growth, broadly and correctly understood. They do not even necessitate reductions in private material consumption from current levels (even though this consumption is historically unprecedented); the focus is rather on steering the fruits of future growth away from further futile increases in conventional material affluence. Thus the choice between the so-called 'American' and 'European' models of work is a real one: it is not that the latter is outdated and unavailable for the future. Similarly, there is nothing to prevent us choosing some combination of options 2 and 3 for the future, providing we recognize that conventional material consumption will be lower than under option 1. But this, I have argued, is no loss to happiness.

It is very tempting here to discuss the detailed policies which could bring about these changes. Some possibilities include: restricting advertising, especially to children; discouraging performance-related pay; raising income tax to reflect the fact that income increases are 'addictive' (because of adaptation) and 'pollute' others (because of rivalry). So the policy ideas are there, but it is too soon for policy wonkery, because there are too many unanswered questions. Some of the questions are obvious – there are many arguments against raising income tax, which will be explored in Chapter 4. At a deeper level, the apparent implication that we can achieve lasting increases in happiness through some combination of options 2 and 3 will leave many readers uneasy. Is it really true that we can realize what sounds like a fundamental shift in the human condition?

The problem is that we have rejected one overarching aim of policy – economic growth – without a word about what would replace it. Since we have used happiness as measured in surveys as the criterion for assessing the success or failure of growth, it might seem obvious that we should pursue happiness directly: let the happiness statistics replace GNP? I turn to this approach in Chapter 5, beginning with an assessment of whether these statistics ultimately mean anything. But suppose, for now, we ignore these statistics. The empirical evidence on the costs of growth, our psychological understanding of adaptation and rivalry, and the phenomenon of positional goods, are together still very persuasive: growth does not buy happiness. And this conclusion fits with generations of philosophical reflection, literary tradition and ordinary experience.

One reason why contemporary Western governments nevertheless pursue growth so enthusiastically brings us finally to the other major myth about growth, that it makes tax-funded 'public services' like health care and education more affordable. In a review of happiness research commissioned by the British government, after acknowledging that growth does not buy happiness, the authors continued, 'However, increases in income that result in increases in tax yield … could be used to fund public services that may themselves enhance well-being.'[34] The argument is straightforward: economic growth means that people earn more and spend more in real terms. Therefore revenues rise from both income and expenditure taxes, even though tax rates remain unchanged. The extra revenue can be spent on improving public services, without having to raise taxes. Growth buys happiness indirectly by enabling better public services. Unfortunately, this argument leads us badly astray because of *Baumol's cost disease*, a phenomenon first brought to prominence by the economist William Baumol in 1967.[35] (Although this faulty argument concerns tax-funded services, Baumol's cost disease itself is equally relevant to privately funded services, as will shortly become clear.)

Baumol's cost disease

Although familiar to economists, you will probably not have heard of Baumol's cost disease. But you should have done. You should have been told: the cost disease radically changes our understanding of services like health care and education. The fact that almost no one outside academic economics has heard of it reveals the shallowness of media debate on the future of these services.[36]

The starting point for understanding Baumol's cost disease is a particular type of service activity which is growing rapidly in advanced economies. This is the personal service sector. Personal services are those where personal, face-to-face, customer-specific work is inherent to the tasks performed. The education, health care and performing arts sectors are all dominated by personal services, but so too are the car repair, household maintenance and restaurant sectors. Some personal services are privately provided, others are archetypal public services. But the public/private distinction is not important here, so in order to see past it, imagine for the moment that *all* personal services are provided by the private sector.

Now for some seemingly bad news: the production of personal services is consuming a sharply increasing share of total resources. Whether measured in terms of the share of resource inputs they consume, or the proportion of income we spend on them, the cost of personal services is growing significantly.[37] This is occurring for two reasons. The first is clear enough: personal services are taking a rising share of our economic resources because we want more of them. One explanation of this is that there is a much wider range of services on offer. A striking example is the explosion in health care treatments and palliative services because of enormous advances in medical science. Other reasons for the growth in demand for personal services include economic forces (for instance, seeking education in order to gain access to skilled jobs), positional concerns (entering higher education), and consumption as a means of self-identity or to signal status (some forms of cosmetic surgery). All these examples relate to education and health but the growth in personal services is not limited to these sectors – the recent expansion in housework and child care services has been startling.[38] The increased demand for personal services is fairly uncontroversial and need not be explored here in any further detail,[39] although it is worth emphasizing that demand has often risen for sensible reasons and not just because we are all hypochondriacs, obese, or want to spend more years being 'student layabouts'. Some commentators seem to suggest that rising demand for education and health is proof of some deeper malaise, that 'things aren't what they used to be', and that we have all gone soft. But I know of no evidence in support of these allegations, and it is difficult to see what could provide it.

The second explanation of why the cost of personal services is increasing inexorably as a proportion of national product brings us to the crux of the cost disease. The key fact is that personal services are very labour-intensive and likely to remain so. In other words, labour productivity (roughly, output per hour worked) grows very slowly in these sectors. To begin with, there are few opportunities to speed things up through standardization. Personal service work is tailored to the individual case or customer – whether repairing a car or a human body. There is an inevitable handicraft element. The outputs are unique. Second, technological improvements tend to be quality-improving rather than labour-saving. Health care is the classic example. New technology often leads to more sophisticated diagnosis, treatment or monitoring; only rarely does it reduce the total labour input required to treat a given condition. Third, and most importantly, high quality personal services are often identified by, and defined in terms of, low labour productivity. If a teacher increases her productivity by increasing her class size, we see this as a decline in the quality of the service provided, not an increase in productivity. Doctors who improve their productivity by spending less time with each patient, but seeing more patients, are rarely applauded either. Insofar as service quality is defined in terms of low labour productivity, productivity improvements are impossible without quality reductions. Another memorable example of intrinsic productivity limitations is one first provided by Baumol: musicians' productivity in 'producing' a live performance of a Mozart string quartet has remained unchanged since it was first composed.[40] Inevitably it still requires four musicians and takes as long to play.

Together these factors explain the relatively low labour productivity in the personal service sector compared with the rest of the economy. To see why this has such a powerful impact on costs, consider the following questions: why, over time and on average, do earnings rise so much faster than prices? How can we afford to pay ourselves so much? The answer is that we pay for increased wages and salaries through labour productivity growth. If earnings rise by 5 per cent but productivity rises by 10 per cent, then labour costs per unit of output have actually fallen, but if, say, teachers' earnings rise by 5 per cent then education costs will rise, unless there has been a compensating increase in teachers' productivity. This is unlikely in an environment where quality is largely defined in terms of low labour productivity. The productivity disparity between personal services and the rest of the economy would not matter if wages and salaries in the personal service sector could be allowed to lag behind the rest of the economy too. However, if pay in the personal service sector falls behind, employers will be unable to attract and retain staff. Inevitably, pay in the personal service sector must remain roughly in line with the rest of the economy – but productivity in this sector lags behind, so the price of personal services ends up rising much faster than the price of goods and services elsewhere in the economy. *This* is Baumol's cost disease.

The cost disease is completely independent of any increase in the demand for personal services. The inexorable logic of rising costs applies even if we do not increase our consumption of personal services over time. So health care costs are going to eat up a rising chunk of resources even without any tendencies towards hypochondria. Simply maintaining *existing* numbers of doctors, teachers, hospitals and schools (and mechanics and plumbers) will cost progressively more in real terms. The insistent, but understandable, demands for more and better services will of course compound the problem.

A little while back I suggested mischievously that, when thinking about the cost disease, we could for the sake of clarity imagine that all personal services are provided by the private sector. The point is that the public–private debate is irrelevant here. Personal services in the private sector suffer from relatively low labour productivity just as much as those in the public sector: the poor productivity performance arises from the nature of the services themselves, not from the fact that they are sometimes provided through the public sector. Indeed, much of the best evidence on poor productivity performance comes from the *private* health and higher education sectors in the US, because productivity is easier to measure for privately produced goods traded in markets.[41] *Personal* services suffer from intrinsically low labour productivity, not *public* services. However, although public provision does not cause the cost disease, it affects the consequences. The cost disease implies that luxury restaurant meals are going to become relatively more expensive over coming years (skilled chefs preparing customer-specific dishes fresh to order, with few opportunities to reduce the number of waiters or chefs without deterioration in service quality), but this is unlikely to trigger a national crisis (except possibly in France). In contrast, in the case of a publicly provided personal service such as the British National Health Service (NHS), the cost disease appears to pose a very uncomfortable choice: either the standards and scope of the NHS are reduced, or taxes go up.

It is at this point that economic growth is usually proposed as an escape from the dilemma. As already noted, growth ensures increased tax revenue without higher tax rates. If public services are going to cost more even at current levels of provision, the suggestion that this extra cost can be met without tax rate increases seems particularly seductive. But Baumol's cost disease shows not just that personal services cost more, but that they cost *relatively* more than other goods and services, so taking an increasing *share* of the resources of the economy. Economic growth means those total resources expand, but a bigger share of this cake means just that – a bigger share, even if the cake gets bigger too. To understand in more detail why economic growth does not help we have to go back to what is driving up the cost of personal services in the first place, namely increased labour costs. The problem is that the same growth that generates higher tax revenues is also associated with rising labour costs in personal services. As mentioned earlier, most economic growth is ultimately driven by productivity improvements: in other words, being able to make more with less.[42] But when average labour productivity rises across the economy, workers in a competitive labour market will soon secure pay increases in real terms. This in turn triggers the cost disease as we have seen: increasing average pay pulls up pay in the personal service sector too, where there is no compensating improvement in productivity. The very productivity improvements which support economic growth also lead to cost increases in personal services. Economic growth may bring extra revenue to pay for public services, but it makes them cost more too. We still face the same uncomfortable choice between public service cuts and tax increases.

Objections and clarifications

This discussion of the cost disease has concentrated on the essentials of the argument, but that leaves it open to some objections. All of them can be addressed by clarifying the basic argument.

The most obvious objection is that this argument assumes that demand for personal services does not fall, despite the persistent increases in their relative price. Surely, as personal services increasingly cost relatively more, people will buy less of them? In fact this need not be so. There are two forces pulling in opposite directions. There is a price effect – as the price of a good rises, we buy less of it – and a less obvious income effect: people simply want more of some goods as their income rises. Luxury items such as exotic holidays and sports cars are obvious examples (milk is one good which clearly does *not* display this income effect). Many personal services, including education, health, household services (cleaning, maintenance) and care for the very young and old, experience increased demand as economic growth raises incomes. It is an empirical question whether this income effect outweighs the tendency for demand to fall as these services become relatively more expensive. Much of the evidence suggests that the two effects largely cancel each other out, implying that demand for personal services remains roughly constant, despite rising prices.[43] As already noted, even if demand is unchanged, the cost disease still bites, because the same level of service provision becomes ever more costly.

Another objection to the cost disease argument is that it ignores recent productivity gains in the personal service sector. Influential recent research – subtitled 'Baumol's Disease has been cured' – has suggested that service sector productivity in the US has accelerated over recent years.[44] This fits conveniently with the fashionable 'New Economy' paradigm: that information technology has brought about a fundamental and permanent increase in productivity throughout advanced economies, and particularly in the US. However, this research does not demonstrate a cure for the cost disease, for several reasons.

First, it still appears that the *personal* service sector is suffering from low productivity, even if productivity in *other* types of service has improved. There are increasingly two service sectors: the one of Wal-Mart and Apple with productivity gains from the use of IT in sophisticated distribution and ordering systems and centralized service centres; and the one of Harvard and the NHS (and your local plumber).[45] Second, all that the cost disease argument requires is a significant difference between productivity in the personal service sector and elsewhere in the economy. Then over time, personal services will become *relatively* more costly, even if they are experiencing productivity gains. Computers may have helped the NHS, but unless they have helped it *more* than they have assisted other sectors of the economy, the productivity gap remains. Third, alleged productivity gains in personal services may be misleading, because they do not compare like with like: they may have been accompanied by a deterioration in the quality of the service. This is especially likely when, as noted above, low labour productivity is implicit in the *definition* of a high quality service. An example is the apparent productivity gain in US education by replacing essay-based assessment with multiple-choice exercises marked by computer: many argue that educational quality is diminished by computerized assessments.

A final objection to the cost disease argument concerns quality changes in the opposite direction. Perhaps much of the apparent cost increase in personal services reflects improvements in their quality, rather than productivity stagnation. It is certainly true that many forms of personal service have improved. The treatment of many illnesses is dramatically better than it was 50 years ago. In some cases better medical diagnosis and treatment implies cost savings as well as quality improvements: if the treatment time is reduced, then cost per illness will have risen much more slowly than cost per patient. Attempts to adjust properly for these quality improvements in aggregate measures of service cost are probably doomed, but again, what matters is the difference between the personal service sector and elsewhere in the economy. Quality improvements have occurred in most goods produced outside the personal service sector too, and have only been imperfectly reflected in productivity data. In any case, quality improvements may change how we look at the personal services – private health care costs more than it used to, but at least your hospital room now has fresh flowers – but they do not remove the underlying cost increase.

Are personal service costs out of control?

This bring us to the fear that 'personal service costs are out of control'. In Europe, where many services like health care and education are publicly provided, it is easy to misinterpret the cost disease as demonstrating that *public* services are inherently inefficient. While the business community and those on the political right may not like Baumol's cost disease because it undermines a standard argument for economic growth, the large public-sector unions and the left are unlikely to be enthusiastic either. So it bears repeating that while there may be problems with public provision which privatization would tackle, these have nothing to do with the cost disease. Privatization would simply shift the inexorably rising cost structures of personal services into private hands. Baumol and his successors found no evidence of productivity improvements that were available, but which for some reason public providers failed to seize. Evidence from the US health care sector shows that private provision can instead be more costly than equivalent public services.[46] Still, even if we set aside the public/private distraction, the 'inefficient' label still sticks to personal services, and stinks. Is it justified?

Inefficiency is relative and depends on the objective; a bicycle is a much more efficient way of converting chemical energy into motion than a car, but less efficient in its use of time to cover a given distance. It would be meaningless to label either cars or bicycles 'inherently inefficient'. Certainly, labour productivity growth in manufacturing is greater than in personal services, but manufactured goods alone cannot heal the sick. Nevertheless, the cost disease implies a large increase in expenditure which many will find alarming, even more so if it is increasing public expenditure because personal services are tax-funded.

However, it is an illusion, subtle and therefore persuasive, that this increase in expenditure is in any respect unaffordable. In the most important sense, personal services are getting *cheaper*. How can this be so, since I have repeatedly emphasized that personal services are becoming relatively more costly? It is true that the real price of these services will continue to rise – that is, the price compared to the average price level across the economy. So we will spend a rising proportion of our income on them. And an increasing *share* of total resource inputs will be devoted to their production. But something can become *relatively* more expensive simply because other goods have become cheaper – it can still itself be less costly than in the past. And so it is with personal services. Since labour productivity is rising in personal services, albeit slowly, progressively fewer hours of work are required to produce the same output. This implies that, measured in terms of labour costs, personal services are becoming cheaper. These labour costs are of course salary payments, so measured in terms of average salaries, rather than average prices, personal services are becoming cheaper. In other words, they are becoming *more* affordable, not less. But since their affordability is rising much more slowly than that of, say, a DVD player, we mistakenly perceive them as less affordable.

It might seem doubtful that there are *any* productivity gains to be had in some personal services: to return to Baumol's extreme example, there appears to be no hope of productivity improvement in the performance of a Mozart string quartet. But after raising this possibility, Baumol continues:

> Yet that is only an illusion. To see why, consider a recent performance by a Viennese group of musicians played in Frankfurt am Main. A trip from their Austrian home base to the German auditorium surely would normally have taken no more than several hours in 1990. But when Mozart made the trip in 1790 it required six days of extreme discomfort (and, at that, Mozart wrote that he was surprised at the speed of the journey). Certainly, technical progress has reduced the number of hours of labour required to provide a unit of the output in question, thus raising the labour productivity of every itinerant performer, even in live performance (and we know that performers are virtually all itinerant).[47]

Even in the most hopeless cases, then, transport improvements (and information technology) ensure productivity continues to creep upward.

There is another reason why the personal services remain affordable despite their rising relative costs – why, indeed, we can afford to continue to expand health care and education services, not merely maintain them at current levels. This is because of continuing substantial productivity growth across the rest of the economy. An increasing share of all resource inputs including labour can be devoted to personal services because fewer inputs are needed elsewhere in the economy to produce the same quantity of manufactured goods. If productivity in the rest of the economy continues along historic trends, as most economists expect it to, then we can afford more of *all* goods, personal services included. It is simply a version of option 2.

Does this mean that economic growth saves us after all? Yes, in the sense that productivity improvements and growth are fundamentally interlinked, but no, growth does not help us escape tax increases. If public services consume a rising share of national product, then this necessitates a rising tax burden (tax as a percentage of GNP) to pay for them. And that in turn entails increased tax rates.[48] The cost disease certainly does not in itself give us a reason to abandon economic growth, but it debunks the myth that growth 'pays' for better public services without tax rises.

The politics of the cost disease is full of contradictions. Politicians of all shades never mention it, because they feel safer portraying a Panglossian world in which public services can be improved without raising taxes. But the public, generally ignorant of the cost disease, nevertheless feels deceived rather than comforted. Yet to some extent, a Panglossian future is available after all. In an economy with productivity growing in almost all sectors, and falling in none, we can afford more of everything (ignoring important environmental constraints which are arguably already beginning to bite). I have claimed that much of this material largesse will leave us no happier, but improved public services provide some exceptions, because at least some of them suffer less from adaptation or rivalry. Service improvements which reduce crime or tackle acute illness are good examples, higher education less so. Thus it is important to overcome the fear that better public services cannot be afforded. Baumol writes eloquently about the communication problem here:

> In *A Connecticut Yankee in King Arthur's Court*, Mark Twain devotes an entire chapter to Sir Boss's unsuccessful attempt to explain the concept of real wages to his primitive hosts. Sir Boss argues with some passion that the monetary magnitudes of wages are irrelevant; that, regardless of their value as expressed in terms of money, wages are really higher only if it takes fewer hours of labor to earn the wages needed to purchase a given set of goods.[49]

The situation is exactly analogous with personal services, although we are presumably no longer 'primitive'. Nevertheless:

> It will not be easy to convince the intelligent layperson that, even though the prices of personal services appear to be rising at a rate that is out of control, in fact the costs of those services (in terms of their labor-time equivalent) are really gradually declining, because of small increases in their labor productivity. One can hardly blame such persons for their reluctance to be taken in by what appears to be pure academic sleight of hand, or mere theoretical gobbledygook.[50]

So the reason for media silence on Baumol's cost disease is clear enough, but by treating us as if we were 'primitive', the media have dragged debate on the public services down to that level. The need for frank discussion of the cost disease is now urgent.

Economic growth revisited

When economic growth takes countries out of poverty, it makes people happier. However, the material affluence made possible by recent decades of growth in rich countries has seen no corresponding rise in happiness. The emerging field of happiness economics is consistent with our intuition, and the insights of philosophy, literature and religion: once we have escaped from poverty, money does not buy happiness. More important than the happiness data (Chapter 5 introduces an overdue dose of skepticism) are the psychological mechanisms of adaptation and rivalry. Their key feature is that they apply more powerfully to some goods – notably income – than others. Some commentators have wrongly suggested that adaptation, rivalry and related social limits to growth are best interpreted as individual failings; the mistaken remedy is self-help and education, while growth-is-good economic policy proceeds as usual. Since its implications are deeply unpalatable at first glance, politicians of all shades adopt the same business as usual response to Baumol's cost disease: they ignore it. Politicians and policy entrepreneurs need not be actively trying to hoodwink the public, but the result is the same: debate is stymied. We must learn to accept the relentless logic of rising relative costs for personal services, whether they are publicly or privately provided. This should be easier if we remember that the cost disease is a by-product of growth rather than inefficiency. And that in absolute terms the public services are becoming cheaper after all. So we have nothing to fear from the cost disease, but it should change the way we think about public services.

Chapter Four

The Politics of Pay

The art of taxation consists in so plucking the goose as to obtain the largest amount of feathers with the least possible amount of hissing. (Jean-Baptiste Colbert, chief minister to Louis XIV, quoted in Stiglitz, *Economics of the Public Sector*)

Moderator: What comes into your mind when someone says tax to you?

Man: Nicking my money.

Woman: Sadness at the end of each month. (Fabian Society focus group)

No one likes paying income tax. And in recent years the voices arguing against it have become much louder. Some now argue against income tax in general, consistently pressing for cuts and opposing all increases, regardless of who pays, the state of the economy, and the fact that rates are lower than historic averages in many countries.[1] In this view, higher income tax is morally wrong and almost always harms the economy. Apart from the economic case against it, the moral argument splits into two separate parts: the argument that taxation is a kind of theft of what is rightfully mine, and the argument that those who earn more generally deserve it. This second argument takes us beyond tax questions and into the broader politics of pay. If we think that those who are highly paid largely deserve their rewards, for instance because they contribute more to the economy, then the greater inequality we now see in most advanced economies is less likely to be seen as a problem. On the contrary, increasing inequality may be a healthy sign, indicating a society where people increasingly get paid their just deserts, as the economy moves closer to a true free market. But if pay inequalities are not deserved, then rising inequality may come to be opposed by most of us, and not just by those who lose out.

The three arguments just mentioned – one economic and two moral – will be examined in detail in successive sections. For the sake of simplicity, income tax is the only tax that will be explicitly discussed, although most of the arguments have a wider significance for debates about fair pay and taxation in general.

Taxation as theft

Although it is tax evasion which is the crime, for many people tax collection feels like a crime too. It seems akin to theft in an important sense: it involves taking something which we own. Income tax is said to be more unpopular than taxes on spending because it is more noticeable; this is true, but does not alone explain its unpopularity – 'tax by stealth', once noticed, is unlikely to be popular either. Income tax is more unpopular because it is more obviously like theft. I own something – my income, salary or wages – part of which is then taken away. Of course some taxation is inevitable, but this does not alter the fundamental principle that my pre-tax income belongs to me. We speak of income as 'earnings' to convey the meaning that it is not just money which comes mysteriously into someone's possession. Earnings are earnt; I deserve my earnings, or at least I am entitled to them, usually in return for work or some other contribution. All this may seem to state the obvious, but it is completely mistaken.

The view that pre-tax income is 'mine' is a very widely held moral judgement. Following the philosophers Liam Murphy and Thomas Nagel, I shall call it the *ownership principle*.[2] Even if not explicitly endorsed, the ownership principle is implicit in the advice of accountants, economists and other tax experts, whatever their political perspective. It provides the starting point for most economic assessments of the efficiency and fairness of taxation.[3] Indeed the ownership principle is so widely taken for granted that it is scarcely recognized as a moral judgement at all, more a fact, or at least an absolute legal right. So before showing *how* it is mistaken, it is worth asking *why* the mistake arises.

In modern societies, we are all born into a legal system where the idea of 'private property' is meaningful: it is defined in detail and protected by law. The legal rules are sufficiently stable and well established that we almost forget they are there, so that what we own effectively becomes a fact of life rather than a legal convention. But occasionally we are shocked out of this delusion. Slave owners in the American South were astonished to be told that their right to own slaves was not a natural right, but a legal right, which could be withdrawn.[4] Similarly, because our post-tax income is so well protected by law, it is tempting to assume that we have a moral or natural right to it. Even if this were true it would not of course imply that we have a moral right to *pre-tax* income. But the slip from post-tax to pre-tax income is an easy mistake to make, especially as it is widely encouraged by politicians and commentators who refer to tax as 'taking away your money', clearly suggesting that we have rights over pre-tax income.

Belief in the ownership principle is also encouraged by deeper misunderstandings. It is widely believed that what we *deserve* depends heavily on our efforts, talents and willingness to take risks. Since pre-tax income is partly influenced by these factors, people conclude that all their pre-tax income is fully deserved. This conclusion is false, because it ignores all the other influences on pre-tax income, many of which, such as inheritance and luck, cannot be regarded as deserved. I will explore these mistaken views about what people deserve in much more detail later. Alongside these philosophical misunderstandings stands a related misinterpretation of economic theory. It is the view that the perfect free market of pure economic theory (and every undergraduate textbook) could, if governments so wished, be introduced into real economies. But the perfect market of the textbooks is a hypothetical model, highly simplified to aid understanding. It should not be interpreted as a starting point for designing tax systems, because it is literally impossible. Here, I shall discuss just one aspect of this impossibility, which brings us to a key reason why the ownership principle is false.

Ownership without tax is impossible

Rights of ownership are meaningless unless they can be enforced, and in a modern society enforcement operates through a legal system, a police force and other institutions of the state. These institutions all have a cost, which can only be paid through taxation. In short, ownership is a legal right, laws imply government, and government implies taxation. The tax and the ownership rights are, so to speak, created simultaneously. We cannot have one without the other.

In principle, there are exceptions: some limited ownership rights exist in simple tribal societies, but there is no taxation. And some empires have avoided taxation at home, funding government through taxation in the colonies. But in practice, the complex forms of ownership in modern economies are impossible without tax funding.[5] It is easy to underestimate the force of this argument, because it might seem that ownership rights can be maintained – the legal framework of private property can be enforced – at relatively little cost. Specifically, it might seem that only a small proportion of current tax revenue is required for this purpose, rendering all other taxation unnecessary, or at least unjustified. This is the view of libertarians, who regard taxation as an infringement of liberty, only justified when it is to pay for a minimal state 'restricted to the narrow functions of protection against force, theft, fraud, enforcement of contracts and so on'.[6] The list of liberties for the state to protect also includes freedom of speech and the right to vote. This minimal state would certainly be radically different to that found in any developed economy. There would be no state-provided health care, no state education system, and no welfare payments. Strict libertarians admit no exceptions here: the critically ill will be left to die unless they have health care paid for by private insurance or charity. The same would be true of those lacking access to food or shelter. Basic education in reading and arithmetic would be optional, and privately funded. Strict libertarianism is an extreme view, endorsed by virtually no one.[7]

But even this minimal state is costly. Apart from the obvious police and legal system costs, there must be military expenditure to protect society itself. Protection of property rights requires not just the ability to enforce contracts and sue for trespass, but the maintenance of complex (and costly) institutions such as patents and stock exchanges. At a more basic level, the protection of physical property from fire, flood and other natural disasters (through communal fire services etc.) is also costly. Protecting freedom of speech and the right to vote involves further costs. In sum, research that has attempted to quantify the cost of maintaining a minimal state suggests that it is misleading to label it 'minimal' at all.[8]

Since the illusion that we could in fact receive all our pre-tax income is so pervasive, it is worth exploring why. One reason is that taxation is often seen as analogous to situations in which there is redistribution from an initial benchmark: for example, when a group of people pays for something collectively (such as a restaurant meal) through contributions from each member. But the analogy is mistaken. A better analogy is with a salesperson employed by a small company, to whom an explicit part of the company's profit can be attributed – the part arising from the sales made by this person. It would be odd to claim that the salesperson 'owns', or is entitled to, that part of the company profit. Even if the company's profit is relevant to deciding a salary or bonus level, the profit *itself* is not the correct benchmark for determining entitlements, because it arises from the joint effort of all employees (and the capital provided by owners or shareholders). The profit only 'belongs' to the salesperson in the sense that they are one of these employees. In the same way, none of us can work in isolation: we must each 'sign up' to a particular legal jurisdiction, and the price is paying tax.

Another reason why the illusion that we can own our pre-tax income is so pervasive is that we forget that what is possible for one person is not necessarily possible for all (economists call it a 'fallacy of composition'). It is clearly possible for an individual to receive all their pre-tax income, and yet have enforceable ownership rights over it, because the rest of us will be paying the tax to sustain the government which can enforce the rights of this lucky individual. But the arrangement cannot be extended to society as a whole. As well as ownership without taxation being impossible in practice, there is a further problem with the ownership principle.

Pre-tax income is not a relevant moral benchmark

Even though the ownership principle gives us rights we could never enforce, it might be thought that these rights are nevertheless relevant to deciding what taxes should be levied in reality. In this view, owning all pre-tax income may be impossible, but it still provides a morally relevant hypothetical benchmark for informing taxation policy. There is undoubtedly a seductive comfort in reassuring myself that I 'really' or 'morally' have a right to something, such as my pre-tax income, even though I could never secure the right. But it is a delusion nonetheless. This is revealed by the self-contradictory nature of any statement of the rights involved, which must be along the lines of 'I am entitled to my pre-tax income, yet the government is entitled to take some of it away to fund the minimal state'. In fact the way of thinking implicit in the ownership principle is faulty, *even if the impossibility of pre-tax ownership is ignored.*

This can be seen by simply asking the question: what taxes should we face? The ownership principle tries to pre-empt, or preclude, debate about the answer by insisting that each of us start by assuming that pre-tax income is 'mine'. But the debate is precisely about deciding 'how "mine" and "yours" ought to be determined; it cannot start with a set of assumptions about what is mine and what is yours.'[9] The ownership principle begs the question.

Suppose, however, that we do not make these question-begging assumptions. Is it still possible that the level of my pre-tax income, while not 'mine' by definition, is a morally relevant benchmark in deciding what taxes we should face? Possible, yes. Plausible, no. There are two reasons why it is highly implausible. First, the pre-tax income benchmark is directly relevant only within the philosophical framework of libertarianism. But libertarianism is itself extremely implausible, as mentioned earlier. Second, even if libertarianism is accepted, pre-tax income is a problematic benchmark.

It should be emphasized that libertarianism does not endorse the ownership principle, for some of the reasons already discussed. For libertarians, there is no straightforward entitlement to all pre-tax income, because some taxes are required to sustain the market system. However, since libertarians believe the government should be as small as possible, it seems that the (unachievable) goal is that we should keep all pre-tax income. It is an idealized benchmark. But why is it ideal? Why choose this benchmark rather than another? The answer offered by libertarianism goes back to one of its founders, the 17th-century English philosopher John Locke.[10] Locke imagined what he called a 'state of nature', a fictional world in which there is no government or legal system. He argued that in such a state we clearly own ourselves, and so we own the fruits of our labour, and so we come to own physical property arising from the free exchange of our labour with others for mutual benefit. These are 'moral' or 'natural' rights of ownership. It is in this government-free world that owning pre-tax income becomes coherent. Libertarians conclude that in a market economy, pre-tax income is a pre-political natural right, not created by government, and so the government has no right to interfere with it.

There are at least two problems here. First, it is far from clear why Locke's state-of-nature thought experiment, as it stands, has any relevance to contemporary market economies.[11] Second, the rights of ownership arising in modern market economies are not the natural or neutral consequences of apolitical market transactions that they might appear. Governments cannot avoid interfering with ownership rights because they play a crucial role in *defining* them. This is starkly apparent in recent cases where governments have introduced controversial ownership rights, such as intellectual property rights over genetic material, or words, signs and symbols in common use. Regardless of how these rights ought to be assigned, it is clear that there is no natural or neutral way of doing so. It is a political decision. But this is just a part of *inevitable* government involvement in defining ownership rights. Suppose a factory's production process leads it to pollute the water of a neighbouring river, imposing a cost on a downstream laundry needing clean water. How much pollution does the factory have the right to emit? And how far should the government legislate to ban cartels and other anti-competitive practices? Left to themselves, firms will always try to subvert competition by colluding or establishing monopolies. Free markets, left alone, hardly ever stay free.

> The upshot is that even if the destitute are left to fend for themselves, it still cannot be said that pre-tax outcomes are simply market outcomes. They are, instead, the returns generated by a market regulated in accordance with a certain set of government policies.[12]

Different sets of policies will lead to different patterns of pre-tax income. None of these patterns have, without further justification, any more claim to be a morally relevant benchmark than any other. There is no single, neutral, pre-tax income benchmark after all. In addressing the question, 'What taxes should we face?', we are no further forward. Whether it is understood in terms of explicit rights or moral benchmarks, the 'taxation as theft' perspective obscures this simple question, tempting us to regard tax payment as a kind of charitable gesture, or even 'a common disaster'.[13] We need to think differently.

Since pre-tax income is at best of limited relevance to answering our question, the focus inevitably shifts to the post-tax distribution of income. This is plausible, because the post-tax outcome is what ultimately affects people. However, the effects do not feed just through the tax system, but extend to all those benefits and burdens which matter, including all forms of welfare payment such as pensions, maternity, disability and unemployment benefits. So our question cannot be addressed in isolation. Whether it is right that the poor face a non-negligible tax burden will depend at least in part on whether there is a matching set of benefits in place, such as the welfare payments just mentioned. The 'common disaster' view of taxation is completely misleading, acting 'as though the tax money once collected were thrown into the sea'.[14] It is not just left-wing welfare enthusiasts who reject this view; in practice, all but the strictest libertarians will look beyond the tax system in isolation when judging what taxes we should face. This is obviously true for those committed to redistribution or equality of opportunity, but it may be less clear for libertarians. However, once it is recognized that market outcomes in reality may not fairly reflect what people deserve or are morally entitled to, then practical libertarianism must confront some awkward dilemmas. For example, libertarians usually hold that people are entitled to do what they like with their money, including leaving it all to their children. But the resulting pattern of unequal inheritance poses libertarian problems: richer children will have many starting advantages in life which do not derive from 'the fruits of their labour'; nor do they appear to deserve them. In such cases, the libertarian decision about what taxes we should face will depend not just on principles pertaining to the tax system but a broader assessment of our entitlements, or what we deserve. In short, there is a widespread consensus among philosophers, including most libertarians, that moral judgements about tax should focus on post-tax income, which will be affected by many factors beyond the narrow structure of the tax system itself.

It is time to sum up. The first problem with the ownership principle was that tax and ownership are defined simultaneously: ownership rights do not exist independently, before taxation. It is now clear that the problem is more general. Ownership rights do not exist before government, even ignoring the issue of taxation. Nothing in this argument rules out appealing to 'moral rights' or 'entitlements' to determine who should be taxed, and how much. But appealing to the right to keep your pre-tax income is futile and misleading, because it is a right which could never be fulfilled. It *is* possible to argue, for example, that government should interfere with market outcomes as little as possible. But the benchmark is not 'no interference whatsoever' because that is impossible in practice. As often in this book, the message is that bad decisions are made not because of factual errors or misunderstanding the technical details (although both play a part), but because of confusion about the underlying ethical principles. If we start from the morally flawed ownership principle, or any related 'taxation as theft' view, we will make flawed decisions no matter how hard we try.

The implications for our thinking about taxation are great, because the ownership principle is so widely believed. Many common views about tax rely upon it, even if they do not appear to do so. And implicit endorsement of the ownership principle is found across the political spectrum. For example, it lies behind all talk about fair taxation being based on ability to pay. The idea is that fairness is achieved when those who are better off pay a greater proportion of their pre-tax income in tax, because they can afford to do so. But since the pre-tax distribution of income is morally irrelevant, it is futile to attempt to define fairness from this starting point. Fairness will instead depend on the post-tax distribution, and vague talk of 'ability to pay' is of no help in deciding what that should be.

Beyond these specific problems, there is a more insidious effect on the language and framing of political debate about tax. The conversation reported at the beginning of this chapter comes from focus group research into British attitudes towards taxation, and captures a commonly expressed view. Many people described tax as a 'necessary evil', suggesting it is seen as morally wrong, despite being necessary.[15] Similar sentiments are even implicit in the technical language of tax experts. This language matters. The share of tax in national income is termed the 'tax burden', as though we would be better off without it. Some taxes are undoubtedly a burden, and should be abolished, but others are essential for public expenditure that almost everyone welcomes. At the very least, those who believe the label 'tax burden' is neutral enough should be willing, for the sake of consistency, to see the term 'public benefits' replace 'public expenditure'. And it is a very short step from the language of tax burden, the ownership principle, and taxation as theft, to the fantasy that tax cuts are inevitably desirable – the fantasy which forgets that they must be accompanied by spending cuts. Of course it is entirely legitimate for politicians and media commentators to press for tax cuts, providing that on each occasion they explain what public spending will be cut to pay for them.

If the case for tax cuts is a moral one resting on the ownership principle, then it is irrevocably flawed. Later I will argue that related moral arguments based on what we deserve are equally flawed. But first I turn to the economic argument, that taxation damages the economy.

Does taxation damage the economy?

Slicing the economic pie

Redistributive taxation is often compared with slicing up a pie: it transfers a portion of the economic pie from rich to poor. The rich receive a relatively smaller slice than they did before tax; the poor a larger one. But unfortunately the effect of taxation is to shrink the overall pie, so that although the relative shares may have altered, in absolute terms the rich have lost more than the poor have gained. How might this mysterious shrinkage occur?

Although there are many arguments about tax harming economic performance, very few of them withstand careful examination. Examples include 'tax increases reduce economic growth' and 'tax increases damage international competitiveness'.[16] That such weak arguments continue to influence debate may be due to the unpopularity of tax in general, or the gut feeling that it is theft, or the fact that those who pay the most tax (whether individuals or companies) are wealthy, and so tend to have the ability and means to complain loudly. These arguments may be popular, but few economists take them seriously, at least in the simplistic form they are commonly posed. It is difficult to make much sense of the concept of 'competitiveness' at all, while the supposed harm that tax does to economic growth has no basis in economic theory, and is not supported by the evidence. The diagram opposite compares average growth rates in various economies over the period 1970–2004 against average taxes, as a proportion of national income. It suggests that there is no link between the two, with similar growth rates being associated with a wide range of tax levels.[17]

A seemingly more promising argument is that excessive income tax on high earners discourages entrepreneurship, innovation and risk-taking among these people, with significant effects on the size of the overall pie. The focus is on the tax rate which determines the financial reward from extra effort: the marginal rate paid on the last dollar of income already earnt, and on the next dollar if income increases. Again, the evidence does not support the argument. On the contrary, the following graphs show that in the US the highest productivity growth occurred at the same time as the highest marginal tax rates were in force.

Of course, this does not show that higher tax rates *cause* faster productivity growth; but there is no straightforward evidence that they reduce it.

Taxation and economic growth

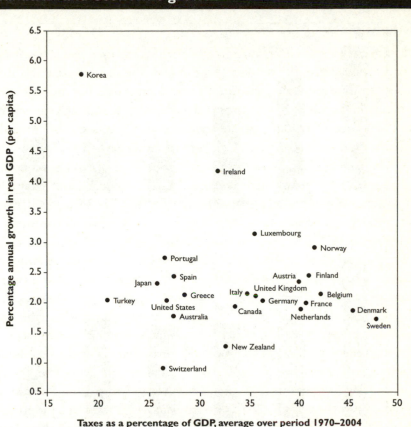

Source: Slemrod and Bakija (2008), p119

The more serious economic arguments about tax start instead by analysing individual choices.

Economists agree that the most important potential effect of income taxation is on the income earner's 'incentive to work'. The argument is that if high taxes or tax increases discourage work, the economy will inevitably be less productive: the overall pie will shrink. From the confident way that some politicians and policy entrepreneurs speak of income tax having harmful effects on incentives, we might imagine that economic analysis is conclusive here. And it is true that economic analysis clearly identifies two different effects of taxation on work incentives – but unfortunately they

Income tax and productivity in the US

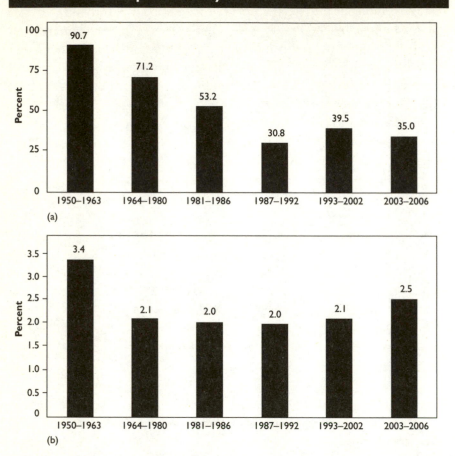

(a)

(b)

Note: (a) Top rate of income tax (highest marginal rate), average over period; (b) annual growth rate in productivity (private sector real GDP per hour worked), average over period.

Source: Slemrod and Bakija (2008), p116

pull in opposite directions, and there is nothing in economic theory to indicate which effect will dominate.

Suppose there is an increase in the marginal rate of income tax. On the one hand, this encourages you to work less, because the after-tax reward for an hour's overtime work, or obtaining promotion to a more highly paid job, or putting extra effort into your business, has fallen. Work has become relatively less attractive. Leisure and other unpaid activities have become relatively more attractive, because the 'price' paid for them (after-tax income forgone by not working) has fallen. Effectively, leisure has become 'cheaper'. Economists term this impact of the tax increase a *substitution effect* because it refers to the general tendency to substitute relatively cheaper things (in this case leisure) in place of others (in this case work) when prices change. On the other hand, the tax increase reduces your overall after-tax income. When people become somewhat poorer, they tend to cut back on non-essential consumption. This includes the consumption of leisure, because that too has a 'price' in terms of forgone income from working. So less leisure is consumed: in other words, people work harder. This tendency to reduce all forms of desirable consumption (including in this case leisure) when income falls is known as the *income effect*. (It is sometimes expressed in terms of the idea that when tax rises, I must work more in order to maintain my 'target income'.) In short, when taxes rise the income effect encourages people to work more, while the substitution effect encourages them to work less.

All this may seem obvious to economists – it is the uncontroversial stuff of introductory textbooks – but others are mystified. Are people really supposed to think in this way? Economists usually concede that the answer is no, but insist that the theory is still relevant: people act *as if* they weighed up income and substitution effects. Yet this reply is hardly convincing. Many people regard the impact of income tax changes on their own pay as relatively minor, and cannot imagine such changes affecting, say, their effort in pursuing a promotion. And even if a tax change is significant, few people see any opportunity to adjust their working patterns in response to it. For instance, if taxes fall, many of us can do little to take advantage of the increased after-tax rate of pay, even if we wanted to do so. These common sense objections to the economic analysis raise some important points. It is true that many people have little discretion over the number of hours they work. And often if they do, their choice of hours will have no effect on their pay, implying a tax change will have no impact on hours worked. For instance, changes in the marginal rate of tax were found to have much less effect on the amount of work undertaken by NHS doctors than self-employed private sector doctors (whose pay depends much more heavily on hours worked).[18] However, in trying to assess the impact of tax changes on work incentives across the whole economy, it is not possible to consider the mass of employee-specific factors. Perhaps all that can be concluded from the theory is that since it is compatible with people working more *or* less in response to a tax increase, both are equally plausible. We must rely on empirical evidence for guidance; unusually for economics, it yields a broad consensus. Tax changes are likely to have very little effect on hours worked.[19] There may be some impact on the decision to take paid work at all (rather than be unemployed or 'inactive'), especially among women,[20] but this impact is not large enough to disturb the conclusion that, overall, tax changes do not much affect the amount of work we do.[21]

To sum up, economic theory is neutral on the effect of taxation on incentives to work. The substitution and income effects act in opposite directions. Empirical evidence suggests that tax changes are likely to have little impact, at least for the kinds of tax changes which have mostly occurred in developed economies in recent years.[22] Given the absence of theoretical and empirical support, it might seem surprising that so much attention has been paid in political debate to the adverse effects of taxation on work incentives. But apart from the political explanations, there is a good reason for this attention. For even if a tax change leaves the amount of work we do *unchanged* overall, because the income and substitution effects exactly offset each other, income tax still 'distorts' incentives to work. Income tax has a distortionary effect on economic activity, separate from any changes it may bring about in the amount of work done, and in turn the size of the economic pie. But if the size of the pie remains unchanged, how could a tax change damage the economy? We need to think of buckets, not pies.

Redistribution: the leaky bucket

The core idea is that if a tax (or a tax increase) leads people to change their economic activities in a conscious or unconscious attempt to reduce their tax liability, then these changes will be harmful, because pre-tax economic activity is disrupted. And pre-tax economic activity is assumed to be valuable to all concerned, otherwise it would not have taken place. Consider Peter the plumber.

Peter the plumber

Peter is self-employed and lucky enough to have a skill in great demand; he can always find as much (or as little) paid work as he pleases. He works full-time during the week, so values his free time at weekends highly, reckoning that he has to earn at least $400 over the weekend to make it worth working then too. But he finds he can earn $500, on which he pays no tax, so he works weekends. However, the government now enforces tax payment on these casual weekend earnings too, leaving Peter with after-tax earnings of $350 from the weekend. So he gives up working weekends.

Setting aside the issue of whether Peter was previously evading tax or merely avoiding it, what do we learn from the parable of Peter the plumber? Had Peter continued to work at weekends, the government would have raised an extra $150 in tax revenue. As it is, the government is no better off. Peter is worse off, effectively $100 worse off, the difference between his lost weekend earnings ($500) and the value of the completely free weekend which he now enjoys ($400). Since no one forced Peter's customers to employ him at weekends, they are probably worse off, and certainly no better off, denied the opportunity to do so. Taken together, Peter and his customers are collectively worse off, even though they are paying no more tax. This difference between the overall negative effect of the tax and the actual revenue raised (in this case zero) is a form of inefficiency caused by the tax distorting people's pre-tax behaviour. But distortionary compared to what? Economics uses the poll tax as a benchmark in assessing distortions, a pure poll tax without any exemptions or deductions, because it has no distortionary effect: there is absolutely nothing an individual can legally do to avoid or reduce liability. In this example, the government could raise the extra $150 (or another amount) through a poll tax without affecting Peter's decision to work at weekends. The poll tax is more efficient in the sense that it can achieve the same 'output' (raising revenue) at lower cost to Peter and his customers.

Of course, poll taxes are politically unacceptable. One of the worst riots in Britain in the 20th century was that in London on 31 March 1990, the day before a poll tax was introduced. The tax is now accepted as a significant contributor to the eventual downfall of Margaret Thatcher, despite her government's attempts to mollify public opinion by naming it the 'Community Charge'. But public disquiet was mild compared to the Peasants' Revolt over a previous attempt at a poll tax in 1381. The Mayor of London, the Lord Treasurer and the Archbishop of Canterbury were all associated with the hated tax and were killed by the protesters. (Perhaps if they had called it a 'Community Charge', they would have escaped with their lives…)

Since it is clearly inconceivable that *all* the tax revenue required in developed countries is raised via a poll tax – even if it seems just about possible to raise some of it that way – distortionary taxation is inevitable. There will be costs in terms of inefficiency across the economy. (This is true even if, unlike the case of Peter the plumber, taxation leaves the level of productive activity unchanged: the level will still be less than it would have been had the same amount of revenue been raised via the non-distortionary poll tax instead.[23]) Poll taxes are politically unacceptable precisely because they impose no distortions – that is, they are unavoidable – and make no distinction between rich and poor. 'Redistributive taxation' is an unpopular idea, suggesting envy to some and clashing with the ownership principle for others, but the history of the poll tax shows that tax which makes no attempt to redistribute is more unpopular still. And as we saw earlier, even a pure libertarian society may unwittingly engage in redistribution in the process of protecting private property. Redistribution, however minimal, is unavoidable.

The lesson of economic theory is that the price we pay for redistributive taxation is the distortionary effect on economic activity and the resulting inefficiency. Redistributive taxation may be likened to a leaky bucket.[24] As we attempt to transfer economic benefit from one place to another, from rich to poor, some is lost in the process. Due to this inefficiency, the total loss imposed on the groups burdened by redistributive taxation is greater than the actual revenue raised (think of Peter the plumber again). And there is more: economic theory shows that the greater the redistribution, the greater the inefficiency.[25] In other words, there is a trade-off between efficiency and fairness. We face an uncomfortable choice between them. How should we strike a balance?

Taxation to maximize happiness

Very few readers will associate 'taxation' with 'maximization of happiness'. But one group of economists have a clear answer to the question of balancing efficiency and fairness. As we saw in Chapter 3, some economists argue that happiness is what matters, not economic growth. Accordingly, they argue that the tax system should be explicitly designed to maximize happiness. They call it 'optimal tax theory'. Whatever we think about happiness as a policy objective (see Chapter 5), optimal tax theory provides a useful framework in which to think about the balance between efficiency and fairness.

The crucial idea is that even if redistribution is a leaky bucket when measured in monetary terms, it may not be when measured in terms of what matters, happiness. This is because of a fundamental principle widely accepted in economics at least since John Stuart Mill, the so-called 'law of diminishing marginal utility'. It states simply that the happiness ('utility') experienced by a poor person from receiving a small extra amount of money will be greater than that experienced by a rich person receiving the same amount. More generally, as a person's income rises, the extra happiness from receiving a little more money diminishes. Returning to redistribution, suppose that an attempted $100 transfer from rich to poor in fact imposes an overall cost equivalent to $110 on the rich, after allowing for the distortionary effect of the tax. Now $10 has 'leaked', but because an extra dollar is worth more to a poor person than a rich one in terms of its contribution to their happiness, overall happiness may have increased. That is, the reduction in happiness of the rich, resulting from their loss of $110, may be less than the gain in happiness of the poor, after receiving $100. Then redistribution would be justified, even if the only objective is maximizing total happiness, and there is no direct concern with alleviating poverty or inequality. In this view, whether redistribution is called for in practice depends on the balance of two empirical factors: the extent to which money is worth more to the poor than the rich, versus the extent to which redistribution involves distortionary monetary costs.

Of course, most of us believe that the case for redistribution is more powerful than this, because we care about poverty. Almost all ethical systems do the same; they include an explicit concern with alleviating poverty or inequality, even if they disagree on much else.[26] Depending on the strength of this concern, the gains of the poorest may have moral or social value over and above the extent to which money is worth more to them. The empirical trade-off between the benefits of redistribution and its costs in terms of inefficiency remains, but the best compromise may now involve transferring relatively more resources to the poorest. So what would an 'optimal tax system' look like? Is it possible to be more specific? Yes, but first we must pin down how 'inefficiency' is measured.

Inefficiency is measured by the magnitude of the substitution effect, because the substitution effect measures the extent to which one activity is substituted for another – that is pre-tax behaviour is distorted – in response to an income tax change.[27] The substitution effect in turn is determined by the *marginal* rate of tax: it is the tax rate payable on additional (marginal) earnings which determines whether a person will work or substitute leisure instead. In short, the inefficiency cost of taxation depends on the marginal tax rate; high marginal tax rates imply greater inefficiency.

The mark of a redistributive tax system is that it is progressive. A tax system is progressive if the proportion of income paid in tax increases as income rises. One way of achieving a progressive system is through people paying a higher marginal rate on successive slices of income, as in most contemporary tax systems in developed countries. But the price of achieving a progressive tax system in this way is the inefficiency cost of high marginal rates on high earners. The economic theory of optimal taxation turns this wisdom on its head. It suggests that marginal rates of tax should be constant *or even falling* as income increases. So high earners might pay *lower* marginal rates of tax than those on middle incomes. Have the economists gone mad? Unsurprisingly this kind of theoretical argument is very attractive to politicians and policy entrepreneurs predisposed to cut taxes for the rich – it appears to have influenced the large tax cuts for the wealthy in the US in recent years.[28] That the argument holds even if we attach extra weight to the happiness of the poor, because of an explicit concern to reduce poverty, serves only to deepen the mystery.

In fact, the theory of optimal taxation does *not* recommend falling marginal tax rates in isolation, but only when combined with a significant 'citizens' income' or 'demogrant' – a fixed sum of money paid by the government to all citizens.[29] Still, the combination remains mysterious. Why does it offer the best compromise between efficiency and fairness? A full explanation is extremely complex; here I shall mention just three key points.[30] First, falling marginal rates generate more revenue than rising marginal rates, all other things being equal. With falling rates, the higher rates apply to the first slices of income, so more people pay tax on some part of their income at a higher rate. The result is that under falling marginal rates, more revenue for redistribution can be raised for the same price in terms of inefficiency. Second, the productivity of high earners is greater (which is why they earn more), so distorting their behaviour through taxation will have a greater effect on productive activity – a greater inefficiency cost. These two points both imply that, for any given amount of redistribution, inefficiency is reduced by having constant or falling marginal rates of tax. But, third, redistribution also implies a progressive tax system, so the proportion paid in tax should rise with income. The *only* way to combine this progressivity with falling marginal rates is to have the first part of income exempt from tax altogether – the citizens' income component. This exemption covers a larger *proportion* of income for those on lower and middle incomes, so they end up paying a smaller proportion of their income in tax, even though marginal rates are falling.

Summing up, optimal tax theory implies that constant or falling marginal rates of income tax as income rises, coupled with a significant citizens' income, offer the best trade-off between efficiency and fairness: that is, the most redistribution for a given efficiency cost, or the most efficiency for a given degree of redistribution. It is a striking result – strikingly unpopular with politicians on the left and right – combining the citizens' income hated by the right with low marginal taxation on the rich, hated by the left.[31] The idea of a citizens' income may seem politically inconceivable, but in fact already exists in Alaska. On the other hand, the theoretical result here should not be naively interpreted as a straightforward policy recommendation. To begin with, it rests heavily on various controversial assumptions. For example, in the second point above, I assumed that 'the productivity of high earners is greater (which is why they earn more)'. But of course high earnings may reflect factors such as luck rather than high productivity. If so, the efficiency cost of taxing high earners will be less – more taxation is justified. More generally, once the assumptions underlying the theory are made more realistic, it becomes increasingly difficult to draw any specific conclusions at all about an optimal tax structure. As far as offering a detailed blueprint for this structure, the theory is at best a work in progress. These pessimistic remarks might seem to cast doubt on the entire exercise. In fact the important lessons of optimal tax theory are general ones, not detailed prescriptions.

The first lesson is that, even if a prescription such as 'falling marginal rates combined with a citizens' income' is not directly applicable, it suggests that imaginative and innovative changes to the tax and welfare system may be called for; efficiency and fairness are not best served simply by tweaking tax rates. The second lesson is that optimal tax theory asks the right questions and adopts the right framework for answering them: it focuses on which *post-tax* distribution will maximize happiness, rather than so-called fair deductions from an irrelevant pre-tax baseline. Tax rates in isolation do not matter, but only their overall effect along with welfare payments to the poor, whether in the form of a citizens' income or not.

Finally, this framework even allows us to question the fundamental compromise between efficiency and fairness which has been emphasized so far. Redistributive taxation may involve little if any sacrifice of efficiency after all. Far from introducing a distortion, redistributive taxation may instead help to eliminate two distortions that are already present. Both these distortions arise from the phenomena of adaptation and rivalry introduced in Chapter 2. Due to rivalry, a rise in *my* income effectively imposes a cost on *you*, because it reduces your relative income. Insofar as my happiness increases, this has been achieved at the cost of reducing yours. But because I typically ignore this effect I am like a polluting firm which ignores the costly impact of its polluting activity on others. This rivalrous effect of an income increase, then, is analogous to pollution. And pollution is taxed to correct this distortion – so income should be too. Turning to the other distortion, people repeatedly but mistakenly believe that future income increases will make them happier, despite the fact that adaptation has always undermined this in the past. So the attraction of higher income is akin to an addiction, and like other addictions (such as nicotine), there is a case for taxing it. Even economists who are enthusiastic believers in 'consumer sovereignty' generally concede that established smokers may continue to smoke, not because it makes them happier, but because they are addicted. Effectively, smokers' choices are distorted by their addiction, and taxation can counterbalance this effect. Similarly, taxing income more heavily can help to counteract its addictive effects.[32]

It is worth emphasizing that these arguments for income taxation are purely concerned with eliminating distortions – that is, with promoting efficiency. They do not rely on moral or political objections to inequality. Put another way, however we choose to strike the balance between efficiency and fairness, adaptation and rivalry imply that income taxes should be higher than we previously thought.

Deserving what we earn[33]

Man: There needs to be a higher tax for the real serious incomes, 'cos my sister's other half is a stockbroker and he gets quarter of a million bonuses a year, and he's paying the same tax level as me – I'm going 'Jesus Christ'.[34]

Although many of us are skeptical that rates of pay in real markets reflect what people deserve, the belief that there is *some* link between rates of pay and just deserts remains widespread. More common still is the view that people *ought* to be paid what they deserve. This is sometimes linked to the idea that if only the economy and society worked as a true free market and meritocracy, then many more people would be able to earn their just deserts. In what follows I argue that, even in principle, it is hard to see how market rates of pay might be justified as deserved. A true free market and meritocracy would not secure this objective. So if people ought to be paid what they deserve, then the pattern of pay is likely to be radically different from anything which might arise in a free market. John Rawls, one of the most influential political philosophers of the 20th century, elegantly captured one of the intractable problems: 'We do not deserve our place in the distribution of natural talents, any more than we deserve our initial starting place in society.'[35] In other words, those born with inherited talent deserve it no more than those born with inherited wealth. In both cases, we are not responsible for our inheritance, so we do not deserve it.

Market rates of pay may fail to give people what they deserve simply because the market is not 'free' in the usual sense – there might be excessive regulation or a monopoly employer or union. But whether markets are free is not our subject here. Rather, the issue is whether free markets can in principle give people their just deserts, so I shall assume that 'market rates of pay' refers to free markets. Two broad arguments will be examined in detail.

Deserving compensation

Some jobs are nastier than others. So some people deserve to be paid more to compensate them for doing nasty jobs. This is the compensation argument. It can be split into two parts:

1   If someone incurs greater burdens or sacrifices in order to do their job, then they deserve to be paid more in compensation.

2   In reality, market rates of pay reflect these burdens.

Together, these two claims support the conclusion that market pay
differences are justified, because they reflect differences in the amount of
compensation people deserve to do their jobs.[36] The compensation
argument is not limited just to explaining why bomb disposal experts and
other exceptionally hazardous or unpleasant occupations command more
pay. The meaning of job-related burdens should be understood much more
broadly. As well as adverse working conditions or danger, jobs involving a
very high degree of responsibility and potential associated stress, or jobs
requiring a long period of prior training, both involve greater burdens in
this sense. For example, police officers often have heavy responsibilities,
actuaries undergo very lengthy training, and surgeons must endure both.
Given the range of possible job-related burdens, the compensation
argument might, at least in principle, be able to justify all the pay differences we see in reality. But do the two parts of the compensation argument
withstand scrutiny?

It looks very unlikely. The second part, that market pay differences in
reality compensate for job-related burdens, is hard to take seriously. Two
people can be doing exactly the same job as each other in two separate
countries, or even in two separate regions within the same country, and yet
be paid quite differently. Such pay differences occur in reality even if (i) the
job-related burdens, such as travel time to work, are identical in the two
jobs; and (ii) the purchasing power of money is also identical: where, for
instance, local housing costs are equivalent in the two locations. The key
reason that pay differences between identical jobs persist, even after
adjusting for these two factors, is a familiar one: market rates of pay reflect
supply and demand. If there is a shortage in a particular area of say, chefs,
but high demand to eat out in restaurants, then chefs will be paid more in
that area, although they sweat no harder over their stoves than their
colleagues elsewhere.

So market rates of pay do not solely reflect differing job burdens. But
perhaps pay differences *partly* reflect the fact that certain jobs involve
greater burdens. It is certainly an appealing idea that a cleaner at a chicken-
processing factory should earn more than a cleaner at the office of a
London bank. But do they? The cleaner who works in London probably
faces higher travel and accommodation costs, but if they earn more than

the chicken factory cleaner, how much of their extra pay reflects just these costs, and how much the forces of supply and demand? The problem lies in separating the deserved pay difference from the undeserved premium due to market forces. Clearly this will be a difficult task in practice, but is it even possible in theory? To answer this question, we must return to the underlying idea of why compensating pay differences could be deserved. Imagine a hypothetical world in which everyone could choose to do any job they liked (regardless of whether they were qualified to do it). In this world, the only way anyone could be persuaded to take an unpleasant or otherwise burdensome job would be if the pay attached to it was higher, to compensate. In general, variations in rates of pay would solely reflect the relative attractiveness of different jobs. We would expect the pay and attractiveness to balance each other out, so that unattractive jobs would be highly paid, while attractive ones would be poorly paid. Effectively, everyone would be equally well off in terms of the overall package of pay and attractiveness in their job. For example, many people would choose the job of a top footballer like David Beckham. If we could all freely choose such jobs, the pay received by top footballers would fall. Football clubs would not have to offer high pay in order to attract people to a job with relatively few associated burdens. In contrast, the pay of chicken factory cleaners would probably be relatively high.

It seems that there is a flaw in the story so far. Hardly any of us have innate football skills equal to David Beckham's, so how could we choose such jobs? But as John Rawls emphasized, we inherit these natural talents, and we are not responsible for our genetic inheritance, so cannot be said to deserve it. Consequently we do not deserve to be blocked from entering certain occupations purely on the basis of our (lack of) natural talent. Such barriers are irrelevant for the purpose of determining *deserved* pay differences due to job-related burdens. This is precisely why our story describes a hypothetical world rather than the real one. It tries to capture the relative burdens of, say, cleaners vis-à-vis footballers, by imagining how much we would need to be paid to tempt us to do one rather than the other, assuming we could choose either. Still, the idea of the relative attractiveness of two jobs when we are incapable of doing one of them remains, at best, hard to imagine. But this difficulty only reinforces the problem facing the compensation argument: even in a truly hypothetical world, we struggle to imagine that part of pay which is deserved compensation for job-related burdens, let alone define or quantify it. Accordingly, the prospects for adequately distinguishing deserved compensatory pay differences from undeserved premiums (due to market forces) look remote – that is, remote in theory, even when the messy complexities of the real world are ignored.

The hypothetical world just described does have the merit of clarifying how pay in real markets fails to reflect deserved compensatory pay differences between occupations. In the hypothetical world there are no undeserved barriers to entering certain occupations, so pay differences are deserved, reflecting people's free choices. In the real world, cleaners are paid much less than top footballers or bankers, but not because cleaning jobs are less burdensome. On the contrary, they may be more burdensome, but cleaners do not receive higher pay in compensation because they cannot usually become footballers or bankers. They have no great football skills, and also lack the education and aptitude to become bankers. In the perfect free market, cleaners receive just enough to prevent them from switching to another job that they could actually get, which does not include playing football or banking. To the extent that cleaners' lack of access to certain jobs is due to genetic inheritance (few football or numeracy skills) or inability to afford higher education (entry requirement for banking), the resulting occupational pay differences between cleaners and footballers or bankers are not deserved. They do not result from free choices for which the cleaners are responsible.

To sum up, pay in the hypothetical ideal world may fulfil the first claim of the compensation argument, because pay differences are entirely due to compensatory burdens. But these are not the pay differences we see in real markets, so the second claim does not hold. Market pay rates clearly reflect undeserved factors too. And it is hard to see how we could isolate and measure that *part* of pay which is deserved compensation, even in theory. It is defined by reference to the job that a person would choose if free to choose any job, but it is far from clear that any of us can even imagine such a choice; I would not be myself if free to choose any job – I am the person who is not free to choose to be a footballer, because I struggle to kick a ball straight.

It might seem that the compensation argument can be saved, because my argument against it relies on Rawls' assertion that natural talents are not deserved. We might believe instead that natural talents, or at least the financial rewards that they make possible, are deserved (perhaps because those rewards depend on our effort too). But even if we hold this view, the compensation argument faces another problem.

It is a problem of pay equivalence, not pay difference. In a free market, if Ann and Bill are doing exactly the same job for the same employer, they will receive the same pay.[37] But they may deserve to be paid differently, because of differing burdens faced in doing the same job. We can see this in how Ann and Bill respond to pay cuts. Neither of them will continue in the job if the overall burden of doing the job, as they individually perceive it, outweighs the pay (ignoring any other job benefits for simplicity). It is easy to imagine how, following a pay cut, Ann leaves but Bill stays: the burden of the job was greater for Ann so the job is no longer 'worth it' for her. This might be because Ann travels further to work, or has to pay for a carer for her elderly mother while absent, or simply because she finds the job more difficult or its responsibilities more worrying. It might be objected that Ann finds the job more difficult than Bill simply because of her lack of natural talent – but in this case, assuming she works as hard, she seems just as deserving. Once we take the idea of job-related burdens seriously, it may be that, depending on Ann's exact circumstances, all these factors count as burdens deserving of compensation because Ann did not choose to incur any of them. This implies that Ann deserves to be paid more than Bill on compensation grounds. But Ann and Bill are paid the same, so again, market rates of pay do not give everyone their just deserts. Perhaps another argument for being paid our just deserts will fare better.

Deserving contributions

The idea at the heart of the 'contribution argument' is straightforward: some people deserve to be paid more because they contribute more. In more detail, if the argument is to justify present patterns of pay, it must make two claims:

1   People deserve to be paid in proportion to the value of the
    contribution they make through their job.[38]
2   In reality, market rates of pay are such that people are paid in
    proportion to the contribution they make.

The contribution argument is probably the most widely held version of the belief that pay reflects people's just deserts. But its popularity may be due in part to confusion with other popular ideas. For example, many people believe in 'payment by results', such as 'performance-related pay'. But the most common argument in favour of it is economic, not ethical: if we pay people by results, this gives them an incentive to generate better results. It is very similar to the familiar incentive argument mentioned in the discussion of taxation: if high earners are allowed to keep what they earn, this encourages them to work harder and increases the size of the pie which we can all share. Whatever we think of these incentive arguments, they are not what we have in mind when we talk of what people deserve. They are not our subject matter here, which is to assess an *independent* ethical argument – the widely held view that people deserve to be paid on the basis of their contribution – not the separate idea that it may be expedient to pay some people more in order to encourage their higher productivity.

So the contribution argument is not as persuasive as it appears at first glance. Much of its persuasive power comes from confusing it with two other arguments for market rates of pay: people who contribute deserve to be paid more than those who do not; and people should be paid by results, as an incentive to generate better results. Indeed, the more we probe the contribution argument, the less clear it becomes that it is really a separate argument at all.

There seem to be two broad approaches to defining 'contribution', one in terms of what a worker gives or inputs, and the other in terms of results or output. It might seem natural to talk of someone deserving to be paid on the basis of the results of their work, but there are at least two problems to contend with. First, since our ultimate purpose is to assess whether market rates of pay are deserved, we cannot measure contributions according to how much people are paid for them in the market. For that would be to argue in a circle: market pay is deserved because it reflects contribution, where contribution is defined as market pay. If the contribution argument is to succeed, it must show that its second claim is true. It cannot simply be *defined* to be true. A way of measuring the value of someone's output, independent of their pay in the market, is needed. Second, the obvious problem with the idea of deserving to be paid by results is that these results, good or bad, may be due to many factors apart from my own input, including pure luck, which I do not deserve. The strength of defining 'contribution' more literally in terms of how much I give or input, rather than as the result or outcome of my work, is that it is more closely connected to my own actions, for which I can legitimately claim credit. However, if we fall back on defining contribution in terms of inputs, we come dangerously close to the burdens of the compensation argument we have already rejected. A surgeon who takes on a bigger case load may be interpreted as making a greater contribution, or bearing a heavier burden of responsibility. More generally, it is far from clear whether working hours measure contribution, or a burden deserving compensation. There may be little conceptual space left between burdens on the one hand and undeserved outcomes or results on the other for a meaningful measure of contribution to squeeze in.

Let me set aside these doubts about the possibility of a separate contribution argument. For it seems that however we measure contribution, the first claim of the contribution argument is difficult to defend. This is the claim that people deserve to be paid in proportion to the value of their contribution. The crucial problem is that the value of my contribution, however measured, will typically depend on various factors for which I am not responsible. And most of us believe that people can only deserve credit for things for which they are responsible.[39] As well as pure luck, other factors which affect the value of my contribution include market conditions (supply and demand for the goods or services which I provide), my training and my natural talents. Clearly we are not responsible for pure luck, but our responsibility for the other factors is controversial: many people probably believe they are responsible for their training, but not market conditions.

Consider Rich, who joins a small software development company just two weeks before a surprise takeover, which results in all employees receiving $20,000 in share options. This may seem like pure luck, so Rich does not deserve the $20,000, but Rich points out that he trained in software development precisely so he could join a lucrative, dynamic sector of the economy where stock option payouts following takeovers are not uncommon. He 'made his own luck' by a particular choice of training, for which he was responsible, and so deserves the high pay associated with his highly valued contributions in this industry. Or so the argument runs. Rob is another employee in the same firm who also receives $20,000; he has worked there much longer than Rich, but only ended up in software development because his aggressive parents pushed him hard into that career. Is he more or less deserving? Both Rich and Rob obtained their jobs on the basis of close links between their employer and the computer science department of the prestigious university they attended. So pity poor Paul, who had the same idea as Rich, but could not afford the fees and attended his local university instead. It has a weak reputation, and Paul is still unemployed. But perhaps he is just as deserving as Rich. The line between luck and responsibility is painfully difficult to draw.

Now consider doctors and nurses. A doctor earns more than a nurse; suppose for the sake of argument that their contribution is unarguably greater. Nevertheless, the pay difference may be undeserved, because some nurses may have wanted to become doctors, but not had the opportunity to do so, for the same reasons as Paul – they could not afford the training. Pay differences seem deserved only if we all have a fair opportunity to earn more; otherwise earning less is not truly our fault, our responsibility. Similarly, someone may fail to gain entry to medical school to train as a doctor because of a demographic quirk that year – lots of young candidates, and few older doctors at retirement age. Had they applied a year earlier, they would have been accepted. Again, the opportunities seem unfairly distributed.

Of course, even if we ignore these worries about the first part of the contribution argument, the link between desert and contribution, the argument depends on its second claim too. This is the claim that in reality, people are paid in proportion to the contribution they make. So for instance, we might grant that doctors deserve to earn more than nurses on the basis of their contribution. But the contribution argument for market pay differences still fails unless doctors and nurses are rewarded in the market in proportion to their contributions. And this is generally not true, because market pay rates reflect supply and demand, as we saw with the compensation argument. If doctors are scarce but there are plenty of nurses, doctors will be paid even more, for instance in comparison to another economy where doctors are less scarce, although the relative contributions of doctors and nurses are the same in both economies.

Economists have a stock reply to this objection. If doctors are scarce, then their contributions will be worth more. Therefore, when market forces reflect this scarcity by pushing up their pay, they will still be paid what they deserve. But assuming each doctor works no more hours, how can their contribution be worth more? Economists believe that the *value* of the hours worked will be greater. They argue that doctors in short supply will prioritize the most important work and ignore the rest, so on average, the work they do will be relatively more important – relatively more valuable – than if there were enough doctors to do it all. This reply clearly rests on debatable premises, such as the assumption that the average value of nurses' work remains the same when doctors are scarce – when instead we might expect them to take on some of the tasks usually performed by doctors. In any case, the economists' reply cannot be generalized. In the case of medical staff, their argument implicitly appeals to an objective measure of contribution (such as patients treated or lives saved), independent of market pay rates, to justify the latter. However, in general there is no objective measure, and economists rely instead on market prices of goods and services to measure the contribution of the person who supplied them. The idea is simple enough: the market price reflects how much consumers are willing to pay for something, which in turn indicates how valuable it is. If market prices *do* measure contribution, and people are paid exactly the market price of the goods and services they produce, then it follows that pay equals contribution, and so the second part of the contribution argument holds. The problem is that there are several reasons why market prices do *not* measure contribution satisfactorily.

To begin with, most goods and services are jointly produced by many people. Although we may know the market price of the product, it is very hard to see how each worker's *share* of that total value could be determined.[40] Second, if market prices measure contribution, then the contribution of an artisan who makes crocodile skin handbags must be greater than that of someone providing advice to the poor on welfare payments. Market prices reflect willingness to pay, and the rich are willing to pay more for most things than the poor, but it does not follow that some goods (crocodile handbags) provide more benefit for the rich than others (welfare payment advice) do for the poor. Finally, consumers are very often not 'sovereign', as we found in Chapter 2. Just because they are willing to pay more for something does not imply that it makes them happier, or serves their goals better than something less costly. Advertising, and the troubles posed by excessive choice, can get in the way. To sum up, for these reasons among others, market prices do not properly reflect contributions, and so the second part of the contribution argument collapses.

The compensation and contribution arguments are the two leading contenders for showing that the significant pay differences we see between jobs are in fact deserved. But neither argument succeeds. Naturally, we resist this conclusion: the idea of 'what we deserve' is so deeply rooted in our ordinary thinking about pay that to abandon it seems unthinkable. Can our ordinary thinking really be so mistaken? We can tackle this question from both ends: first, ideas of desert may be more popular than they deserve to be; second, we do not have to think the unthinkable after all.

Why ideas of desert may be more popular than they deserve to be

My argument is illustrated by the previous sentence: we often talk of what 'deserves' to happen, but we mean no more than 'it ought to happen'. The talk of desert is just an assertion which begs a question; it does not refer to any distinctive, fundamental ethical concept which all would acknowledge, such as freedom or justice. Desert may be another basic ethical category like these, but its widespread usage in ordinary life does not necessarily count as evidence. So it remains elusive. And it is certainly not a timeless ethical absolute, because the ancient Greeks had no notion of desert at all. In Sophocles' *Oedipus Rex*, Thebes was cursed with plague and drought because Oedipus married his mother. It was irrelevant to the Greek value system that Oedipus was a righteous man who did not realize what he was doing.

Turning to more specific beliefs about deserved differences in pay, the most popular basis for this is probably effort: the view that some people deserve to be paid more because they try harder, they exert more effort. But measuring effort is an intractable problem.[41] Someone's achievements can usually be observed, but how much are they due to effort, rather than factors such as luck or innate talents? And 'hours worked' is not a satisfactory measure of effort either, because some people work hard, others lazily. This brings us to a more fundamental objection to the effort-based view of desert. The willingness and ability to exert effort may itself be heavily influenced by genetic inheritance, and family upbringing, rather than reflect a choice for which the worker is responsible.[42] Beyond the simplest (and increasingly rare) work tasks, 'laziness' may not be entirely due to conscious choice. I may simply lack the imagination to realize I could work differently – in a more efficient and intensive way.[43] So it may be neither fair nor practicable to base judgements of what we deserve on the effort we exert. Once we recognize this, then ideas of desert lose much of their popular appeal.

Why we do not have to think the unthinkable: Pay differences are justified

Some people may deserve to be paid more. This statement might seem to contradict the conclusion I have just reached about the compensation and contribution arguments. But the conclusion was that *existing* market pay differences are not deserved. This does not rule out the possibility of justifying as deserved another, fairer pattern of pay. Nevertheless, the most obvious means of justification, our differing levels of effort, is problematic for the reasons I have just suggested.

If we set aside effort-based justifications for differing pay, then there is still one argument left. It is the incentive argument mentioned earlier. Good performance is rewarded with higher pay; this acts as an incentive to encourage good performance. And socially valuable occupations should receive greater rewards in order to attract the most able people to work in them. In both cases, we might say that pay differences are deserved – but that description would be a mistake. As emphasized above, the incentive argument is not an argument about desert at all, so pay differences are not deserved. Nevertheless, they are justified because everyone benefits, that is, overall happiness is increased.

This incentive argument does not support excessive inequalities in pay. Instead we face a trade-off akin to that concerning optimal taxation: some pay inequality may be justified insofar as overall happiness increases *enough*. And as well as overall happiness, we may be especially concerned with improving the lot of the poorest. Pay inequalities which make the rich much richer and leave the rest of us untouched are unlikely to be justified. We return now to a different incentives argument, that concerning the link between tax and incentives to work.

Tax, ethics and economics

The standard economic argument about tax and incentives to work is built on a crucial assumption: if income taxes rise, there is a fall in the benefit to the individual from working. So there is less incentive to work because the benefit from doing so has fallen. But this assumption may be faulty, because tax increases pay for improvements in public services. What if people also consider the wider benefits from improved public services, rather than reacting to tax increases in isolation? The overall benefit from working may now be the same as before the tax increase, although some of it now comes in the form of improved pensions, health care, education or other gains from increased public expenditure. And if the overall benefit from working remains unchanged, there is no reason to expect the incentive to work to have decreased. Most economists will find this possibility so bizarre as to be scarcely comprehensible. It is obscured altogether by the orthodox economists' tale of workers thinking in terms of changes in 'the price of leisure' and balancing the income and substitution effects. Non-economists will doubtless find that tale more bizarre. Once we set it aside and begin with an open mind, it does not seem so implausible that workers might take the broader view of tax changes suggested here. Consider the following scenarios.

Suppose Ann chooses to commit x per cent of her income to a pension. After pension contributions, her short-term marginal benefit from an extra hour worked is now smaller. However, we do not expect this to have a distortionary impact on her incentive to work, because overall the benefit from working is as large as before. It is just that some of this benefit has been saved for retirement. Suppose instead that the x per cent contribution is to a *compulsory* pension, funded through income tax. Again, there seems no reason to assume that the rewards from working are necessarily affected because some of them are compulsorily ring-fenced for the future. Suppose finally that a tax increase of x per cent is used to pay for improved public services. Now there are at least four factors affecting whether Ann feels the overall benefit of working is as great as before. First, whether she sees taxation as a kind of theft in line with the ownership principle; second, whether she wants the public service improvements made possible by increased taxation; third, whether she trusts that they will actually happen; fourth, whether she sees any link between the tax increase she faces and service improvements: after all, access to public services is not (usually) dependent on paying a tax contribution. If Ann ceased paid work or otherwise stopped paying tax, public services like health care and education would still be available to her. Clearly, everything depends on how increased taxes are perceived.

Economics takes a much narrower view. Essentially it adopts a very negative interpretation of the fourth factor mentioned above. Even though collectively we cannot have increased public expenditure without paying higher taxes, *Homo economicus* is assumed to consider his own circumstances alone. From this individualistic perspective, if public services are available whether or not the individual pays tax, then tax is a pure cost, with no benefit in return. I know of no economist studying the impact of tax changes on work incentives who has considered the possibility outlined here – that people may see public expenditure as a form of benefit in kind, akin to a pension. And yet there are several reasons to take it seriously. To begin with, in the *Homo economicus* view, since tax payments are completely disconnected from public service benefits, people only pay tax because of the penalties facing tax evaders. But empirical evidence suggests people pay more tax than this view would imply;[44] similarly, there is evidence from laboratory experiments that people contribute more to a 'public good' which provides collective benefits than *Homo economicus* would do.[45] And once people realize that they must pay tax, it is psychologically much easier to accept this by associating the payments with public service benefits;[46] rather than following *Homo economicus,* restlessly calculating whether it is worth evading tax, based on the probability of being caught and the size of the punishment.

The empirical study of attitudes to taxation is still in its infancy.[47] It has focused on whether taxpayers will try to evade tax, given the opportunity. The argument here suggests that the study should be substantially broadened to include taxpayers' views about the link between tax and public expenditure benefits. It would connect the argument about tax and work incentives with the debate about attitudes to taxation more generally. If tax increases are seen as tied to public service improvements, and these in turn are understood as benefits in kind, like pensions, then the relationship between tax increases and incentives to work will be very different to that portrayed in orthodox economics. For any given level of income tax, the adverse effects on efficiency are likely to be lower if taxpayers do not regard their pre-tax income as 'owned'; if they strongly associate taxation with public expenditure increases; and if they believe that their taxes will be spent wisely by government.

There is an important general lesson here. The standard economic efficiency argument is much too narrow. Policy entrepreneurs often present it as a reliable scientific relationship between tax and incentives. But in fact the relationship depends heavily on the wider context of ethical judgements about ownership, whether taxpayers act like *Homo economicus,* and whether they trust government to turn increased taxes into improved public services. Again, we have ethical economics: the economic arguments about taxation cannot be separated from the underlying ethical debates. Chapter 2 introduced *Homo economicus,* ownership was discussed in this chapter; questions of trust in public services are addressed in Chapter 7; in the next chapter it is time to look in more detail at the obvious yardstick for policy, happiness.

But first I summarize the arguments of this chapter. Three widely held beliefs about pay have been examined: that we own our pre-tax income, that income taxation generally damages the economy, and that differences in market rates of pay are, or could be, justified as deserved. I have argued that all three beliefs are mistaken; it is difficult to overstate the implications. Many people would see their work pay in a new light and, as a result, think about their working lives in a very different way. For example, if high market rates of pay are not deserved, then high pay should not be seen as a signal of achievement to the extent it is at present. A truly open debate about taxation might finally be possible, one not tainted with the view that income tax is in some sense immoral. We do not own our pre-tax income. And since patterns of pay in the market are not the sacrosanct reflection of what people deserve, there can be no presumption that they must be protected from infringement by taxation.

Chapter Five

Happiness

You will never be happy if you continue to search for what happiness consists of. You will never live if you are looking for the meaning of life. (attributed to Albert Camus)

The happiness of society is the end of government.
(John Adams, Thoughts on Government[1])

How can I be happy? How can you be happy? What makes for a good life? In case you were still wondering, this book does not offer recipes for happiness, nor will it tell you how to win friends and influence people. I say this straightaway, in the hope that it will prevent cynical readers from moving on to the next chapter in disgust.

Their tut-tutting is not entirely surprising. The idea of research into 'happiness' strikes many people as bombastic, even absurd. Why not, they ask, tackle the meaning of life in the next chapter, and polish off 'achieving world peace' in the chapter after that? They need not worry. My ambitions are reassuringly humble. Chapter 3 introduced a limited, albeit crude, notion of happiness defined in terms of satisfaction levels measured in surveys. Part of my task in what follows is to defend the conclusions reached there – to show that happiness surveys make enough sense to be taken seriously. But I shall go further, and explore what is valuable in the economics and psychology of happiness. There *is* something valuable, but great philosophical leaps must be made to reach it, leaps we may not be prepared to make. However, we should not object to philosophical athletics in general, because any satisfactory story about happiness will require them. There is no way to avoid making explicit moral judgements if we are to gain an understanding of happiness which is deep enough to help determine the details of practical policies. The economics of happiness is inescapably ethical.

Measuring happiness

As soon as we look beyond the happiness surveys, the cynics seem to be right. The happiness economists and psychologists have grand ambitions: happiness can be defined neutrally, scientifically, objectively, they insist, with survey responses being merely fallible estimates of the true happiness score. A leading pioneer of this view is Daniel Kahneman, the Nobel Prize-winning psychologist introduced in Chapter 2.[2]

Kahneman introduces his discussion of 'objective happiness' by asking how we answer the kind of question about happiness that we often ask:

> 'How happy was Helen in March?' In the context of an informal conversation this question would usually be understood and answered with little difficulty. If we know Helen well and saw her often in March, we probably believe we know whether she was happy then, we almost certainly believe that *she* knows whether she was happy then, and with even greater certainty we believe that she knew it then… As soon as we take on the scientific role, we are no longer sure of what the question means… The aim of this chapter is to narrow the gap between lay knowledge and professional ignorance.[3]

Life must be very simple for Kahneman and his colleagues if they really have this 'lay knowledge'. Imagine that Kahneman's wife is called Helen. Many of those tiresome misunderstandings of marriage are avoided. No 'leave me alone. Can't you tell I'm feeling miserable?'; and no need for time-consuming reflection on one's life: 'things seem to be going well, but am I happy? Is this all there is to life?' Or 'we're going to have a baby/get married. I'm delighted, of course, but scared. Aren't I just supposed to feel happy, without reservations? Or is this what true happiness feels like?'

There is professional ignorance *and* lay ignorance: it is very difficult for someone to assess even their *own* all-things-considered happiness, and the ignorance only deepens when it comes to assessments by an external observer. Much of our greatest literature takes this ignorance as a starting point in grappling with the human condition. Other literature and ordinary thinking doubt that there is any meaningful thing called overall happiness, subjective or objective, to be discovered or measured. But before pursuing this skepticism any further, we should examine with an open mind the case for happiness as understood by happiness economists and psychologists, our 'happiness experts' hereafter. The evidence is powerful enough to unsettle the most wizened old cynic. No more tut-tutting.

Happiness facts

People who in surveys report themselves as happy are:

- more likely to smile
- more likely to be assessed as happy by their friends and spouses
- more likely to be assessed as happy by an interviewer who they do not know
- more likely to initiate contact with friends
- more likely to respond to requests for help
- less likely to die
- less likely to attempt suicide
- less likely to suffer psychological illness
- less likely to be absent from work.

This is a long and impressive list, and there are no doubt many other items which could be added to it, all of which correlate self-reported happiness with elements of, or ingredients for, happiness as we intuitively understand it.[4] But correlations are just that: an association between self-reported happiness and, say, contacting friends, which does not imply causation. Extroverts are more likely to initiate contact with friends, and may be more likely to report themselves as happy too – this would explain the correlation, but it does not show that what is meant by 'happiness' is being measured. Nevertheless, the sheer number and range of these correlations suggests that self-reported happiness may be meaningful after all. At the very least, those who consider themselves happy when responding to a survey are more likely to behave in the ways listed above, behaviours that we associate with happiness.

But does reported happiness relate to a real phenomenon? Happiness experts have been greatly influenced by recent research in neuroscience. The actions indicative of happiness listed above are not just correlated with self-reported happiness; they are correlated with particular brain activity too. And this same brain activity is also correlated with people's reports of positive feelings and memories. In a range of experiments, people have been shown pleasing images, such as a picture of a smiling baby or a humorous film clip. The result is that their left prefrontal cortex becomes more active (as measured by various scanning techniques), while their right prefrontal cortex becomes less so. Conversely, if the stimulus is negative – a deformed baby or a disturbing film – then the right side of the brain becomes more active, the left side less so.[5] Even when they are not exposed to a stimulus, people differ in the pattern of their brain activity. Given that left-side brain activity seems to be associated with positive stimuli, we might expect people with more dominant left sides to report more positive feelings, with dominant right-siders reporting more negative feelings. This is indeed the case. Turning to the list above, dominant left-siders are also more likely to smile and be assessed as happy by their friends, while right-siders smile less and are regarded as less happy by their friends. Left-siders purposely given the flu virus were less likely to get ill, too.

All this evidence seems to correlate brain activity with positive/negative feelings and behaviours, and these in turn are correlated with self-reported happiness, but is there a more direct link? At least one widely discussed experiment suggests there is. All the experimental subjects – victims might be a better term – had a very hot pad applied to one of their legs. The pad was exactly the same temperature for everyone, but people gave very different reports of the level of pain. Nevertheless, the differing reports were highly correlated with brain activity, again suggesting that such reports are meaningful.[6] Still, this experiment might seem worrying for the defenders of happiness surveys because it demonstrates so clearly that the same objective stimulus is described differently by different people. So when people are being asked to state their overall life satisfaction, a harder task than reporting the intensity of a one-dimensional pain, can we be sure that their reply will relate to their objective brain activity, or will they use different words to describe the same satisfaction? Of course, the interviewer with the clipboard could attach electrodes to the respondent's head to monitor their brain activity, but try picturing this in the middle of a crowded shopping street...

The happiness experts have conducted interesting research on a closely related issue – whether people speaking different languages will describe the same satisfaction fundamentally differently. Switzerland is a particularly good place to test this, because there are German-, French- and Italian-speaking groups in a small and relatively homogeneous country. They answer the happiness question in different languages, but all report similar levels of happiness. All the Swiss are happier than their neighbours speaking the same language in Germany, France or Italy.[7] In another study, a group of Chinese students each answered the same happiness question twice, two weeks apart, once in Chinese and once in English. Their answers in each language were highly correlated, with the average level of happiness being nearly identical on the two occasions.[8] Happiness experts conclude that language need not be a barrier to measuring happiness and so comparisons between countries are legitimate. Yet the nagging question remains: can happiness be measured? And if it can, is that what these surveys are measuring? With its breezy optimism the happiness experts' reading of the evidence ignores some awkward objections.

To begin with, it is easy to pick holes in the neuroscience. As ever, the problem is not the science itself, but the interpretative spin put on the results. To begin with, the core of the neuroscientific research is a set of correlations which do not demonstrate any causation. There is little understanding of why external stimuli are associated with increased brain activity, so there is no basis for assuming causation. And even the correlations are less robust than they appear, because of the assumptions which have been made to derive them. For instance, most of the research adopts the 'subtractive method', in which measurements of brain activity in the control condition (when there is no stimulus) are subtracted from measurements in the experimental condition (when the stimulus is present). This is controversial, because it assumes that what is happening in the brain in the two conditions is essentially identical except for the mental process of interest. Some psychologists also question the underlying theoretical framework behind these experiments, which treats different cognitive processes as neatly separable into activities occurring in different parts of the brain. This concern is provocatively summarized by the title of William Uttal's recent critique, *The New Phrenology*.[9] There is a plausible alternative framework which assumes instead that different parts of the brain usually interact with each other, and even simple processes are handled by multiple regions. Any relationship associating particular processes (such as happy feelings) with specific locations in the brain is not sufficiently constant over time to allow the subtractive method to work.

Nor are the locations sufficiently constant across people to support the generalized conclusions which have been drawn.[10] At the very least, the neuroscience cannot be treated as any kind of 'proof' of the existence of objectively measurable happiness.[11]

Regardless of the state of the neuroscience, the happiness experts face other challenges. Do the survey questions mean the same thing to different people? As well as the Swiss and Chinese research suggesting happiness means the same thing in different languages, it is striking that whether surveys ask people how 'happy' they are, or how 'satisfied', or to give their life a numerical score, the ranking of countries remains unchanged.[12] It seems that the exact question wording may not matter, because the question elicits essentially the same reply in each case. However, this explanation leaves the door open to another possibility: different question wordings draw the same response, but that response is not comparable across countries. This seems likely, because words like happiness do *not* mean the same in different countries.

This should hardly come as a shock. Experienced travellers know that the same words have very different connotations in different languages and cultures. The title of the film *Lost in Translation* captures the problem perfectly. Having a close friend from a different culture is even more revealing, because the different meanings are most apparent in words which express feelings, emotions or judgements. In the business world, when complimenting an employee or a product, Americans will typically be much more effusive with praise than their East European counterparts. These cross-cultural differences run deeper than many realize, particularly with a concept as overloaded with meaning as happiness.

Perhaps the most devastating message from linguistics is that the question, 'how happy are you?' is almost incoherent in many languages, akin to asking 'how female are you?'[13] In French, Italian and Russian, the words for happy, *heureux, felice* and *scastlivyj* are absolute, not quantitative matters of degree. They are very close in meaning to the words for happiness: *bonheur, felicità* and *scastie,* words used to denote an existential condition which is absolute and rarely achieved, not a transitory feeling. In English, *happiness* sometimes still has these connotations, but *happy* has been degraded by excessive use. The *Collins-Robert English–French Dictionary* gives these examples: 'I'll be quite happy to do it'; 'I'm happy here reading'; 'I'm not happy about leaving him alone'. In every case the

French word *heureux* has not developed these extended meanings, and the Dictionary suggests completely different words and phrases for the translation. It is no surprise that *happy* is spoken over twice as often in English as *heureux* is in French. An obvious implication of these differences is that English speakers may be more likely to declare themselves happy than the French, because they think of the everyday feelings of contentment and being at ease, as well as the rarefied idea of happiness. They are happy to declare themselves happy. Or as Nietzsche put it in *Maxims and Arrows,* 'Man does not strive after happiness; only the Englishman does that.'

Of course our use of language does not obey dictionary definitions: it should be the other way round. The dictionary guidance reflects usage which in turn reflects cultural norms. In her memoir *Lost in Translation,* Polish-born Eva Hoffman describes her departure from Poland aged 13 with her parents:

> [My classmates] choose melancholy verses in which life is figured as a vale of tears or a river of suffering… This tone of sadness is something we all enjoy. It makes us feel the gravity of life and it is gratifying to have a truly tragic event – a parting forever – to give vent to such romantic feelings.

Two years later she experiences another parting for ever from teenage friends, this time in the US:

> 'It was great fun knowing you!' they exclaim… 'Don't ever lose your friendly personality!' 'Keep cheerful, and nothing can harm you!'

Different cultures do not just understand happiness differently; they have very different ways of expressing it, and of expressing sadness. There are countless other examples, but it might seem that while wallowing in cultural relativism we have forgotten the physiological evidence. Self-reported happiness is well-correlated with smiling in all countries – so surely happier nations *are* happier, because their populations smile more. But is a smile in one country just as significant as a smile in another? An American woman who married a Pole and moved to Warsaw observes:

Americans smile more in situations where Poles tend not to… In
American culture, you don't advertise your daily headaches; it's bad form;
so you turn up the corners of the mouth – or at least try – according to
the Smile Code.[14]

The correlation between self-reported happiness and smiling does not
demonstrate that happiness means the same in different countries – but it
does reflect the fact that the tendency to smile, and the tendency to be
outwardly cheerful, describing oneself as happy, are both driven by the
same cultural norms.[15]

So the cross-country comparisons of happiness are not quite what they
seem. It may be more difficult to describe oneself as happy in some
countries, because the word is taken to mean an existential condition which
is much more difficult to attain, or the words 'happy' and 'happiness' may
effectively mean the same thing in different cultures, yet people in some
cultures are much less willing to describe themselves as happy. In principle
as well as practice, these two possibilities may be impossible to separate.

To illustrate the problems, turn back to the striking scatter diagram in
Chapter 3 (see page 51), showing many East European countries clustered
on the left-hand side with low income and happiness levels. Part of the
explanation may be that 'being happy' in these countries means a much
more exalted state, much harder to reach, and people are in any case not
so accustomed to talking cheerfully about life. This is not to deny the
relevance of economic and political factors too: life under Soviet-style
communism and its immediate aftermath made people miserable. But
considering the cross-country happiness comparisons in isolation is
misleading. There is a cultural and linguistic dimension to the story. If
hypothetically we could define happiness in objective terms, standardized
across languages and cultures, cross-country happiness comparisons might
look rather different.

We return from this speculation to the nagging questions: *can* we define
happiness objectively? Even *within* a language and culture, can happiness
be measured? And if it can, is that what these surveys are measuring?

Our happiness experts generally agree on the answer – back to Bentham.
The 18th-century utilitarian philosopher Jeremy Bentham believed that
happiness consists in the greatest balance of pleasures over pains, both
defined quite broadly. Happiness involved maximizing *utility,*

that property in any object whereby it tends to produce benefit, advantage, pleasure, good or happiness, (all this in the present case comes to the same thing) or (what comes again to the same thing) to prevent the happening of mischief, pain, evil, or unhappiness to the party whose interest is considered.[16]

Kahneman's approach is very similar, basing his definition of objective happiness on 'instant utility', again understood broadly to include any pleasure/pain or good/bad experience. Objective happiness is defined as the average level of this instant utility over a period of time. The idea is that each moment of experience has a 'good' or 'bad' value, and objective happiness over the period is a weighted average of these good and bad values, with longer experiences receiving more weight and shorter experiences less.[17] Among economists, at present the most well-known and influential advocate of happiness economics in Britain is Richard Layard. He also adopts Bentham's view of happiness (with one reservation to be discussed below).

So in principle the happiness experts are clear about what they are trying to measure, so-called objective happiness, the average utility of all moments of experience over the relevant time period. In practice they usually rely on self-reported happiness, the subjective assessments obtained from asking people how happy they are in surveys. The problem of course is that this subjective data may drift far from the objective happiness that supposedly lies behind it. Indeed, there are so many psychological theories about why the survey responses may not reflect the respondent's objective happiness that it is difficult to know where to begin. I shall mention just a few of the possibilities.[18]

To begin with, when a person is asked to report their happiness with their life as a whole, their answer may be overly influenced by their current mood. There is plenty of evidence: for example, people are less likely to report themselves as happy when the weather is bad, although drawing the respondent's attention to the weather will reduce this effect. Mood is much more likely to influence answers to overall 'how happy are you?' questions rather than narrower questions such as 'how happy are you with your work?' It seems that people subconsciously fall back on their mood when the question is harder to answer. In a famous study, the performance of the German soccer team in the 1982 World Cup affected Germans' general life satisfaction responses, but not their reported satisfaction with work and income.[19]

Even if people are not swayed by their present mood, their answers to happiness questions will be more influenced by information and memories which are readily *available,* in the sense described in Chapter 2: memories of recent events and recently used information will be more available, as will particularly vivid or striking memories. Some students were asked 'how happy are you?' before being asked 'how many dates did you have last month?' A second group was asked the same two questions, but the question order was reversed. The correlation between the two answers was much higher when the dating question was asked first, because the dating information was much more available to this second group, and so significantly affected their responses.[20] Chapter 2 also introduced a particular type of availability effect known as Peak-End evaluations. People remember any experience in terms of the extreme moments and the final moment of the experience. They do not, as Layard and Kahneman would like, take the average of *all* moments of an experience, adjusted to reflect the *duration* of each moment. We saw a memorable example of Peak-End evaluations in Kahneman's famous colonoscopy experiment.[21] Recall that half the patients had the colonoscope deliberately left stationary inside them for an extra minute, causing them to experience mild discomfort for this period, but less pain than earlier in the procedure. Nevertheless, their later evaluation of the whole experience was much more favourable, because they focused on the end moment, which was less painful. Kahneman commented: 'A clinical application of such an intervention could be justified if it increased patients' willingness to undergo further colonoscopies when their treatment required it.'[22] Less controversially, the colonoscopy experiment shows that people can judge 'objectively worse' experiences more favourably than less unpleasant ones, a worrying result for attempts to measure happiness based on self-reports.

Self-assessments of happiness that have managed to dodge these unwelcome influences face a final obstacle. People must be honest and candid in reporting their self-assessments. *Candour* is a better description of what is required: it is not so much that people set out to lie; rather they hesitate to state how happy they feel if, for instance, the interviewer is severely handicapped.[23]

One response to these concerns is to adopt a different measurement technique altogether. The *Experience Sampling Method* involves respondents carrying palmtop computers around with them; the computer prompts them at random moments to record their happiness. It brings to life a dream of the 19th-century utilitarians: that a person's happiness or hedonic state might be measurable at any moment using a 'hedonimeter'. The happiness experts are very enthusiastic about the Experience Sampling Method, since it looks set to track objective happiness quite closely. There are still drawbacks, including the high cost of the technique, the unwillingness of people to tolerate this time-consuming intrusion into their lives over long periods, and the danger that frequent self-assessment of momentary happiness will itself affect a person's happiness.[24] But a deeper concern emerges once we realize what measurement of objective happiness involves. Each momentary report is a kind of gut reaction: someone is unlikely to consider their situation deeply when interrupted in the middle of some activity in their everyday life. The difficulty lies not just in the hurried nature of the judgement, and arises with the usual survey method of measuring happiness too. Consider the standard happiness questions again:

Taken all together, how would you say things are these days – would you say that you are very happy, pretty happy, or not too happy?

On the whole are you very satisfied, fairly satisfied, not very satisfied, or not at all satisfied with the life you lead?

(And overleaf the shameless version, less commonly used, but still widespread.)

The fundamental problem with all these questions is that they ask us to reduce the astonishingly rich diversity of human feelings down to a single number, phrase or pantomime face:

Suppose that you have just won the Nobel Prize; this surely merits the smiliest face. But suppose also that you have just lost your family in a car crash; this surely warrants the frowniest face. So, how happy are you? There is no coherent answer – unless you are supposed to combine these points by picking the indifferent face in the middle![25]

Smiley-face sampling

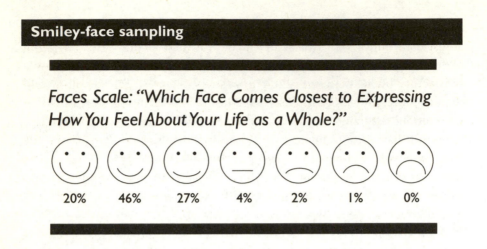

Faces Scale: "Which Face Comes Closest to Expressing How You Feel About Your Life as a Whole?"

20%   46%   27%   4%   2%   1%   0%

Note: The scale and data are from *Social Indicators of Well-Being: Americans Perceptions of Life Quality* (p207 and p306), by F. M. Andrews and S. B. Withey, 1976, New York, Plenum. Copyright 1976 by Plenum. Reprinted with permission.

Source: Andrews and Withey (1976)

The usual happiness surveys pose exactly this kind of absurd conundrum; the Experience Sampling Method resolves it, but in an equally absurd way. If you recorded a high score after hearing of the Nobel Prize, and a low score after learning of the crash, then your happiness would be assessed as the numerical average of the two. Effectively, you are assigned the indifferent face in the middle. If this kind of smiley-face sampling brings us closer to measuring objective happiness – as the happiness experts define it – then perhaps it is not what we should be trying to measure after all.

Another way of approaching the question is to imagine a happiness psychologist such as Kahneman assessing his own happiness, presumably able to avoid all the measurement problems already mentioned. Would Kahneman's self-reported happiness accurately track his objective happiness? Maybe not. As he acknowledges, 'the standard for the judgement of happiness is not obvious at all. Most people describe themselves as happy, but the meaning of this finding is unclear because the phrase "neither happy nor unhappy" has a distinctly negative connotation.'[26] Of course Kahneman would not be deflected by the negative connotation if answering one of his own questions, but still, the meaning of the neutral point on the happiness scale is unclear. More precisely, the problem is that its meaning in terms of objective happiness may change. Just as people adjust their notion of a satisfactory income as their income rises, reflecting their rising aspirations, they may also adjust their overall notion of a satisfactory life as their overall circumstances change. Such people would require more, and more intense, pleasures to report the same level of life satisfaction: they are on a 'satisfaction treadmill'. Subjective and objective happiness have become detached; the former remains constant while the latter improves. Kahneman insists, however, that 'it is objective happiness that matters. Policies that improve the frequencies of good experiences and reduce the incidence of bad ones should be pursued even if people do not describe themselves as happier or more satisfied.'[27]

Wait a moment. Surely a crucial part of the rationale for happiness research is that it avoids making these judgements. The whole tradition of consumer sovereignty, and the ingrained opposition to paternalism among most economists, sees happiness research as attractive precisely because it claims to sidestep the messy, unscientific and open-ended business of arguing about values. Happiness is self-evidently an important goal of public policy – plausibly *the* most important – so we can concentrate on maximizing happiness without becoming mired in philosophical debate about what counts as happiness. It is whatever people say makes them happy, or so the argument goes.

But it is now clear that even the happiness experts do not really follow this script. Kahneman states that self-reported happiness is biased if it 'is affected by a factor that is normatively irrelevant'.[28] That is, irrelevant according to the normative judgement of the happiness experts. Some of these judgements are entirely uncontroversial, others less so. It might seem unarguable that, when measuring overall happiness, we should seek to filter out any immediate mood effects. However, if people are in a happy mood because their national soccer team has performed well, should we ignore this? Politicians frequently justify expenditure on national sports teams on the grounds that their success will be good for the national mood. More controversially, it is far from clear that Peak-End evaluations should be ignored. Kahneman's suggestion that doctors should manipulate Peak-End evaluations (for example by artificially prolonging a surgical procedure) illustrates the moral complexities. On the one hand, the fact that Peak-End evaluation might lead someone to prefer longer unpleasant experiences to shorter ones suggests that such evaluations should be given little moral weight. Accordingly, manipulating them does not matter – and is morally justified if it leads patients to accept the treatment they need. On the other hand, this manipulation seems paternalistic and arguably undermines the dignity and autonomy of the patient by misleading them. More generally, if good peaks and ends to, say, a holiday, give someone happy memories and make them feel happy, why should so-called objective happiness, which treats every moment equally, be more important? Again, if someone is on a satisfaction treadmill, then they truly do not feel more satisfied as their circumstances improve, so why insist that they are objectively happier?

To answer these questions affirmatively, to justify shoehorning how people actually think about happiness into a particular model of objective happiness, requires a philosophical argument after all. Objective happiness as defined by Kahneman and endorsed by Layard and other happiness researchers is not simply a tidy version of self-reported happiness with any obvious errors stripped out. It is not just subjective happiness data, correctly measured. The rationale for favouring their version of objective happiness over raw survey data is just as 'value-laden' as the rationale for adopting an explicitly philosophical conception of happiness, such as that based on Aristotle's *Ethics*.[29] The scientific study of happiness comes laden with unavoidable philosophical baggage. It is now time to unpack it.

Before that, it is worth emphasizing why such a philosophical exploration has proved necessary. The happiness experts all agree that self-reported happiness should be a goal of government policy, or at least an input into government decision making, along with measures of education, health, crime and so on.[30] This modest role for self-reported happiness seems surprising, since presumably the appeal of happiness as a goal is that it is all-inclusive. It *incorporates* concerns with health and crime; it should not have to compete with them for the government's attention. This puzzle forces us to ask why, and to what extent, happiness matters. To repeat, it is not a measurement problem. Suppose we could measure objective happiness infallibly, perhaps through a refined version of smiley-face sampling – so what? Why would this measure of happiness matter?

Why does happiness matter?

Without exception, all the happiness economists and psychologists mentioned so far have looked to utilitarianism for philosophical support.

They take utilitarianism to begin with the *Greatest Happiness principle*: the right action is the one that produces the greatest overall happiness, with happiness understood as the objective happiness defined above. The complex debate about utilitarianism has been running since Bentham first proposed his principle of utility and, in the nature of philosophy, resists a neat resolution. Here I shall explore some features of utilitarianism which the happiness experts emphasize as desirable, and which have major practical implications. This exploration in turn helps to uncover which aspects of happiness matter, and why.

Happiness as good feelings[31]

The fundamental problem with this view of happiness is that it conflicts with many of our strongest intuitions about the meaning of happiness. The strongest of all is probably the intuition that our happiness concerns what our life is *really* like, not merely how it seems to be. The most famous illustration of this intuition is a thought experiment, *The Experience Machine*, conducted by the philosopher Robert Nozick.

The Experience Machine

Suppose there were an experience machine that would give you any experience you desired. Super-duper neuropsychologists could stimulate your brain so that you would think and feel you were writing a great novel, or making a friend, or reading an interesting book. All the time you would be floating in a tank, with electrodes attached to your brain… Would you plug in?[32]

Another example comes from the film *The Truman Show*, where the hero lives all his life (until the last scene) without realizing that he is living inside a TV show: his 'friends and family' are actors; every moment is broadcast to the world through hidden cameras; his town was specially constructed for the show. These examples are memorable, but more everyday examples are easy to find. If happiness is just a feeling, then being deceived by someone I love does not count as making me unhappy, provided I never become aware of their deception. Surely this shows happiness cannot be just a feeling?

The happiness experts are unperturbed. Layard's view seems to reflect the maxim 'what you don't know can't hurt you':

> In Aldous Huxley's *Brave New World* people take *soma* to make themselves feel better. This idea was meant to sound revolting and threatening. However, people have used drugs such as alcohol from the beginning of time. But most of the drugs we have found so far can have bad side-effects. If someone finds a happiness drug without side effects, I have no doubt that most of us will sometimes use it.[33]

This passage is interesting for three reasons. First, it shows that seemingly obscure philosophical distinctions can be relevant to current drug policy debates. Second, in a survey of 1000 Australians asked 'If there was a legally available drug that could be bought over the counter, that made you feel happy and did not have any side effects, do you think there would be occasions when you would take it?', 73 per cent of respondents answered 'definitely' or 'probably' not.[34] So 'happy pills' may be less appealing than Layard believes. Third, Layard avoids condemning 'recreational' drugs without side effects, but suspiciously fails to recommend them. But if happiness is just a feeling, then Layard should not merely avoid condemning them, he should actively encourage taking these drugs, on the grounds that total happiness would increase. It is inconsistent to embrace a *general* principle – the pursuit of happiness as good feelings – yet introduce exceptions whenever its implications make us squeamish. (Of course most drugs *do* have significant side effects, so Layard cannot be interpreted as condoning consumption of these.)

A better defence of happiness as good feelings might argue as follows: the examples of The Experience Machine, *soma* and the person being deceived by a loved one all show that we care about more in life than our immediate feelings. We do care about what our life is really like, but this is a broader concern than our happiness. However, that broader concern is necessarily evaluative: it involves moral judgements about what matters in life. The advantage of defining happiness solely in terms of good feelings is that it makes happiness a scientific matter of fact, obtained by measuring our feelings.

I have already mentioned one problem with this argument: even the happiness experts do not treat happiness as a non-evaluative matter of fact.

They do not define happiness in terms of the raw data, but make evaluative judgements – for instance that smiley-face sampling is better than Peak-End-based memories of experiences. If we set this problem aside, there remains a more subtle difficulty. If happiness is defined in non-evaluative psychological terms – if the happiness of a person at a particular time is just a fact about them, like their temperature – then we still need an argument for why this fact matters. There is no more reason for government policy to target people's happiness than their temperature. David Hume's famous philosophical dictum puts the point concisely: 'you cannot get an "ought" from an "is"'. If happiness is a purely factual matter of measured feelings, then we need a separate argument for why we *ought* to be bothered with it. In other words, how is the Greatest Happiness principle, the view that the right action is the one that produces the greatest overall happiness, to be justified?

Greatest Happiness as the single ultimate goal

Layard justifies the Greatest Happiness principle as follows:

> The problem with many goals is that they often conflict, and then we
> have to balance the one against the other. So we naturally look for one
> ultimate goal that enables us to judge other goals by how they contribute
> to it. Happiness is that ultimate goal because, unlike all other goals, it is
> self-evidently good. If we are asked why happiness matters, we can give
> no further, external reason. It just obviously does matter. As the American
> Declaration of Independence says, it is a 'self-evident' objective.[35]

This passage contains two arguments.

Greatest Happiness is a self-evident, obvious goal

We have seen that people care about more than happiness as good feelings. Their concern is broader – what will make their life go as well as possible. However, in terms of language, many people still use the H words to refer to these broader concerns, so for example, they say they would be 'unhappy' being deceived by a loved one, even unknowingly. This may help to explain why 'Greatest Happiness' may seem such an obvious goal: the word 'happiness' includes whatever I think it should include. If people use the word as a peg on which to hang their views about what makes life go best, no wonder 'Greatest Happiness' is a self-evident goal. But this is simply a different use of the term; it is no argument for the Greatest Happiness principle. Layard's reference to the American Declaration of Independence may rest on the same equivocation; Thomas Jefferson's ideal of happiness was certainly much broader than mere feelings.[36]

One overall goal is better than several

I will shortly argue that Layard's preference for one goal is based on a misguided and ultimately futile desire to sidestep politics in favour of science. But first a more basic objection: despite appearances to the contrary, the Greatest Happiness principle does not involve only one goal after all. Many, perhaps most, philosophers believe that even if happiness is narrowly defined in terms of feelings, these are so diverse that the pursuit of happiness amounts to the pursuit of more than one goal. The crucial idea here is that many feelings do not just differ in degree (more or less intense), but in kind too. They are intrinsically different, so cannot be boiled down to a single thing. If happiness is defined in terms of several intrinsically different feelings, pursuing it involves pursuing several goals. This is why happiness survey questions seem to many people naive, crass, absurd or even impossible to answer. Smiley-face sampling is no better. Both measurement techniques require diverse feelings – winning a Nobel Prize and learning that loved ones have been lost in a car crash – to be aggregated and reduced to a single number.

Both Kahneman and Layard went back to Bentham, and that is where the trouble began. Recall that Bentham lumped together 'benefit, advantage, pleasure, good or happiness', and similarly treated 'mischief, pain, evil, and unhappiness' interchangeably. The 19th-century philosopher John Stuart Mill is perhaps the most famous advocate of the idea that some feelings fundamentally differ in kind. Mill was Bentham's godson; he was brought up by a stern father to carry forward Bentham's utilitarian legacy; he was educated intensively, reading Greek philosophy at the age of four; he began his life as a philosopher as Bentham's greatest champion. But in his early twenties he entered a two-year period of deep depression, probably in part due to feeling unloved by his parents and discouraged from expressing his emotions. It is now widely believed that Mill's philosophical views changed because of the painful understanding of happiness which that period gave him. Mill came to reject Bentham's crude simplification, arguing instead that there are deeper or higher pleasures (and pains). The pleasure of eating an ice cream is intrinsically different in kind from the pleasure of time spent with a loved one or close friend. The philosopher Martha Nussbaum explains: 'Bentham did not value the emotional elements of the personality in the right way; he oversimplified them, lacking all understanding of poetry (as Mill insists) and of love (as we might add).'[37]

Much of Mill's discussion of higher pleasures points the way to a substantially broader conception of happiness than provided by the Greatest Happiness principle. But if Mill, one of that principle's most famous advocates, rejects the idea that there is just one kind of feeling, then at the very least, we should be doubtful about assuming there is. This difficulty is central to questions such as 'How happy was Helen in March?' and similar problems involving overall happiness judgements about ourselves and others in real life. It is not just that the question is hard because it requires a mass of disparate information to be considered; we suspect that there is no unqualified single word or single sentence answer – let alone a single number. The different dimensions of happiness are essentially incomparable; the closely related idea that some good things or benefits are incomparable with money (that is, their value is not measurable in terms of it) will be a recurring theme in Chapters 6 and 7.[38]

Greatest Happiness as a fair goal

At first glance the Greatest Happiness principle is supremely fair. My happiness counts just as much as, but no more than, yours. The principle implies that a change which leads to my happiness increasing by more than yours falls would count as an improvement. At first glance, this might seem right, but what if I was already very happy and you were already miserable? Many utilitarian philosophers (and happiness experts) conclude that Bentham's formulation should again be modified. *Distributional weights* should be used: changes to someone's happiness (up or down) should weigh more heavily if they are relatively unhappy than if they are already happy. This modification is to be welcomed, and does not undermine the feasibility of the Greatest Happiness principle.

Greatest Happiness as a neutral scientific goal

There is little doubt that our happiness experts prefer a Greatest Happiness principle rooted in science to one emanating from politics. For example, the Nobel Laureate economist Amartya Sen's 'capabilities approach' to well-being involves multiple objectives, rather than a single happiness goal. Layard comments: 'In [Sen's] view, conflicts between these objectives should be resolved through the political process. I am more hopeful that *evidence* can be brought to bear, evidence that tells us about how achieving these objectives affects people's feelings.'[39] And Layard clearly believes in a form of scientific progress in application of the Greatest Happiness principle, based on accumulating knowledge: 'The analysis is always difficult, but it will become easier as our knowledge progresses.'[40] Layard is especially candid, but there is no evidence that other happiness experts disagree. What might the 'scientific' implementation of the Greatest Happiness principle look like in practice?

Consider a relatively uncontroversial idea: discouraging smoking through high cigarette taxation. Layard argues that high tax is justified here because smoking works against a person's long-term happiness.[41] But even supposing there is complete agreement on *long-term* happiness as the single ultimate goal, it is far from clear that heavy taxation of cigarettes will increase long-term happiness. While quitting smoking may mean someone lives a longer and healthier life, they may be very unhappy doing so, and miss the pleasure of a smoke thereafter. Chapter 2 showed that with self-control problems such as smoking, people's preferences pull them in opposite directions. They cannot decide what will make them happy, no matter how hard they scrutinize their preferences. The observing happiness economist will not do any better: it is no use trying to measure something which is not there. Scientific observation alone cannot uncover what is best for someone, if they do not know themselves.

Of course this focus on the happiness or otherwise of smokers ignores the unhappiness that smoking can bring to others, but against this, some passive smokers may be happier knowing that their neighbour has the freedom to smoke. This is plausible if the passive smoker fears anti-smoking legislation might lead next to restrictions on alcohol, or gun ownership, or some other activity which makes *them* happy. My aim here is not to defend smoking (I favour high cigarette taxation) but to show how restricting discussion to implementation of the Greatest Happiness principle ignores many widely held ethical intuitions: no mention of freedom (to smoke), or duty (not to harm others) was allowed above. Another example is more general. As mentioned above, Layard rightly proposes giving more weight to reducing the misery of an unhappy person than increasing the happiness of an already happy one. And he recognizes that the choice of weights is a value judgement.[42] Of course the way to make the implementation more 'scientific' is to pass the controversial value judgements back to the previous stage where the Greatest Happiness principle is first agreed upon – secure agreement on the distributional weights at that stage as well. But what is involved in this mysterious stage where tricky ethical disagreements are supposedly resolved? Assuming dictatorship is unacceptable, several thousand years of philosophy has uncovered only one answer: political debate.

So in practice, the combination of the Greatest Happiness principle and happiness psychology artificially silences debate by excluding anything which cannot be incorporated into the happiness maximization calculus. And it invokes additional political and moral judgements – often opaquely and implicitly – in order to reach operational policy recommendations. Regarding these additional judgements, the Greatest Happiness principle, far from being a complete overarching philosophy, has very little to say. We need what might have been suspected all along: a less simplistic and more nuanced philosophy.

Beyond self-reported happiness

Talk of philosophy suggests to many people nowadays a concern with the individual – a private ethic of 'how to live' – rather than political affairs. This view of philosophy may reflect the widespread cynical view of politics as unprincipled, amoral squabbling over shares of a cake: politics and philosophy don't mix. In contrast, the Greatest Happiness principle is a first step towards an open, explicit recognition that ethical debate must be at the heart of contemporary politics and economics. But as I have argued, it does not go far enough. So my focus in what follows is public ethics, guidance for the conduct of public policy.

As ever, we need to start by asking the right question. There are no objective facts about people's happiness levels, because assessing happiness is unavoidably a matter of both moral and technical judgement. Any attempt to make this assessment entirely scientific cannot succeed and risks leaving out what truly matters to people's lives in pursuit of a narrow version of happiness (feelings alone). With such an implausibly narrow view of happiness, and the evidence about it limited to controversial surveys, doubts about its importance inevitably arise. The happiness experts are forced to ask, 'What good is it?' and justify their focus on self-reported happiness by appealing to correlations with good health, better performance at work, higher income and so on.[43] But this appeal is absurd and contradictory; contradictory because happiness experts elsewhere argue that self-reported happiness is the overarching ultimate goal, not a means to other ends; and absurd because happiness is profoundly more important than this. Justifying the pursuit of happiness because it correlates with higher income makes the same mistake as justifying the value of good health and education by arguing that they help people become richer. It may be true, but it misses the point. Education and health matter for their own sake, and as means to more important ends than material wealth. The same is true for happiness, only more so. The way out of this confusion is to begin by asking, as Aristotle did, 'How ought we to live?'

The question is still about happiness: Aristotle *defined* happiness (which he termed *eudaimonia*) as living in accordance with an answer to this question. The unashamedly moral aspect of this question immediately draws attention to those lives where pleasure is undoubtedly experienced but where something is wrong or missing. The person hooked up to the Experience Machine is one example; the sadist's life contains others. For Aristotle, such people cannot be happy because a good life cannot involve evil pleasures, and must be *lived,* not simply experienced through a machine. Aristotelian approaches to happiness are usefully labelled 'objective list' theories, because they defend a list of things which are good or bad for people, regardless of what people immediately want.[44] It is the objective facts about these states of being or achievements which matter, not just our subjective experience of them. Some psychologists, influenced by Aristotelian approaches and dissatisfied with the view of happiness presented by Kahneman and Layard, have proposed an alternative, psychological well-being (PWB).[45] PWB attempts to measure happiness in terms of numerical measures of autonomy, personal growth, self-acceptance, life purpose, mastery and positive relatedness. As objective lists go, this is vaguer and hence less repugnant than one drawn directly from Aristotle, who lived in a time when slavery and the subjugation of women were part of the moral fabric of society. There are many problems with the PWB approach,[46] but the most important is the obvious one: who decides what is on the objective list and on what authority? Life is probably more complicated than in Aristotle's time; certainly the citizens of modern developed nations hold a much wider range of views about the good life than the citizens of ancient Greece. My objective list might not suit you. To take just one example, consider the difficult choices almost all of us face in dividing time between our working and private lives. If Ann seeks a promotion, this may bring increased job satisfaction and greater financial security, but it reduces the time Ann has available for friends and family, and she may be more tired and stressed during these periods. Ann decides not to pursue the promotion, because the quality and depth of her personal relationships is central to her idea of a good life. But others might take the promotion, because for them career achievement is an even more important value on their objective lists.

These are just the kinds of practical dilemmas with which we must all wrestle in thinking about happiness, in shaping our own understanding of what it is to live a good life. Fortunately, in matters of *public* ethics we can, and should, largely avoid taking sides in these debates. That we *should* do so is straightforward – to avoid the worst kind of meddlesome paternalism. That we *can* may be less obvious. The trick is to combine some of utilitarianism's neutrality about the nature of the good life with some of the concreteness of objective list approaches, straddling the gap between Bentham and Aristotle. Consider again the problem of public policy on smoking. On the one hand, we wish to avoid interfering with widely perceived freedoms (to shorten your life by smoking); on the other we need more policy guidance than to maximize self-reported happiness.

Mill's doctrine of higher pleasures is one attempt to find this balance. Given its central place in happiness debates, and the practical implications at stake, it should be no surprise that it remains a hot spot in moral philosophy. There are two fiercely contested interpretations. First, Mill emphasizes the *dignity* of a person choosing how to live; it effectively works as a gatekeeper preventing the choice of a life devoted solely to the more banal lower pleasures.[47] Second, Mill suggested that activities involving higher pleasures would be undervalued by people before experiencing them, but once experienced, a competent, fully informed person would prefer higher to lower pleasures. This second interpretation is related to the idea of 'perfect preferences' introduced in Chapter 2. The idea is much more defensible here, as part of understanding how we *ought* to live, than as a way of justifying consumer sovereignty. Both interpretations of Mill have been developed further in recent years. The first interpretation suggests the crucial point that happiness does not involve good feelings alone or items on the objective list alone, but both: only when they are combined is dignity respected.[48] Evil pleasures and machine-induced deceptions do not bring happiness, but neither does having someone else's idea of the objective good things in life foisted upon you. In light of this, and developing the second interpretation, there comes a focus, not on developing an objective list of the good things in life, but on an objective list of the *means* to these good ends. This is where it becomes so much easier to make progress with public than private ethics.[49]

While people's pleasures, preferences and views about the good life are strikingly diverse, their basic needs and preconditions for a good life have something in common.[50] More precisely, needs, preconditions and means to good ends may differ in detail across individuals, but they have enough in common to form a basis for public ethics. In guiding policy, the aim is to give people the basic resources and capabilities to pursue their own idea of a good life. Education is a good example of such a resource. According to Sen's objective list of 'capabilities', adequate education is an essential part of developing various capabilities to lead a good life: for example, it is essential to a person's development of his or her powers of imagination and ability to reason.[51] A more utilitarian approach justifies education by arguing that it is something we would all want, if we had perfect preferences; the effect of education is to lead us to have preferences about our lives which will be more satisfying than the ones we would have had otherwise. We can ignore the finer philosophical distinctions of these different hybrid theories; what is more important here is to show how they differ in practice from the Greatest Happiness principle.[52]

First, there is an open and unashamed reference to value judgements, ideals about what a good life involves. The happiness experts try to sidestep these, but in practice must make ad hoc judgements which are often hidden because they are implicit. For instance, they would need to decide whether requiring children to study science to age 16 (or beyond) would bring a gain in happiness to society sufficient to outweigh the boredom of children forced to study science. This decision would be made uninformed by an explicit discussion of the kind of education we all require to lead a fulfilling life (however we define happiness). In contrast, the hybrid theories draw on a thorough understanding of the basic needs and interests we have in common; this leads to a comprehensive understanding of the merits of education, including its role in supporting emotional development, artistic understanding, logical thinking, political awareness, recreational and play skills, and other means to good ends. This richer account of education should facilitate policy making, and the rationale is relatively transparent.

Second, as the above example suggests, the Greatest Happiness principle is in one sense more paternalistic than the hybrid theories, not less. Crucially, it adopts a particularly narrow view of the good life – happiness as good feelings – and favours policies which pursue it, even though many of us may reject this concept of happiness. It might seem that, if there is disagreement with the resulting policies, this should register in happiness surveys, leading to abandonment of such policies after all. But this is a mistake: I can report a high score in a happiness survey while believing that our lives in this society are not going well. Indeed, I can report a high score while believing that *my* life is not going well. Self-reported happiness measures just a *part* of what matters in life, so maximizing it does not guarantee that we avoid failure in the things that matter to us. Suppose, for example, that we want to live in a society where opera performances, or small local soccer teams, or rare bird species, are protected or subsidized. The hybrid theories leave plenty of room for justifying these things. Opera might be appreciated by someone with perfect preferences, while local soccer might be an anchor holding together the thriving community which everyone needs. The exact details of the justificatory discussion are not my concern here: the point is that the hybrid approach invites such a discussion, while with happiness economics as it stands we simply have to hope that the pleasures of opera, local football and rare birds will be well tracked by happiness surveys.

This raises a third distinction between the hybrid theories and happiness economics. The Greatest Happiness principle requires governments to maximize happiness scores provided by experts who interpret the raw data, leaving a limited and uncertain role for politics. Layard refers to the principle as determining legal rights and constitutional rules, and helping decide what to do when these laws conflict.[53] This appears to give the principle a kind of super-legal status above politics. But in a democracy there must be an essential role for disputing the happiness scores provided by experts, and arguing over the distributional weights. And what if the Greatest Happiness principle unambiguously recommends policy *X*, yet people vote for *Y*? Since adopting the principle must presumably be a democratic choice, so too must its rejection. The problem is that by refusing to engage with politics, the Greatest Happiness principle has nothing to offer in its defence in such cases. If happiness as good feelings is at best just a part of what makes life go well, then there seems no reason to prioritize it. In contrast, politics is central to the hybrid theories. There will be ongoing debate about the underlying preconditions or means to good ends which society should promote. The debate should never be closed, because views will evolve over time.

It is easier to make progress with public ethics than private ones, because although we all have different views of the good life, public ethics can and should remain largely neutral between them. However, it is tempting to believe that we can apply the hybrid theories to individual lives: the idea that happiness does not just involve good feelings or items on the objective list, but both, seems particularly attractive at the personal level. Unfortunately there are a number of problems with the hybrid theories in this context, arising from the utilitarian side of their parentage. Both utilitarianism and the hybrid theories have *impersonal* goals – happiness, achievements and so on – but most of us believe that as individuals we should not live like this. We should be biased towards family and close friends, putting their interests and happiness above those of a complete stranger. Perhaps too, we should do the right thing, act out of duty or moral obligation, regardless of the consequences; such dilemmas are the stuff of great literature. And no one would want to live like Gradgrind in Dickens' *Hard Times,* who made every choice, however small, on the basis of a cold, calculating analysis of the resulting pleasures and pains. Gradgrind would be no more admirable if, following some hybrid theories, the satisfaction of perfect preferences was calculated instead. These points are worth making, not just to explain my reluctance to offer advice in the manner of a self-help manual about how you ought to live, but because they also suggest why principles of personal ethics might not transfer across to public policy making. Governments ought *not* to be biased towards particular people. They ought *not* to act out of duty regardless of the consequences, because arguably their only duty as a public body rather than a private individual is to consider the consequences of their actions for all of us. Indeed, they ought to be coldly calculating, taking account of all consequences of which they are aware, since the scale of public policy implies that even some of its relatively minor consequences may still have major effects.[54]

In this respect at least, the utilitarianism of the happiness experts remains a good starting point for public policy making. It should not be abandoned altogether in favour of a Ten Commandments-style list of moral principles, because that approach is ill-suited to public ethics for precisely the reasons it is attractive at the personal level.

Building a happier society?

Chasing happiness may seem like a fool's game. Happiness is elusive because it is like sleep: it only happens if you're not trying to make it happen. Although there is some truth in this fatalistic view when it comes to individuals pursuing their own happiness, it need not trouble us when seeking a happier society. As I have just suggested, lessons about the pursuit of our own individual happiness do not necessarily apply to policy making at the level of society. The problems are different. This is especially true of measuring happiness.

Given the apparent absurdity of attempting to quantify our own happiness, it is tempting to dismiss as meaningless the collective measures of self-reported happiness relied upon by the happiness experts. But difficulties in the measurement of individual happiness need not render aggregate self-reported happiness data useless. Essentially random measurement errors and biases at the individual level may cancel out over large populations; or if errors affect all individual measurements equally, measures of *relative* happiness will be unaffected – and these are generally the only sensible measures to use. At the very least critics who reject self-reported happiness data should be obliged to give reasons why, in a particular policy context, they are unreliable. For example, if the claim that 'money doesn't buy happiness' is at stake, then the critics need to show that the data contain systematic distortions – such as the rich being systematically less likely to report themselves as happy than the poor, other things being equal. It is not enough just to argue that the data are imperfect. In some cases of course there *are* systematic distortions – particularly when international comparisons of happiness are attempted –

so the happiness data should be read with a large dose of skepticism. But they are not worthless.

Debate over the findings of happiness economics has been preoccupied with these measurement issues. Implicit in the debate has been the assumption that if happiness is very hard or impossible to quantify, then it is at best of limited relevance to public policy making. Happiness matters when we can put a number on it. There are several errors here. That happiness may be very hard to quantify does not make it meaningless, impractical or irrelevant to policy making. In particular, if unreliable happiness data fail to undermine economic growth as a policy goal, this is not the same as a justification of the latter. The pursuit of growth would still lack a positive justification in many circumstances.

On the other hand, even if happiness could be accurately quantified, all the most important problems remain. This becomes clear if we suppose, hypothetically, that we have flawless data on self-reported happiness, free of measurement problems – call it 'perceived happiness'. What then? Should we, as many of the happiness experts seem to suggest, explicitly strive for a society in which perceived happiness is maximized?[55] The philosophical concerns raised in this chapter imply that a government policy of maximizing (perceived) national happiness would face many objections in practice. Perceived happiness can conflict with what we think is important in life or beliefs about how we should live. Here are just a few examples. Having children may decrease self-reported happiness yet nevertheless increase parents' sense of meaning and purpose.[56] Some people may perceive themselves as happier living in ways which many others regard as harmful or immoral. Racists may be happier in segregated communities. Holiday hedonists may be happier taking six return flights a year, regardless of the environmental damage. Even setting these ethical objections aside, we may doubt that perceived happiness is always a reliable guide to the kind of happiness it is supposed to reflect. It is far from clear that we should regard Peak-End evaluations as unwelcome distortions of our memories of experiences, but if we do, then in principle we could avoid them by relying on moment-by-moment reports of our happiness on palmtop 'hedonimeters'. However, these hedonimeter readings would still be vulnerable to phenomena such as the satisfaction treadmill: perceived happiness fades as we become accustomed to it. If perceived happiness is all that matters then this adaptation should be ignored, implying for instance that there is less need to help the very poor in developing countries, insofar as they are accustomed to their deprivation. On the other hand, taking full account of adaptation seems equally troubling. It implies that some accident victims should be given less compensation than others, if we can predict that they will adapt to their misfortune more readily.[57] Finally, whose happiness counts? Presumably governments are supposed to prioritize the happiness of their current citizens, but should they simply ignore the happiness of foreigners and future generations?[58]

As well as these philosophical concerns about maximizing happiness, there are some straightforward political ones. Any government adopting an explicit, overarching policy of maximizing perceived happiness must confront its relationship with democratic politics. As I have argued, the Greatest Happiness principle cannot stand above politics. Another problem is what economists call *Goodhart's Law*.[59] A succinct definition is: 'when a measure becomes a target, it ceases to be a good measure'. So once governments target aggregate measures of self-reported happiness, these measures cease to track 'true' happiness. Goodhart's Law can be thought of as the application to human society of Heisenberg's Uncertainty Principle in quantum physics. Put simply, measuring a system generally disturbs it.[60] In human society, an important reason is that people manipulate data once it matters to them. Lobby groups, policy entrepreneurs and assorted cranks would be drawn to happiness data like moths to a flame. They would unscrupulously mine and manipulate the data until it appeared to support their ideas. And of course governments would be tempted to jump between measures of happiness in an attempt to demonstrate a large increase.

So for both political and philosophical reasons, an explicit policy of maximizing perceived happiness would be a mistake. Nevertheless, happiness economics has something to offer. It represents a giant improvement on the non-philosophy of maximizing economic growth. Although the rest of us may long ago have realized that growth does not buy happiness, many economists are still convinced that it does (partly for the reasons suggested at the start of Chapter 3). Perhaps the most important contribution of happiness economics has been that economists have finally begun to change their minds. The consensus has shifted. This is enormously significant, although further progress will not be easy. As one happiness economist put it:

> Some economists and policy makers will go to their deathbeds ignoring
> these data. The numbers are too scary. They imply that clever people
> have for decades given the wrong advice to governments and citizens...
> The best evidence now suggests that growth does not work.[61]

Even if not all economists – and the governments they advise – are yet
convinced, the debate has at last begun. Environmentalists and other
radical critics have been warning for decades about the dire consequences
of excessive growth, but their focus has been relentlessly negative.
Happiness economics is more of a Pied Piper than a Prophet of Doom. It
offers a positive vision for a better society. In case this sounds like an empty
platitude, happiness economics has many concrete implications, such as
recognizing that 'labour market flexibility' can bring misery through loss
of job security and the erosion of communities as people move more
frequently between jobs.[62] Other implications include giving the reduction
of unemployment relatively more priority, and low inflation relatively
less;[63] and the proposal outlined in Chapter 4, that income tax should be
increased to reflect the 'polluting' effect of higher income on the happiness
of others.[64]

The problem remains that self-reported happiness is too flimsy a
justification for these ideas. Without a developed moral argument, they are
too soft a target for defenders of the growth orthodoxy. As it stands,
happiness economics is just a beginning. I have argued that it is time to
move beyond narrow and misleading measures of self-reported happiness
and focus on enabling people to pursue their own vision of a good life.
Governments preoccupied with economic growth think of themselves as
neutral between these differing visions, but they are not: implicitly they
favour materialistic ways of life, because economic growth only measures a
narrow form of material progress. Happiness economics avoids this bias,
but as we have seen, it is a form of ethical economics: happiness measurements are not based just on how people feel but inevitably involve ethical
judgements. These judgements are presented as simply ensuring
scientifically valid measurements, but they are evaluative nonetheless. Self-
reported happiness is not solely based on self-reports. Beyond this, there
are ethical judgements every step of the way – for instance in the choice of
distributional weights. So happiness economics is not a science. To
develop, it must become part of politics, not a science outside politics and

potentially in conflict with it. Happiness economics is only a beginning, and that it is considered such a radical challenge shows up how withered mainstream economic and political debate has become.

The study of happiness is not the only area of economics suffering from economists' continuing science-envy and obsession with measurement. The limits and perils of monetary measurement (putting prices on human life and nature, the 'audit culture', performance-related pay, and so on) are the underlying themes of the next two chapters.

Chapter Six

Pricing Life and Nature

Say that politicians could build a roundabout for $9 million and save one life. If the roundabout does not get built, it means that the politicians valued that life at less than $9 million. (Bjorn Lomborg, the 'Skeptical Environmentalist'[1])

Just between you and me, shouldn't the World Bank be encouraging *more* migration of the dirty industries to the less developed countries?... The measurement of the costs of health-impairing pollution depends on the forgone earnings from increased morbidity and mortality. From this point of view a given amount of health-impairing pollution should be done in the country with the lowest cost, which will be the country with the lowest wages. I think the economic logic behind dumping a load of toxic waste in the lowest-wage country is impeccable and we should face up to that. (Lawrence Summers, then Chief Economist of the World Bank, in an internal memorandum of 1991 that was subsequently leaked[2])

At first glance, it is hard to imagine that these problems have anything in common. Yet the economist's response to them shares a crucial common element, a way of thinking that increasingly determines the way governments, businesses and individuals approach most decisions. The common element is quantification in terms of money. The clearest example of this way of thinking, and one central to debates about the environment, is cost–benefit analysis. Cost–benefit analysis (CBA) may sound technical, but its essential idea is very simple: when making a decision we should express all the advantages and disadvantages of each course of action as benefits and costs in terms of money. The total benefits and costs can then be calculated, and the best action is the one that maximizes 'net benefit', that is, total benefits minus total costs.

CBA has a seductive basis in common sense. In our daily lives we often weigh up the pros and cons of various options when making a decision. CBA seems to be nothing more than a developed, scientific version of this weighing up process, with all advantages and disadvantages measured in terms of money to enable comparison. But the extra step from an intelligent, common-sense weighing up of the pros and cons to a comprehensive monetary valuation of all of them is a huge one. It conceals important assumptions about valuing life, uncertainty and the future, including:

● Human life can be indirectly given a monetary value.
● A given amount of money is worth the same to everyone.
● Outcomes in the future matter less.
● Uncertain future outcomes always have a quantifiable probability.

This chapter will explore these ideas in successive sections, not just because they deserve uncovering and questioning, but because monetary quantification as a way of thinking has profound implications for how we act. For example, many people believe that we have so far done much too little to address the threat of global climate change. Part of the explanation may be that we are thinking about the problem in entirely the wrong way. Our preoccupation with quantification may prevent action until the right numbers are available, and by then it may be too late.

This suggestion may sound like scaremongering. Surely current global policy on climate change does not rest on highly controversial assumptions about matters such as the monetary value of human life? It is hard to disentangle the forces behind complex policy decisions, but at the very least the assumptions listed above are not only of obscure technical interest. They may determine the future of climate change policy – and therefore the extent of climate change: 'Given that cost–benefit approaches certainly had some influence on President Bush Jr in his decision to withdraw from the Kyoto Protocol, the numbers matter.'[3] And we have seen that monetary quantification is equally central to more local matters, such as building roundabouts. It has crept into most aspects of our lives. It is difficult to overstate the influence of a way of thinking that has spawned a price tag on babies and human organs for sale in markets; ubiquitous numerical performance targets in the workplace; and government-sponsored online betting sites to predict terrorist attacks. We will meet some of these examples in the next chapter. But here I focus on environmental matters where many of the underlying problems with quantification arise in a particularly stark and challenging form. Before examining them in detail, it is worth taking a glimpse at policy debate on climate change in order to see exactly how the issues arise and how crucial they have become.

Climate change battles

The key organization charged with advising governments across the globe on climate change policy is the Intergovernmental Panel on Climate Change (IPCC). The IPCC has argued fiercely over the monetary valuation of human life – the argument nearly tore the IPCC apart. The argument was not about the notion of monetary value of human life itself, but the numbers involved. The standard view of market economics is, unsurprisingly, that the monetary values put on life, or decreased risk of death, should reflect values in markets. Economists argue that we can deduce how much people care about an increased or decreased risk of death by observing their behaviour in markets. In particular, they study the job market and observe how much extra people must be paid to persuade them to take a dangerous job. An alternative method is simply to ask people, in surveys, how much they would be willing to pay to reduce some specified risk, or how much they would require in compensation to tolerate some new risk. For example, people might be asked how much more tax they would be willing to pay for reduction in some hazardous pollutant in city air; or how much money would be the minimum acceptable compensation for tolerating the siting of a hazardous waste dump nearby. For the climate change debate, the key issue is that all these methods imply that life is valued less in poor countries: the decreased risk of death, arising from policies that reduce climate change, attracts a lower monetary value in poor countries. Compared to rich countries, the extra wage earnt in dangerous jobs will be lower, and so too will the amount people are willing to pay to avoid an increased risk of death. Poor people are worth less, on any measure of their value reflected in market prices or surveys.

In drafting the second IPCC report, most governments completely rejected this view, but a group of economists insisted that the report should include it: 'A careful reading of the fine print revealed that they were valuing lives in rich countries at $1,500,000, in middle-income countries at $300,000, and in lowest-income countries at $100,000.'[4] The final report heavily qualified this approach, but not because any consensus was reached: 'The outcome of it all was that the IPCC is very reluctant to engage in that controversy again because the proponents on both sides are still there and obviously still willing to have another fight if the opportunity was given to them.'[5] And in preparing subsequent reports, the IPCC has attached less importance to ubiquitous monetary valuation. But many economists are dissatisfied, and their arguments have been invoked as part of attempts to discredit the IPCC and the Kyoto Protocol. In July 2005 a British House of Lords committee published an influential report on climate change that pressed the IPCC to 'monetize' *all* costs and benefits, and give more prominence to such measures. It acknowledged that the controversy over the monetary valuation of life had been an obstacle, but dismissed such objections and explicitly sided with the economists.[6] In its conclusions and media summary, the House of Lords committee went on to question the independence of the IPCC, arguing that its membership and findings were being driven by external political pressures.[7]

Against this view, I shall show that attempts to monetize all costs and benefits inevitably involve ethical judgements of just the sort that are vulnerable to political pressure. If we want the IPCC or other advisory bodies to stick to the science, the clamour to measure all impacts in terms of money should be resisted; many impacts should be left in their natural units, such as 'lives lost'.

The authors of the highly influential *Stern Review* on climate change repeatedly indicate that they favour the latter approach. Most clearly:

> Our preference is to consider the multiple dimensions of the cost of climate change separately, examining each on its own terms. A toll in terms of lives lost gains little in eloquence when it is converted into dollars; but it loses something, from an ethical perspective, by distancing us from the human cost of climate change.[8]

Nevertheless, they do go on to 'convert into dollars', presenting detailed analyses that monetize impacts of climate change very widely, including all direct impacts on human health, lives lost and the environment. Admittedly, the *Review* reports *both* monetary and non-monetary assessments of the impacts of climate change, and this is an improvement on including monetary measures alone. But it can still be misleading. So for example, the *Review*'s summary states that:

> [I]f we don't act, the overall costs and risks of climate change will be equivalent to losing at least 5 per cent of global GDP each year, now and forever. If a wider range of risks and impacts is taken into account, the estimates of damage could rise to 20 per cent of GDP or more.[9]

The impression created is that the damage from climate change might conceivably be as low as 5 per cent of GDP – unsurprisingly the 5 per cent headline figure received the most subsequent media attention – and only if more doubtful, uncertain or less significant impacts are included does the damage rise to 20 per cent. Readers must wait till Chapter 6 of the *Review* to discover that the impacts excluded by the 5 per cent figure are, in fact, arguably the most important of all: the impacts on human health, lives lost and the environment. The *Stern Review* shows the controversy over monetary valuation to be very much alive. It leaves crucial questions unanswered by favouring non-monetary assessments, yet emphasizing monetary ones; and by measuring lives lost and environmental impacts in terms of money, yet suggesting they are optional or peripheral for inclusion in monetary measures of damage.

Another assumption of CBA is that outcomes in the future matter less. The economists' technique for giving future costs and benefits less weight is called 'discounting', and it continues to arouse controversy, for reasons to be explained later. In taking these reasons seriously, the *Stern Review* is a major improvement on previous practice in CBA, which largely ignored objections to discounting. Indeed, the *Review* attracted substantial flak from some economists for arguing that in comparison to standard CBA the scope and magnitude of discounting should be restricted. This occurred despite the *Review* devoting much more attention to economists' arguments that it discounts too little, than the opposite view of philosophers and others, defended below, that it still discounts too much.[10]

Turning to the question of whether uncertain future outcomes can always be given a probability, the debate has been less vociferous but remains very active. The House of Lords report complained repeatedly that the IPCC does not provide probabilities of various possible future climate change impacts, and pressed it to do so.[11] But attributing probabilities in the face of pure uncertainties which preclude them is a dangerous pretence that we know more than we do. The *Stern Review* is more balanced, explicitly recognizing that some probabilities in the science of climate change are unknown.[12]

Beyond these technical wrangles, we must confront the basic question: should climate change policy be made using CBA? For most economists, the answer is obvious; after all, CBA is just a systematic weighing up of pros and cons, they argue. This view may seem entirely reasonable – until we think of many other areas of government policy. Whether the issue is abortion or foreign policy, it is hard to take seriously the view that policy decisions in these areas are best made using a full CBA, partly because that is obviously not how people reason about such decisions. At every step there are complex ethical considerations which cannot be captured in monetary expressions of benefit and cost. It might seem absurd to suggest that abortion law be determined on the basis of such monetary measures, but most of us find *equally* absurd the prospect of determining climate change policy through attaching monetary values to human life. Economists and policy makers in government may disagree, because they are more familiar with CBA applied to climate change than to abortion or foreign policy. But of course that is no argument for distinguishing them.

Once we grant, as almost all of us do, that CBA is no help in deciding matters like abortion, the question becomes: what are the appropriate limits of monetary quantification? While the doubts about it may be more vivid in climate change debates, exactly the same issues arise elsewhere. Elsewhere? Almost everywhere. Monetary quantification is a way of thinking about almost any choice, large or small, which increasingly pervades every aspect of private life as well as public policy. For instance, can the services provided by schools and hospitals be measured in monetary terms? Even if they *can,* is this always the best way to assess them? Questions like these are the subject of the next chapter: I mention them here for two reasons. First, to try to convey to enthusiastic supporters of climate change CBA and other forms of valuing nature a hint as to why some of us object – we see no more justification for climate change CBA than foreign policy CBA. Second, to show that in focusing on the mechanics of monetary measurement, I have not forgotten to ask whether we should be doing it at all. But this bigger question is much better approached once armed with a sense of what monetary quantification involves, so I shall begin with the mechanics.

Valuing lives

An economist who has persevered this far (less surprising than it sounds, because many of them are doubtful of some applications of CBA) will probably be furious with my repeated assertion that CBA and related practices require 'the monetary valuation of human life'. Most economists insist that CBA involves no such thing, that my assertion is actively misleading. The textbook view is that CBA values *statistical lives,* not plain ordinary ones. Consider for instance the valuation of life adopted by the US Environmental Protection Agency, $6.1 million.[13] This number was obtained by examining the link between pay levels and workplace risks, as mentioned above. If someone must be paid an extra $60 to compensate them for undertaking a job or task involving a risk of death of 1 in 100,000, then economists *describe* this evidence as revealing that the value of a statistical life is $6 million. This is simply $60 multiplied by 100,000. The arithmetic logic is the same as for insurance: if I am prepared to pay up to £30 to insure a bicycle against theft, and I believe that the chance of theft is 1 in 5 (an optimistic underestimate in my home town, Cambridge), then this shows that I 'value' the bicycle at no more than £150. So terms such as 'value of life' are in a sense misleading, because life is not valued directly.

However, the jargon 'value of a statistical life' is hardly an improvement. Once we have realized that 'the value of a statistical life is $6 million' is simply shorthand for 'people require an extra $60 to tolerate a risk of death of 1 in 100,000', then the jargon may no longer mystify, but it continues to mislead. The reason is that in practice CBA is almost always used to evaluate policies that will affect many people. If a proposed environmental regulation for drinking water would reduce the risk of death per year from drinking it by merely 1 in 1 million, but the entire population of Britain is affected (say, 60 million people) then the regulation would on average save the lives of 60 people per year. Suppose we assume that the value of statistical life in Britain is £1 million, then we obtain a 'benefit' from this regulation of £60 million. Suppose, however, that such a regulation would be very costly to implement, say £80 million. CBA would recommend we do not adopt the regulation, even though on average 60 lives will be lost. CBA claims only to value 'statistical' lives, but if enough people are affected, statistical lives add up to real lives lost. The valuation of statistical lives can lead to the sacrifice of real lives, on the grounds that the cost of saving them is too great. In some cases this may be the correct decision, but nevertheless the rationale is exactly equivalent to putting a straightforward monetary value on life, without the 'statistical' smokescreen. So in what follows I shall refer without apology to CBA 'valuing life', and drop the 'statistical' qualifier.

So much for the terminology. How are the numbers obtained? There are other methods, but by far the most common techniques for valuing life in CBA have already been briefly mentioned – 'wage differentials' and surveys.

Contingent valuation surveys

Individuals are asked in surveys how much they would be willing to pay to avoid risks, or how much they would demand as minimum compensation for tolerating them. In both cases, the risks are described through hypothetical scenarios, and the numbers people provide are *contingent* on them responding as if the scenarios were real. Many economists regard this as the biggest weakness of the approach. People may provide a number without much thought, because the question is mysterious and 'making a mistake' in answering it has no consequences. Many people questioned in these surveys simply refuse to answer, either because they object to a market research approach that seemingly treats life like washing powder or cornflakes, or because they struggle to make any sense of the question.[14] It is unsurprising that almost all the valuations of life used in policy making reject this method.[15]

Wage differentials

Suppose there are two jobs, identical in every respect, except that one involves some dangerous task, exposing the worker to, say, a 1 in 10,000 risk of death each year. In a free market, economists assume that any observed difference in pay between these two jobs must be entirely due to this extra risk. Wages in the riskier job are higher only because the employer must offer more money to persuade workers to tolerate the risk. This is the wage differential, and it measures how much workers care about a risk, how much they are willing to forgo to avoid it. Or so the argument goes. I find that non-economists react to this approach with incredulity, although it forms the basis for a large majority of the monetary valuations of life which enter CBA, and which in turn have a heavy influence on decision making in both public and private sectors. For example, the guru of wage differentials analysis is Harvard Professor Kip Viscusi, who was influential in persuading the Bush administration that much existing environmental regulation is wasteful, on the strength among other things of his numbers.[16] So it is worth briefly summarizing the flaws in the wage differentials approach – at least for those economists and others who still take it seriously. First, and most obvious, the wage differentials literature simply assumes that workers consciously weigh up risks against wages. There is no mention of any research – such as interviewing workers – to support this implausible assumption. Even if these workers *wanted* to act like *Homo economicus,* in reality they are often unaware of the extent of the risks they face. Second, the wage differentials argument assumes perfectly free markets. In reality, workers end up in risky jobs not because they have freely chosen them, but because there is no alternative. They may lack the skills or mobility needed to obtain other jobs. Third, the wage differentials logic does not generate estimates of the attitude to risk of the population at large. At best, it shows how those in dangerous occupations value risk – but not the attitude of everyone else. And clearly, those in dangerous occupations may be there precisely because they are more tolerant of risk than the average.[17]

On the basis of this brief glimpse at how the numbers emerge, it is tempting to dismiss the monetary valuation of life without further comment. However, as elsewhere in this book, I set measurement problems aside, partly because a fuller discussion of them demands a deep understanding of the arcane details. And better measurement techniques may appear shortly. It is problems with the underlying framework for valuing life, rather than measurement difficulties, which deliver the fatal blow.

To begin with, there is an absurdity at the heart of the monetary valuation of life. It arises from the attempt to value life by examining increased risks of death. Suppose a policy or other government action (or inaction) was going to lead to the death of an identifiable person, John. Clearly the monetary value that John would place on his own life would be infinite. This would be consistent with the theory behind CBA too. There is no amount of money that John would be willing to accept as compensation for his death. So because of John's death alone, the costs of this policy are infinite, and it would fail the cost–benefit test. And yet CBA in practice often approves polices that will on average result in many deaths. This is possible only because the identity of those who will die is unknown, so there is no particular individual like John. Consider a policy that the government knows will on average lead to the death of, say, 60 people (such as the hypothetical example mentioned above, involving a decision not to adopt a drinking water quality regulation). The government knows that for any of these people, no amount of money is enough to compensate them for their death. So the costs of the policy are truly infinite in monetary terms. However, because of ignorance about the identity of the victims, it is possible for such a policy to pass the cost–benefit test. But it is absurd that ignorance should make a difference here. What matters is the numbers who will die, not whether we know their identity. The 'value of a statistical life' is a sleight-of-hand device to conceal this absurdity. If a proposed policy were presented as 'causing the death of 60 people on average, but we do not know who', it would be very hard for cost–benefit analysts to persuade their audience that a monetary value could be put on this harm. Instead, the harm is represented as a loss of statistical lives, or increased probability of death. But it is still the same loss, and we should not be deceived into believing it can be valued in terms of money.

This argument against valuing life in terms of increased risk of death is based on the work of the Oxford philosopher-economist, John Broome.[18] He first identified this absurdity in valuing life in the late 1970s, and it has been hanging like a sword of Damocles over CBA ever since. No cost–benefit analyst has yet proposed a satisfactory answer to the problem – instead some supporters of CBA have recently put forward another version of it. Suppose that everyone in a country faces an increased annual risk of death of 1 in 10 million, for instance because of climate change. If, somehow, we could obtain a number for how much individuals are each willing to pay to avoid such a risk, it would probably be very low, perhaps zero, because the increased risk is so small. But since everyone faces the risk, on average significant numbers will die – for example, 26 Americans. And this is the average impact; depending on how the risk manifests itself, there could be a catastrophe in which many more would die. Yet CBA, based on the sum of individuals' 'willingness to pay', would imply that the cost of such risks to life is approximately zero.[19] This absurd conclusion becomes even starker when low probability risks of catastrophe are considered, such as those posed by climate change.

By revealing some of the absurdities which emerge, these philosophical arguments provide a compelling reason to abandon attempts to place monetary values on life. However, the practice is so entrenched that it will not be displaced by philosophical arguments alone. Yet if these are set aside, and it is assumed that life *can* be valued in terms of increased risk of death, valuing risk is itself plagued with difficulty. The difficulties extend to all kinds of risks, not just risk to life, so deserve discussion in their own right.

Valuing risks

In CBA if two different risks each pose an identical probability of harm to life or limb, then the risks themselves are deemed identical. They are termed 'statistically equivalent'. This raises an immediate problem. All statistically equivalent risks may be equal in the eyes of a statistician or cost–benefit analyst, but not for the rest of us. Probability is far from being the only thing that matters.

Considering only probabilities, you are much more likely to be harmed by having an X-ray in hospital than by living near a nuclear power station. But many people regard nuclear power as riskier than hospital X-rays, because they understand risk in a much broader sense. Risk has qualities as well as quantities. A risk is perceived to be much worse if it is involuntary, unfamiliar, unfair, irreversible or uncontrollable – risks from nuclear power are widely believed to have all these worrying attributes. Similarly, travel by air is perceived to be riskier than travel by car. Once in the air the risks we face are unfamiliar and completely out of our control, but nevertheless on any reasonable measure the probability of harm from air travel is lower. Widespread attitudes to risk cannot be dismissed as gut reactions which people discard after a moment's thought, because there is now overwhelming evidence that they arise systematically and predictably.[20]

Scientific experts often respond to this evidence with frustration. At the very least, they note that political concerns (for example, with fairness) are being muddled with objective scientific assessment. They believe, rightly, that the public are usually ignorant about the reversibility and controllability of a risk. And they doubt that 'familiarity' should be a relevant consideration at all. In short, experts often regard lay judgements about risk as irrational. A powerful exponent of this view is not a scientist, but a US Supreme Court judge, Stephen Breyer, who argued that policy decisions involving risk should be made by an elite cadre of civil servants, isolated from any political, media or popular influence.[21] Breyer's proposals were explicitly adopted by the Bush Administration.[22]

Although the view that ordinary people are irrational is often tinged with arrogance, it should not be dismissed any more quickly than the lay opinions which it scorns. Most of us accept that we struggle to think about complex risks in any coherent manner – especially if they involve uncertain small probabilities of potentially catastrophic outcomes – so it is hardly surprising that instead we fasten on to more accessible clues such as the familiarity of the risk. Moreover, the interest of the media is in spinning a story, often knowingly inducing panic, rather than promoting rational judgement. Politicians have their own biases too, particularly a tendency to ignore hazards which will play out only after the next election. Against this background, decision makers turn to CBA for guidance, but CBA is caught in a dilemma between scientific and lay judgements about risk.

On the one hand, as we have seen, market economics is built on the principle of consumer sovereignty. In this spirit, it is no more acceptable to dispute lay preferences about risk than preferences for chocolate over strawberry ice cream. If CBA in general, and the valuation of life in particular, is supposed to be built on preferences expressed in markets, then it should reflect ordinary attitudes towards risk, even if people favour activities involving a much higher probability of harm (passive smoking) over those where the probability is low (living near a nuclear power station). Considerations of reversibility, controllability, voluntariness and familiarity lead people to regard risks with an *equal* probability of occurring as *unequally* risky. It is easy to imagine other differences between these 'statistically equivalent' risks too, so there should be no presumption that two statistically equivalent risks can generally be treated alike in CBA.

All risks are context-specific, so monetary valuations of life should vary: they will be just as context-specific as the associated risks. There will not be a uniform monetary value of life.

On the other hand, although context-specific valuation is sometimes defended by supporters of CBA,[23] it faces major practical difficulties. Context-specific values cannot be obtained using wage differentials, and they substantially increase the cost of the valuation process itself. Wage differentials are by definition context-specific – but a different context to the one under consideration. They concern the risk faced by a particular group of workers in a particular job, not the risk being evaluated in the CBA. So the numbers must be obtained through the controversial survey approach. If, instead, a uniform value of life is assumed, the actual number can be obtained simply by making minor adjustments to values of life used in previous cost–benefit analyses. Expensive new investigations or surveys are not required. This 'benefit transfer' approach is very common. For example, cost–benefit analyses of planned new roads in Britain always start with a 'valuation of a prevented fatality' of £1,145,000.[24]

But the most revealing problem with context-specific valuation is that it begs the question of why we should place monetary values on life at all. Cost–benefit analysts repeatedly insist that the most important function of valuing lives is to ensure consistent policy making, with the price of inconsistency being unnecessary deaths.[25] They point to policies which had high financial costs but saved few lives, yet were adopted, and contrast them with policies which were not adopted, yet involved a lower cost per life saved. The conclusion drawn is that, within a given budget, governments should save many more lives by focusing their efforts on those policies with the lowest cost per life saved. At first glance, this consistency argument may seem compelling. It implicitly rejects context-specific valuation, instead adopting a single uniform figure for the monetary value of every life. This seems to imply all people are worth the same, which fits with our ethical intuitions. But more precisely, it implies all people are worth the same amount of money, which does not fit at all. Against the consistency argument, a policy that costs more but saves fewer lives can be justified, provided that other relevant factors come into play. Although the number of lives lost is very important, it is usually not all that matters. Perhaps the policy would prevent particularly painful deaths or avoid involuntary risks.

The consistency rationale for valuing lives collapses if the value of life is context-specific in this way. Does the monetary valuation of life then serve any purpose? It is hard to see what that could be. For example, putting a monetary value on pain or voluntariness, in order to determine the context-specific value of life, simply shrouds important judgements behind a quantitative veil. The hard work in making the decision is in these judgements – for example in judging that the avoided deaths would be sufficiently painful to justify the relatively high cost. The context-specific value of life represents these judgements; it does not help to *make* them. And it obscures them.

So CBA faces an intractable dilemma in valuing life as risk of death. An influential supporter of CBA, who has recently argued for context-specific values of life, is right in saying that they are the only way of being true to the underlying theory of consumer sovereignty. This approach 'takes the current theory *very* seriously – more seriously, in fact, than do those who now use it'.[26] But that is because the practitioners have rejected the context-specific valuation of life. It makes the process impractical and extremely costly, and completely undermines the consistency rationale for attaching monetary values to life in the first place.

In fact the problem facing CBA is much broader, because the same dilemma arises in another way. We have seen context-specific valuations arising from statistically equivalent risks being perceived differently. They can also arise when truly identical risks are faced by different people. This returns us to the IPCC controversy over people in poor countries being assigned a lower monetary value. Suppose the inhabitants of two countries, one rich and one poor, each face an identical risk of death from climate change. Even though the risks are identical, economists' standard techniques will give different valuations of life in the two countries, because incomes differ. These context-specific valuations, built on market choices and the idea of consumer sovereignty, suddenly seem much less democratic. While the second IPCC report adopted different values for lives in different countries, the third report instead calculated an average of these different values (approximately $1 million) and assumed that to be the value of life in all countries.[27] Which is the better approach?

There is little consensus among cost–benefit analysts on this crucial issue. On the one hand, money is worth more to poor people – the law of diminishing marginal utility explained in Chapter 4. Therefore any given expression of willingness-to-pay or monetary valuation from a poor person (whether via surveys or market prices) should count for more, because money is worth more to them. That is, the values actually reported by poorer people through surveys or market prices should be adjusted upwards to give them greater weight and make them truly comparable with valuations from richer people. The result would be adjusted valuations of life in rich and poor countries which are closer, even if not typically identical across countries. A rough practical approximation of this adjustment process might simply adopt a uniform value of life in all countries, say $1 million.

On the other hand, it is unclear exactly what this $1 million figure means in practice. It certainly does not imply governments in poor countries are willing to pay $1 million per head of population towards tackling climate change. Tragically, there are many poor countries where the threat of climate change, no matter how serious, is simply less worthy of resources than pressing problems of HIV/AIDS, malnutrition and lack of clean drinking water. Economists critical of the uniform value approach argue that the $1 million figure misrepresents the importance of climate change to poor countries, skewing priorities towards rich country concerns. They conclude that it is anti-democratic and favour different values of life in different countries. However, this conclusion reflects a particular version of democracy, one that endorses dumping toxic waste in poor countries, along the lines of the chapter epigraph. On this view, if poor countries are willing to accept the waste because rich countries are paying them enough, then it would be anti-democratic to block this expression of poor country preferences. The problem, of course, is that many poor countries do not feel they have a choice at all. Talk of preference and choice is fanciful when most of the population is struggling to subsist.

Again, we have 'on the one hand' and 'on the other'. No wonder President Truman asked exasperatedly for a one-handed economist. My conclusion here is that *both* approaches are flawed. There are intractable problems, whether we adopt uniform or context-specific values of life.

To some readers, it might seem that the above arguments against valuing life in monetary terms are unnecessarily long-winded. After all, almost all cultures and religions include absolute prohibitions on taking human life. The position is more complex when actions involve passive 'letting die' rather than active killing, and more complex still when the actors are governments rather than individuals – at least if there is ever such a thing as a just war. Nevertheless, many people clearly endorse an ethic in which saving human life has absolute priority; a CBA that weighs up the value of life saving against other benefits is obviously wrong.

I do not assume an ethical framework along these lines. In this respect at least, I share the view of most economists, who struggle to see how such an ethic is compatible with many reasonable decisions which governments regularly make. Governments often decide to subsidize opera performances or sporting events, even though the money could otherwise save lives if spent on health care. Another example: 'The French government knows that a few people die in accidents every year solely because of the avenues of trees lining the roads; yet we do not think it monstrous that they have decided not to sacrifice such beauty.'[28] There is no clash of noble values here, no tragic choice between life and liberty; it is salutary to be reminded that lives are knowingly sacrificed for relatively humble ends such as opera, sport and tree-lined avenues. As economists put it, we often 'trade off' life in return for other benefits. And if we are willing to trade off life, then we are undoubtedly willing to make trade-offs when less is at stake. In the next chapter I shall argue that there are fundamental ethical problems with the practice of monetary valuation and closely related ideas about trade-offs, but my arguments do not assume that certain things, such as human life, have some kind of intrinsically superior moral status.

Although the discussion so far has concerned *human* life, CBA faces major problems valuing non-human lives too. CBA is frequently used to value animal lives, for example when a planned road through a forest will entail the destruction of a particular animal habitat. There are distinctive difficulties here, especially if the species is endangered. The habitat in question may be one of the few remaining on Earth, and its destruction might significantly increase the risk of the species becoming extinct. In putting a price on this increased risk, CBA must effectively value the whole species. Although the difficulties here are substantial, they are minor when compared to those faced by more ambitious examples of pricing nature on a global scale, for example attempts to put monetary values on biodiversity and ecosystem services. Many of these valuation exercises make astonishing assumptions: an influential early attempt to value global ecosystem services attempted to combine the 'production benefits' (e.g. timber from forests) with the 'consumption benefits' (e.g. pleasure in walking through a forest) and the 'system functional benefits' (e.g. carbon absorption by the forest), in each case adding up all the benefits from all the ecosystems on Earth, in order to obtain a *single* overall monetary value.[29] These breathtaking attempts to calculate the monetary value of everything have rightly been ridiculed by most economists, so they are not discussed in what follows.[30] The arguments here focus on showing that relatively easy exercises in pricing nature – for instance as part of a CBA on whether to build a new road through a forest – still face severe problems. One important set of problems concerns valuing the future.

Valuing the future

There are two distinct challenges that arise when making a decision with consequences extending into the future: uncertainty, and comparing outcomes that occur at different times. In policy contexts, five to ten years from now is generally the future in question. As consequences extend further into the future, decisions become even more difficult. Uncertainty becomes pervasive, and it is harder to compare outcomes which are very far apart in time. Again, climate change policy illustrates both problems vividly. Many of the costs involved in tackling climate change must be incurred now, but the main benefits will not be felt for 30 years or more. And estimating both the benefits and costs is fraught with uncertainty, not just in the underlying science, but because of complex feedback effects. For example, the scale and rate of climate change will affect economic growth and the speed of technological innovation, both of which in turn influence emissions levels, feeding back to shape climate change.[31]

A skeptic might acknowledge that the benefits and costs of reducing climate change are uncertain, but query whether they are really any *more* uncertain than other difficult problems. It is a misleading question, because the important distinction between different situations of uncertainty is not one of degree, but kind. It is a distinction between risk and uncertainty.

Risk versus uncertainty

If the effect of some action or decision is not certain, but we know the numerical probability of each of the possible outcomes, then there is *risk* (regardless of whether the outcomes are good or bad). In this sense, there is risk when tossing a coin. We do not know whether the outcome will be heads or tails, but we do know that the probability of each is 1 in 2, or 50 per cent. But if we do not know the probabilities either, it is a situation of *uncertainty*. (I shall occasionally refer to 'pure uncertainty' to emphasize this special usage of the word, distinct from its 'not certain' meaning in ordinary language.) The concepts of risk and (pure) uncertainty both take for granted that all the possible outcomes are known. Sometimes, however, we are ignorant about those too. Sadly, current climate change policy must be formulated in this state of ignorance. We do not know the probability of the various climate impacts associated with, say, the 'do nothing' option. Neither do we know the likely magnitude of these impacts. We do not even know whether we are aware of all the major impacts arising from 'doing nothing'. Uncertainty and ignorance are more widespread than they might appear. They do not arise only when there is an absolute blank in our knowledge, but also because experts fundamentally disagree about probabilities or impacts. If these disagreements cannot be resolved, then we face uncertainty or ignorance or both.

Why does the distinction between risk, uncertainty and ignorance matter? The answer is that if we treat a problem as one of risk when in truth we face uncertainty or ignorance, we will often go badly wrong. We will be acting as if we know all the possible outcomes and their associated probabilities, when in fact we may know neither. If there is uncertainty, then any probabilities we use in quantitative analysis must be invented. This is one instance of a more general problem of spurious quantification, attaching numbers to things when there is no scientific basis to do so. In all these cases, the outcome of the CBA or another quantification exercise will have a misleadingly reassuring precision. Decision makers may understandably take this precision to mean that they can confidently rely on the recommendation of the CBA, when in fact it is no more reliable than the dubious numbers on which it is based. The situation is reminiscent of an apocryphal story about weighing hogs in Texas.

> Down there, they put the hog in one pan of a large set of scales, put rocks in the other pan ... until they exactly balance the weight of the hog. Having done that very carefully, they guess how much the rocks weigh.[32]

Calculation does not confer precision. On the contrary, dubious numbers are infectious: adding a dubious number to a reliable one yields an equally dubious number. Nevertheless it might seem that imperfect quantification is better than no quantification at all. If a bad decision is likely to be made because something is imperfectly quantified, then it is just as likely – seemingly more likely – to be made if it is not quantified at all. If there is danger of a bad decision because we ignore all the caveats and arbitrary assumptions made in quantifying some relevant factor, then that danger is surely increased if we simply ignore it altogether.

The first objection to this argument is obvious: just because some factor remains unquantified does not mean that we must ignore it altogether. It will be ignored *within* a CBA or similar exercise, but it can still receive full consideration in the broader decision-making process. Supporters of CBA maintain that even then qualitative factors may be ignored; they seem less concerned that the limitations of the numbers might be overlooked.[33] But this is surely the opposite of what will happen. The caveats – the limitations of the numbers – are often complex technical issues, hidden from immediate view. They are not pros or cons, but qualifications and assumptions about the measurement of those pros and cons. In contrast, a qualitative pro or con can be readily understood. In a research or consultancy report, qualitative considerations can be included in the 'Executive Summary' of an otherwise quantitative analysis. Yet because of its complexity, proper discussion of the caveats behind the numbers will rarely reach the summary. Indeed it may not get beyond the footnotes to the main text.

Talk of 'imperfect' quantification is also misleading. It suggests the possibility of perfect quantification: there is a correct number waiting to be found, if only we can uncover it. Then it would seem plausible that our imperfect estimate of this truth conveys some useful information. The number may be inaccurate, but it differs from the truth in predictable and systematic ways. But in the messy world of decision making, perfect quantification is usually a myth. Many attempts to quantify involve arbitrary assumptions. In 1996, TWA Flight 800 crashed near Long Island, New York. Shortly afterwards, Robert Hahn, an influential US economist and policy adviser, tried to estimate the costs and benefits of improved airport security. The benefit estimate was based simply on the number of deaths caused by terrorism up to that time, and the research concluded that the costs of improved security outweighed the benefits.[34] Then there was 11 September 2001: that awful day could hardly have been anticipated five years earlier – but nevertheless, it was supremely foolish to use the past as a reliable guide to predicting future levels of terrorism. The situation was one of uncertainty, not risk. Inventing a number in such cases simply encourages a deluded sense of predictability and control.

Yet the myth of perfect quantification seems extraordinarily deep-rooted. Why is the belief that a true numerical answer exists, that something is being measured, so widespread? This is a very broad question, so we shall focus on just one aspect of it, namely the practice of quantifying uncertainty and ignorance – inventing probabilities when there is no basis to do so.

The practice is widespread among economists because many of them believe that, no matter how extreme the uncertainty, effective probabilities always exist. This view is termed 'subjective Bayesianism' (hereafter *Bayesianism* for short), from the Reverend Thomas Bayes, an 18th-century English mathematician.[35] Its implications are startling. Bayesians believe there is no such thing as pure uncertainty in the sense I have defined it. They assert that we always use probabilities, consciously or otherwise, when outcomes are not certain. The issues are more clearly depicted in simple gambling games than messy real-world choices; the Ellsberg Paradox (see box opposite) is a classic illustration.

If you think in terms of probabilities, then choosing A in the initial choice would show you believe box A contains fewer black balls. So now that the prize has switched to the black ball, you should choose box B. (By similar reasoning, if you chose B initially, you should now choose box A.) And people who act as if they think in terms of probabilities would do likewise. But in experiments just like this, most people choose box A initially, and do not change their choice once the prize is for black. This is unsurprising if people do not attribute probabilities to the balls in box B. People like to know the odds they face, so they choose box A in both cases rather than the pure uncertainty of box B. But Bayesians think this is inconsistent, irrational, puzzling behaviour. Hence the name, the Ellsberg 'Paradox'.[36]

Many economists who reject Bayesianism are nevertheless influenced by it, holding a parallel view about how we *should* choose: they believe that the only rational way to think about uncertainty is in terms of probabilities. For example, when conducting CBA, many economists not only favour attaching probabilities to all uncertainties, but also see this step

The Ellsberg Paradox

Suppose there are two boxes, each holding 100 balls, which are either red or black. Box A holds 50 red and 50 black balls; in box B the mixture is unknown. A ball is to be drawn at random from one box, but you can choose the box. You win $200 if the ball is red. Which box do you choose?

Bayesians assume that, if you pick box A, this shows that you believe it contains more red balls than box B, and vice versa – in other words, you think in terms of probabilities. Even if you explicitly deny thinking this way, Bayesians are undeterred. They assume your decision is the same as it would be if you *did* use probabilities. Bayesians say we act *as if* we used probabilities.

Now suppose you win $200 if the ball drawn is black, but the boxes are left unchanged; will you change your choice of box?

If you think in terms of probabilities, then choosing A in the initial choice would show you believe box A contains fewer black balls. So now that the prize has switched to the black ball, you should choose box B. (By similar reasoning, if you chose B initially, you should now choose box A.) And people who act *as if* they think in terms of probabilities would do likewise. But in experiments just like this, most people choose box A initially, and do not change their choice once the prize is for black. This is unsurprising if people do not attribute probabilities to the balls in box B. People like to know the odds they face, so they choose box A in both cases rather than the pure uncertainty of box B. But Bayesians think this is inconsistent, irrational, puzzling behaviour. Hence the name, the Ellsberg 'Paradox'.[36]

as unavoidable, if the decision is to be rational. Rational choice, they insist, requires that we *must* attach probabilities, explicitly or implicitly – so it is better to be explicit about it. But in the absence of a developed argument behind these assertions, and given the strong evidence from the Ellsberg 'Paradox' and related experiments that this is *not* how people think, the influence of Bayesianism on CBA and policy making is unwelcome. It is a clear case of the economic-theory tail wagging the policy-making dog. Or as the joke puts it: when confronted by a successful policy, economists are prone to ask: 'That's all very well in practice, but how does it work in theory?'

Returning from the Ellsberg experiment to real-world policy making, the *Stern Review* on climate change abandons strict Bayesianism, but remains wedded to an analogous and misleading quantification of the uncertainties. Rather than demanding probabilities for all the unknowns, it assumes we know the precise range of possible probabilities, *and* can put numerical weights on these possible probabilities according to factors such as 'which probability might be more or less plausible.'[37] The result of these assumptions is a kind of quantitative pseudoprobability attached to each uncertainty. This insistence on quantifying the unquantifiable still implies that we know more than we do, and forces inherently qualitative views about catastrophic risks and the like into an unhelpful quantitative framework.

We turn next to the other major challenge facing attempts to value the future: comparing outcomes that occur at different times. The problems of dealing with pure uncertainty in this context are largely set aside for the sake of simplicity.

Discounting

Discounting concerns the idea that future costs and benefits should have less weight in our decision making than present ones. The most basic argument for discounting is termed 'pure time preference', the view that happiness, well-being or satisfaction now is preferred to the same amount of it later. This preference is familiar enough in individuals – we call it impatience. But to justify discounting, the observation that individuals *are* impatient needs to be transformed into an argument for why society *ought* to be impatient. This transformation requires several steps, each one of them open to objection: individuals may show pure time preference, but nevertheless this is irrational; even if it is rational, it does not follow that *society* should similarly favour the present; even if such a social preference is legitimate within generations, it is unjust across them (because future people must pay the price of our past impatience). So it is hardly surprising that almost all philosophers reject pure time preference applied to society.[38] A moral framework cannot claim to be fair if it treats the happiness of some people as less important purely because of when they happen to be born. Impartiality across generations is essential to any plausible ethical theory. The economists who first developed CBA agreed.[39] Frank Ramsey, who introduced the concept of discounting to economics, nevertheless described pure time preference as 'a practice that is ethically indefensible, and arises merely from the weakness of imagination'.[40]

Despite the arguments against it, and the opposition from philosophers and eminent economic theorists, practical CBA in both Britain and the US almost always assumes some pure time preference.[41] I return to the issue below, but for the moment set it aside for the sake of clarity: assume future happiness is worth just as much as present happiness. Even if this is true, future monetary costs and benefits may not be worth as much as present ones. This brings us to a much more persuasive argument for discounting, a discounting of monetary costs and benefits rather than happiness itself.

Is receiving $100 now worth the same as receiving $100 in one year? Of course not, because $100 received now could be deposited in a bank, and assuming an interest rate of 5 per cent, $105 will be available in one year. Put another way, $105 in one year cannot be worth more than $100 today, because the latter can always be converted into the former. In the jargon, we 'discount' future monetary values to make them comparable with monetary values today. If $105 in one year is discounted using a discount rate of 5 per cent, then it becomes equivalent to $100 today. An interest rate defines how a present sum of money is converted into a future one; the same discount rate defines the reverse process. The larger the discount rate, the more we discount the future, that is, the less it matters to us. But even a low discount rate has a dramatic effect on our valuation of costs and benefits in the distant future, because the discounting is repeatedly compounded. Consider discount rates of around 3 per cent, and a 200-year time horizon, both of which are widely used in cost–benefit analyses for climate change policy. Although 3 per cent is generally regarded as a suitably low discount rate, $100 in 200 years is worth only 27 cents today. And estimation of the present value of benefits and costs is extremely sensitive to the discount rate. If the rate is increased to 4 per cent, the same $100 in 200 years shrinks to just 4 cents – about seven times less important.

A parallel but deeper version of the argument for discounting starts by explaining why we can grow our money in this way – why banks offer positive rates of interest. The answer is that they can do so because someone else wishes to borrow money from the bank and pay a positive rate of interest for the privilege. And the borrower is willing to do *that* because there are productive opportunities in the economy. The borrower can invest the money now, and produce more in the future, the surplus being more than enough to cover the interest charges. In a fundamental sense, the borrower's capital investment is productive. For example, trees purchased now, and not felled for timber, will grow and yield more timber in the future. Technological improvements will allow more manufactured goods to be produced in the future than the present, from the same quantity of inputs. Generally, if we forgo consumption now and instead invest to generate consumption in the future, we will be able to consume more later. As noted in Chapter 3, this process is at the heart of economic growth. But if economic growth means there will be more consumption in the future, then extra units of consumption will be worth less – the law of diminishing marginal utility again. A unit of extra consumption in the future will be worth less to us, because we will be richer and consuming more then, due to economic growth. Since future consumption is worth less in this sense, it is discounted.

This version of the argument for discounting reveals the assumption that there will be more consumption in the future. While this may be true of some goods, certain goods will be just as scarce, because economic growth cannot generate more of them. Stocks of fossil fuels do not increase through economic growth, nor do environmental assets such as beautiful countryside. On the contrary, consumption of these 'non-renewable resources' is likely to decline as we progressively use them or build over them. This implies that future consumption of what remains of our non-renewable resources will be worth as much or more to us. The discount rate for these goods should therefore be zero or negative. Another example is the saving of life. Lives saved in the future are presumably just as valuable as lives saved now, even if more lives are saved in the future.[42] So some costs and benefits should not be discounted, such as those associated with future lives saved (or lost), or non-renewable resources. Yet current practice in both Britain and the US almost always ignores this distinction.[43]

There is a broader objection to discounting which applies to all costs and benefits affecting future generations. The problem is that future generations are disenfranchised.[44] As we have seen, the basis for calculating the discount rate is the interest rate, which is set in financial markets. At least in principle, this market-determined interest rate reflects our preferences – specifically how impatient we are. But the preferences of future generations are represented only insofar as current generations care about them. Future generations are disenfranchised in just the way that women are in societies where only men have any direct say in decisions. This may seem like the point about impartiality between generations that I made above. But that concerned whether, thinking ethically and impartially, we should discount the future. The argument here is that, no matter what the ethically correct discount rate is, in practice we should not use market interest rates as a guide to it, because only the present generation has any influence on interest rates. Even though current generations may care about the future, they care less than future generations would if they could express their preferences directly. Obviously, it is inevitable that only current generations make decisions – in *that* sense future generations are unavoidably disenfranchised – but it is less obvious, and not inevitable, that this bias is reinforced by using market interest rates to determine discount rates.

Some economists have begun to acknowledge these objections to discounting. They have become increasingly uneasy about the practice, especially in cases such as climate change, where significant impacts fall on future generations, and the extreme and implausible effects of discounting into the distant future become relevant. Martin Weitzman, probably the most influential economist in the field, reflected candidly: 'to think about the distant future in terms of standard discounting is to have an uneasy intuitive feeling that something is wrong, somewhere'.[45] And faced with a complete lack of consensus on appropriate discount rates for the distant future, he resorted to surveying over two thousand economists for their opinions.[46] But rather than abandon discounting, the economists have, characteristically, embraced a technical modification with great enthusiasm. This new approach to discounting is seen as answering the skeptics, and has swiftly turned into British Government policy.[47] It proposes that discount rates should decline over time, rather than remain constant as in standard CBA. This implies that although each time period still matters less than the preceding ones, the distant future matters much more than it does under conventional discounting.

Several reasons for adopting declining discount rates have been advanced. They all rest on a mathematical phenomenon that confounds our intuition. It cannot be briefly explained, so I shall just state it here: if there is uncertainty about how much weight to give to costs and benefits in the distant future, and we address this uncertainty by adopting an 'average' weight, this does *not* imply use of an average discount rate, but a much lower one.[48] For example, suppose we are unsure whether to use a discount rate of 1 per cent, 10 per cent, or any whole number in between. The effect of choosing any of these rates on costs and benefits in 100 years' time can be calculated. We might expect the average of these effects to be equivalent to using an average of the discount rates. That is, an average of 1 per cent, 2 per cent, 3 per cent and so on up to 10 per cent: the average of these numbers is 5.5 per cent. But this is false. Far from obviously, the average effect is actually equivalent to a much lower discount rate of just 1.61 per cent. Until very recently, economists made exactly this mistake. Faced with uncertainty, they simply adopted an average rate, constant over time. It is now understood that if there is doubt about the appropriate discount rate, the effective discount rate should be much lower, and it should decline over time.

Two sources of doubt about discount rates seem possible – economic and ethical. Regarding the former, the argument for discounting depends on continuing economic growth, and determining rates of economic growth in the distant future is akin to gazing into a crystal ball. The appropriate discount rate will be uncertain because economic forecasting is uncertain. Turning to ethical doubts about the discount rate, recent research has interpreted them as a form of uncertainty. For example, a 'materialist' might favour a high discount rate, while a 'conservationist' would favour a low one.[49] The 'correct' rate is effectively uncertain. The argument of the previous paragraph is then applied to show that when considering the distant future we should not average the high and low rates, but adopt declining discount rates over time in order to average the weight given to the two ethical positions. This approach is popular among economists because they believe it enables ethical worries about discounting to be incorporated in a standard CBA framework. If they are correct, the implications are more radical than most economists might like. If one of the ethical views is that the discount rate should be zero (i.e. the future matters just as much as the present), then this approach implies that the discount rate should decline over time towards zero. Skeptics about discounting should welcome this, and also welcome the implicit recognition it gives to competing ethical views. But the overall approach is a bizarre one. Trying to average the implications of 'materialist' and 'conservationist' views is akin to the person who, because they are unsure whether to become a Christian or a Buddhist, decides to be a Buddhist on Mondays, Wednesdays and Fridays, and a Christian on Tuesdays, Thursdays and Sundays (with Saturday off for shopping).

The right way to resolve ethical disagreement is through open debate, and the technical fix of declining discount rates is no substitute. We have seen that there is a limited argument for discounting some costs and benefits, but not those associated with fossil fuels, or beautiful landscapes or saving lives. The argument collapses entirely in cases such as climate change, where impacts affect future generations. Should we abandon discounting in such cases? The advocates of discounting offer two final reasons why we should not.

First, they claim that if we do not discount the future at all, and are completely impartial between generations, this implies an excessive sacrifice by the present generation: we should reduce our income to a subsistence level now for the sake of future generations. The reasoning is that any sacrifice now will be outweighed by the benefit to future generations, because investments made now will grow and yield greater benefit in the future, and there are many future generations who will benefit. This argument for discounting fails, partly for technical reasons,[50] but mainly because it misunderstands the purpose of discounting. The purpose is to calculate how much future benefits and costs are worth in present terms, rather than to decide how much we should leave for the future. Discounting cannot resolve this ethical dilemma. Too many of the arguments for discounting reflect a muddling of economic and ethical reasons for discounting. The result is obviously confusion.[51] If on the one hand we wish to be impartial across generations, but on the other we do not wish to commit those presently living to excessive sacrifices, the solution is to apply some kind of constraint on present sacrifice, preferably one emerging from, and made legitimate through, an open political debate. This is not a novel suggestion. It has already happened, but CBA – and with it the operation of much government policy – simply ignores it. The constraint is called 'sustainability', and the debate 'sustainable development'.

Second, some economists believe we should carry on discounting because they sidestep the ethical dilemma between obligations to present and future generations. They simply assert that we should, in a democracy, be concerned only with the views of the current electorate. Insofar as the current electorate cares about future generations, then governments should respond to that concern. And if people are impatient – in other words, show pure time preference – government policy should reflect that too. These economists take the strong evidence that people are impatient in their everyday decision making as directly relevant here.[52] This democratic defence of discounting might seem persuasive, but faces an immediate practical problem. Just because people are impatient in their everyday decision making, it does not follow that they want the government to be impatient on their behalf when making climate change policy. They elect governments to make good decisions on their behalf, not mimic their own mistakes. And there is evidence that people perceive their own impatience as mistaken. In many countries people vote for some form of compulsory saving for pensions. But why vote to constrain yourself? Either you do not trust yourself to save enough towards your pension, or at least you believe that others cannot be so trusted. In others words, you believe that you or others are too impatient. More generally, as we saw in Chapter 2, it is very difficult to read off people's preferences from their everyday choices, and there is much evidence that people regret their own past decisions and would wish to have acted otherwise. That is one reason why democracies mostly operate indirectly via elected representatives rather than using an endless stream of referendums. This brings us to a more basic objection to the democratic defence of CBA.

Governments can either do what people want, or do what is, on balance, for the best. The democratic defence of CBA aims it squarely at showing what people want. It implies that CBA is a kind of glorified opinion poll. But we already have the political process as a way of representing what people want. If the public, through the political process, disagrees with the recommendation of a CBA, is CBA supposed to take precedence? Of course not, because that would subvert democracy. The recommendation provided by the CBA cannot be regarded as emerging from a democratic process, because it depends on important assumptions made by economists, not the public. We have seen these assumptions at work influencing the choice of discount rate or the monetary value of life, and there are many more assumptions buried in the details.[53] Economists determine the CBA recommendation, not the public. Many economists largely acknowledge this, and respond by stressing that CBA in practice is an *input* into the democratic process, providing guidance on what is best. But then CBA cannot also be a democratic decision-making device in its own right, for the sake of defending discounting.

Life beyond monetary measurement?

It is sometimes suggested that there is no alternative to CBA and other forms of monetary measurement. I have already hinted that sustainable development may provide an alternative decision-making framework for environmental issues. There is no space to discuss this framework in depth here, but it is worth a brief look at just one aspect of it, to illustrate how it can provide a real alternative to CBA.

A key concept in sustainable development, particularly in discussions of climate change, is the precautionary principle. There are many versions of the precautionary principle in circulation, and its status in European law is confused.[54] But the essential ideas are easy to summarize. The strongest case for 'taking precautions' arises when (i) there is pure uncertainty about the future; and (ii) at least one possible outcome in the future is catastrophic. Then it seems entirely reasonable to act now so as to prevent catastrophe occurring, if at all possible. More precisely, we should choose the course of action with the best 'worst-case' outcome. There is little doubt that the threats posed by climate change meet both conditions (i) and (ii). These conditions have been endorsed by specialists in a number of disciplines, and can even be given a solid theoretical basis in orthodox economics.[55] But clearly they leave many questions unanswered: what are the costs of ensuring that catastrophe is avoided? And who bears them? Some economists argue that poor countries would end up bearing a significant share of the costs of mitigating climate change – if they are right, then mitigation is less attractive. Is there a realistic possibility that if we spend less on addressing this possible catastrophe, we might instead be able to avoid other hazards, not catastrophic but still grave? Perhaps more information is available. Even if probabilities are unknown, there may be some rough knowledge of the likelihood of catastrophe. A more radical response to the lack of information is to delay making a decision. If we do so, is significant new information likely to emerge? Or even new options? Or will our options diminish – will there be irreversible losses from delay?

Faced with these questions, and others, the precautionary principle is clearly just a beginning. But it is one that launches us in a very different direction from CBA and other forms of ubiquitous quantification. It is not only that these questions cannot be answered by CBA, which cannot accommodate pure uncertainty; more revealingly, many of these questions are not even relevant as far as CBA is concerned. There is no direct consideration of justice and fairness between and across generations, and problems are understood in static terms, that is, where fixed options are evaluated as means of achieving fixed aims. But we do not make our everyday decisions in this rigid, unimaginative and mechanical way – and neither should policy makers. As we have all learnt from experience, intelligent decision making requires a flexible willingness and ability to reconsider both our aims and our means of achieving them, in light of new knowledge. This new knowledge may not just come from outside; more often, it emerges in the process of trying to make a decision and contemplating the available options. For instance, we may decide that all the apparent options facing us are deeply unattractive, so we try to refashion the choice, either by revising our aims, or by striving to develop new options altogether. In particularly difficult cases, we may need to go through several iterations of this process, progressively revising means and ends. In principle, CBA is compatible with these revisions, but in practice it works against this dynamic process.[56] CBA is such a complex, time-consuming and costly process in itself that it would be unworkable to repeat the entire process whenever new options or aims are contemplated. Since CBA emphasizes the evaluation of given options against given aims, it is easy to forget that neither are rigid and unalterable. This emphasis reflects the underlying economic theory of rational choice that we met in Chapter 2: it takes both preferences and options as given, and has nothing to say about their origins. In contrast, it is central to the precautionary principle that both are likely to evolve over time, so we take precautions now in order to preserve flexibility for the future.

This brief glimpse at the precautionary principle aims just to illustrate that alternatives to CBA already exist. But the focus here has been on a critique of various practices of quantification, because that way of thinking remains overwhelmingly dominant, and exploring it has yielded some important insights. Before summarizing these, it is worth emphasizing what my arguments do *not* claim.

It is always worth clarifying the pros and cons of the various options facing the decision maker. It is the extra step to quantifying all these pros and cons, particularly in terms of money that is often objectionable. When making choices, people often speak of 'weighing up the costs and benefits', but not all costs and benefits are understood in monetary terms, so the process involves no more than comparing the pros and cons. The argument here is *not* that the fewer pros and cons we monetize the better, but simply that the scope of monetary quantification has limits. For example, we stray beyond these limits when we try to value lives, or perform valuations in the presence of pure uncertainty, or attempt to express an essentially ethical 'trade-off' between the interests of present and future generations in terms of a discount rate. There are other limits, too, which will emerge in the next chapter.

It is also clear that these limits cannot be entirely specified in general terms. They are context-specific, depending on what is being quantified, when and where, and by whom. When making decisions, it is appropriate for a private company to express more impacts in monetary terms, because it is usually driven by an overarching *monetary* goal – profit. The goals of government, representing the people, should be more complex. More generally, the crucial ideas underpinning monetary quantification have been borrowed from the private sector, from markets. Consumers make free choices in markets, revealing how much they value things by the prices they pay (or so the theory goes). Cost–benefit analysis and other practices aim to mimic this valuation process. So it is unsurprising that monetary quantification is more at home in the private sector. Outside the market, whether in political, social or private life, other values and purposes prevail.

While relying on this distinction, I have tried to remain as neutral as possible about these values and purposes. Specifically, my criticisms of quantification do not depend on rejecting the underlying value framework which many of us share with economists: choices should be made on the basis of their consequences – no options are ruled out in advance according to a Ten Commandments-style list of moral principles. So I do not assume, for instance, that human life has a superior moral status and can never be sacrificed for other benefits. After all, governments often explicitly choose to spend money on opera and sport rather than health care.

Although the emphasis has been on monetary quantification, non-monetary quantification is equally mistaken in cases of pure uncertainty, and discounting non-monetary future impacts is no more defensible. Regarding valuing life, a non-monetary but comprehensively quantitative alternative, 'Quality-Adjusted Life Years', has become influential in health policy, but has had relatively little impact elsewhere. It has technical advantages and disadvantages compared to monetary valuation, but ultimately it fails for reasons analogous to those undermining its monetary rival.[57]

Democracy, objectivity and economic science

We have seen that the valuation of life in terms of risk of death is absurd: people think about risks in ways which reject the rationality assumed by CBA, uncertainty often prevents quantification, and discounting is ethically indefensible. These objections have been considered in isolation, but gain further strength once it is realized that monetary valuation often compounds the problems, one on top of another. Lives are valued, values are discounted, so lives are then discounted, even though in almost all ethical systems, a life in the future is just as important as a life now. Powerful as they are, we must look behind these objections if we are to use them as a point of departure for making difficult choices about, say, climate change policy. The problems with quantification reflect an essential dilemma.

Attempts to quantify are torn between democracy and objectivity. So practices such as CBA can be justified either because they aim to inform and improve decision making, or because in a democracy they reveal what people want. But not both. If economists defend discounting on the grounds that it reflects the preference for the present over the future we display as individuals, then on what basis do they ignore our individual preferences for certain risks (travel by road) over statistically less likely ones (travel by air)? This tension between what we ought to prefer according to economic theory, and what we actually prefer, arises repeatedly in the debate over quantification. It is just one instance of the deeper conflict between two views of how decisions should be made: an objective and technocratic approach, which claims to be rational and efficient, and a subjective and populist approach, which claims to be democratic. But when filtered through orthodox economics and its influence on decision making, both views fail to live up to their promises. The technocratic approach is not objective, or neutral between competing values or political claims, because the economists impose their own controversial values about rationality and efficiency on the decision-making process. For example, rationality requires that uncertainty always be translated into numerical probability, and efficiency requires that toxic waste be transported to poor nations. Turning to the populist approach, it is not democratic, because it caricatures democracy as consumer sovereignty. Democracy involves much more than fulfilling consumer preferences; it requires education and debate which help to create and transform those preferences. And as citizens rather than consumers we elect representatives to make decisions on our behalf, not simply elicit our preferences through referenda or focus groups – or CBA.

In light of this dilemma, what role, if any, does quantification play? Beyond rejecting the specific forms of quantification which have been the focus of this chapter, there are some general lessons.

To begin with, the worry that CBA and other quantification techniques may produce inaccurate numbers misses the point. It is not that CBA is flawed in consistent and predictable ways which we can detect and remedy. Rather, perfect quantification is a myth. For many outcomes, impacts or considerations, a true numerical measurement does not exist, so the numbers we produce cannot be good estimates of it. Since there is no true number to be found, the search for one often becomes desperate, searching in ways which will definitely lead to numbers, regardless of their relevance. It is reminiscent of the drunkard who searched for his wallet under the street light, not because he lost it there, but because that was the only place he could see. Or as John Maynard Keynes possibly commented: 'I would rather be vaguely right than precisely wrong.'[58]

Second, the values that emerge from economic theory provide too flimsy a platform for policy advice. The idea that value-free economic advice is possible is another myth, but chasing it has left economics with minimalist values which are too denuded of ethical content to support practical conclusions. As we have seen, the gap is filled with ad hoc assumptions which are often left unstated. This implies that techniques such as cost–benefit analysis embody the values of the analysts, and they therefore undermine democracy insofar as they replace democratic political processes. So, third, quantification can be at most an aid to decision making rather than a replacement for it.

A crucial reason why the values of economists have remained hidden inside their economic advice is that, repeatedly, they attribute their own values and ways of thinking to the individuals and institutions they study. For example, Bayesianism attributes to people a probabilistic understanding of uncertain future outcomes, regardless of whether they think in this way. Similarly, many economists interpret criticisms of discounting as arguments for discounting at 0 per cent.[59] But there is an important difference: the criticisms are accompanied either by a rejection of CBA, or a demand that discounting be limited in scope, with rates determined by explicit ethical debate. They do *not* recommend 'business as usual, except for a 0 per cent discount rate'. A final example comes from the economists' argument that all of us regularly put monetary values on life (and everything else) in the course of our day-to-day activities. When you take a dangerous job, or delay having your car brakes or heating boiler checked, or even cross a busy road to save money by shopping on the other side, economists attribute to you a monetary sum that you would accept in return for an increased risk of death, and then infer a monetary value that you place on your own life. 'Individuals behave in accordance with real prices where prices exist, and *as if* prices exist in areas where they do not.'[60]

These processes of attribution are not attempts to conceal economists' imposition of their own values: they reflect an honest, or at least unconscious, belief among many economists that people actually behave as *Homo economicus* does. But the result is the same – objections are neutralized or emasculated. So a final, important lesson is that economics must accept alternative ways of thinking for what they are, rather than treat them as if they have already been seamlessly incorporated into standard economic analysis. In the debate between *Homo economicus* and alternative ways of thinking, there is no hope for progress until economists accept that the alternatives are exactly that – distinct alternatives.

Chapter Seven

New Worlds of Money: Public Services and Beyond

George Bernard Shaw to a lady at a dinner party: 'My dear, would you spend the night with me for £10,000?'

Lady: 'Well…'

Shaw: 'How about £100?'

Lady: 'What kind of person do you think I am?'

Shaw: 'My dear, we have already established that. We are merely haggling over the price!'[1]

'What is a cynic? A man who knows the price of everything and the value of nothing.' (Oscar Wilde, *Lady Windermere's Fan*, Act 3)

This chapter looks at the effect of introducing money into new contexts. The idea of introducing money should be broadly understood. Obviously it includes turning things into commodities: making goods, services and activities available to be bought and sold for money. But also it includes the introduction of prices or monetary values where no buying or selling is possible: as a way of quantifying things in terms of money, usually for the purpose of measuring their social worth or moral importance. 'Buying and selling' includes every case where an agreement is made to exchange money for something. If I am offered extra pay in return for promising to do a part of my job that was not previously monitored or measured, then that aspect of my work is now directly sold to my employer for the first time. It is a new commodity.

The introduction of money into new contexts, turning things into new commodities, is very significant for economics. The domain of economics is commonly understood to be those areas of life involving money. In truth, economics has a much broader scope; an economics in which the only values are those expressible in monetary terms is a distorted, one-sided version of the subject. When money and 'commodification' is extended into new areas, then the domain of this distorted vision of economics can expand. The domain of labels such as 'efficient', 'uneconomic' and 'value for money' grows, while the part of life in which these considerations are at most of secondary importance in determining the right thing to do will contract. So the spread of money into new contexts is closely related to the spread of particular forms of economic thinking. Critics denounce it as 'economic imperialism', while many economists see it as inevitable and refreshingly honest, because they believe the conversation between George Bernard Shaw and the lady captures an essential truth: everyone and everything has a price – we are just too ashamed to admit it. Still, almost all of us recognize that problems can arise when we attempt to treat things as commodities inappropriately.

Since the problems of commodification are complex and subtle, varying across contexts, a grand universal theory of what is wrong will not work. So in what follows I shall look at one context in detail: what in Britain and most of Europe are called 'public services', especially education and health care; here 'public services' means publicly funded services, services funded by taxation or state-organized insurance schemes. These services may involve direct public provision – where the government actually owns and operates the schools and hospitals – or the government may pay the private sector to provide them. Although the terminology and public–private mix are somewhat different in the US, many of the same issues arise in US education and health care provision. The focus here is on the wider lessons, rather than the detailed nuts and bolts of British public services. Along the way we shall see how standard economic thinking in general, and practices of commodification in particular, have distorted attempts to improve public services. And I shall develop an alternative analysis based on what is distinctive about the domain of public services compared to the market for ordinary goods and services. Later in the chapter I look beyond the public services and return to the problems of commodification more generally.

Some problems of commodification

Harmful effects on the buyer or seller or the thing being traded. Markets in babies and body parts are classic examples here. The sellers would mainly be desperate people vulnerable to exploitation. Another example is child labour.

Unpredictable effects of introducing money. Financial incentives often have surprising effects. For example, it might seem that with a free market in babies, supply would equal demand, so there would be no unwanted, unadopted babies. But because many of the women conceiving for money would probably be poor, ill or addicted to drugs, it is likely that their babies would be less desirable for potential buyers. Whether the number of unwanted babies would rise is impossible to predict.[2]

Erosion of community values. Citizenship rights are by definition equal while market outcomes are always unequal. We define and preserve our sense of community and common citizenship by keeping some things outside the market, and ensuring that they are provided equally to all; examples include police protection, freedom of speech and basic education. For the same reason some duties are imposed equally on all citizens, such as military service or jury duty; we cannot pay to be exempted because that would impose a lesser burden on the rich.

Understood broadly, 'commodification' of the public services involves various overlapping activities, including privatization, introducing markets and copying commercial practices from the private sector. Here I have space to discuss only two activities which are central to the idea of commodifying public services. First, a 'choice culture' which assumes the economic theory of the consumer applies to public services as well as ordinary market commodities: it attempts to turn public service users into the sovereign consumers of Chapter 2. Second, an 'audit culture' of targets, incentives and quantitative measurement, which attempts to package up public services into bundles of commodities with clearly demarcated boundaries and values measured in terms of money. Focusing on these activities directly rather than the abstract idea of commodification also allows me to avoid using ugly language like 'commodification'.

The choice culture

Recent governments on both sides of the Atlantic have been seduced by the mantra of 'choice'. In the US much of the current debate focuses on school choice, while in the UK a range of policies has been used in an attempt to widen choice in both education and health care.

The first argument for widening choice is very simple: it is what public service users want. Politicians of all shades who support widening choice point to opinion poll evidence of strong support for increased choice. But appearances are deceptive. To begin with, surveys may show support for choice although there is little real desire to choose. In one survey, 65 per cent said they would want to choose their treatment should they fall ill with cancer, compared with only 12 per cent of actual cancer patients who want to do so.[3] The Blair Government was impressed by a survey asking people whether they would want to choose a hospital for treatment. Fifteen per cent said they would want to make the choice alone, 23 per cent said they would prefer their doctor (GP) to choose, while 62 per cent said they would want to choose, subject to advice and guidance.[4] However, it may be mistaken to interpret this latter group as wanting any more choice: they may simply want to decide *jointly* with their doctor, which is what most doctors believe should happen in any case.[5] When service users exercise choice in practice, their motives are no easier to interpret.[6] If those around me can choose a school for their children, or a hospital for treatment, I may exercise the opportunity to choose too, not because I welcome increased choice, but simply because I fear being left with a poor school or hospital after everyone else has taken their pick. It is not even clear that in their survey answers and elsewhere, ordinary people understand the word 'choice' in the same way as enthusiastic politicians and policy entrepreneurs. Many of us use a phrase like 'choice of hospital' as shorthand for 'getting my first choice of hospital' – or at least 'getting a hospital I want'. But policy entrepreneurs advocating wider choice use it to mean 'more than one hospital to choose from', even if the chooser finds all of them unattractive. The debate about widening choice involves this second meaning, increasing the number of options, and I shall follow this usage in what follows. (Of course, for its supporters, widening choice is also supposed to make all the options better in the long run, a claim I shall return to shortly.)

The argument for widening choice because of its popularity is a red herring. Proposals with overwhelming popular support are often not adopted by government, while policies which are extremely unpopular are pursued instead. So even supposing there is strong public support for some policy, that fact alone does not justify it, and it rarely explains why politicians advocate it. We must look for an underlying philosophy. In this case, politicians from a wide range of standpoints seem to regard widening choice as an end in itself.[7] Widening choice is regarded as morally desirable, regardless of any other effects it may have. This assertion deserves examining, because it has been explicitly made and widely taken for granted.

The only possible philosophical basis for the assertion is libertarianism. Libertarians believe that liberty almost always has priority over all other moral values, so increasing liberty through widening choice is good in itself. However, libertarianism cannot be invoked to justify widening choice of public services, because it objects to the very existence of most of these services. As we saw in Chapter 4, libertarians regard coercive taxation as an infringement of liberty, only justified when it is to pay for services strictly necessary for maintaining the state and enforcing the law (limited military and police forces). No other services should be funded by government, so the debate over widening choice is irrelevant.

Many other political philosophies support extending freedom of choice, but always as a means to some more fundamental end. More choice is not an end in itself. In *On Liberty,* John Stuart Mill argued that individuals should usually have decision-making power over their own lives – but only insofar as they are the best judges of their own happiness. The ultimate goal of Mill's utilitarianism, and more generally the hybrid theories advocated in Chapter 5, is happiness or well-being. Extending choice is simply a means to that end. This brings us to the central argument for widening choice: that it will improve overall happiness, regardless of whether it is desirable for its own sake. The argument follows Mill. If individuals are the best judges of their own happiness, then their happiness will be increased by letting them make choices which affect their lives. So the argument is an old one, given a modern gloss when translated into contemporary economic jargon: consumers are sovereign, so their welfare will be maximized by fulfilling their preferences. More bluntly, it becomes the slogan 'choice increases efficiency'. But it is still the same argument.

The policy lesson is that the allocation of public services should work more like markets for ordinary consumer goods. Consumer sovereignty reigns supreme in markets for goods such as cars, coffee and washing powder, so it should work in the market for public services too. Or so the argument runs. In Britain, probably the most influential architect of public service reform has been the economist Julian Le Grand, an adviser to Tony Blair, who has advocated widening choice on essentially these grounds. The link is clear from his emotional language: widening choice is supposed to turn service users from helpless 'pawns' of a monolithic system into sovereign consumer 'queens'.[8] But as we saw in Chapter 2, consumer sovereignty is very doubtful even for choices over ordinary products, and many of the same problems arise in public services, only in more extreme form. The key point is easy to state: services like health care and education are very different from cars, coffee and washing powder.

Complexity and importance

The main difference is the complexity and importance of the services involved. In the idealized story of consumer sovereignty, consumers make 'informed choices' based on full information about the various options facing them. Economists accept that it is much harder to make informed choices about which hospital to use for a particular treatment, or which school will be best for your child, than which washing powder to buy. There is much more to know, and the options (for example, different schools) vary in multiple and complex ways. Economists label the problem one of 'imperfect information', but it goes much deeper than this jargon suggests. It cannot be solved simply by providing more information, because much of the information requires specialized training to interpret – the kind of training which doctors and teachers receive. We have all experienced that daunting, sinking feeling when, overwhelmed with information, we must make a very important decision, but feel unable to do so. This often results in bad decisions. Of course the problems are not limited to publicly funded services. Elderly people in the US have recently had that sinking feeling when trying to choose between various extremely complex drug plans offered through Medicare 'Part D', provided by private insurance companies.[9] And a classic US study by the Rand Corporation found that if people pay medical expenses directly (rather than having insurance) they spend less overall, but this is not the result of setting sensible priorities – people simply cut back across the board.[10]

Lack of training to understand, sift and interpret information is one reason; another is our emotional response to important but difficult decisions. There are few more important decisions than health care choices that may literally make the difference between life and death. Choosing a school for your children is also a major decision. So what happens in these cases? It is very difficult to make a calm, informed assessment of the options when you have already 'set your heart on' a particular school for your child, no matter how unlikely it is that they will ultimately secure a place. Similarly, health care decisions are often made at times of great anxiety or stress. The difficulty is exacerbated by our lack of experience in making such decisions.

Another feature of many choices concerning services such as education and health care is short-term pain or cost, followed by potentially great long-term benefits. Chapter 2 showed how this combination invites self-control problems, where we struggle to make the sacrifice now for future benefit. And when we choose emotionally, when stressed, self-control is even harder to maintain. I may prefer to let my doctor decide whether I should have chemotherapy, because all I can think about is the short-term misery it will bring, even though I know it offers the (uncertain) chance of prolonging my life.

It is all very different from buying washing powder. The differences are not just due to lack of information, but also the impossibility of filtering and evaluating that information without professional training, lack of experience in making decisions about public services, and the emotional challenges posed by very important decisions. Faced with all this, our newly empowered queen may struggle to exercise any real sovereignty and instead make disastrous mistakes. Le Grand may have had Elizabeth I or Boadicea in mind when adopting the queen metaphor, but Anne Boleyn may be more apposite.

Others are affected

In the supermarket we do not need to look beyond our nose – we can often choose just with our own interests in mind. In contrast, choosing public services always has implications for others. Most obviously, we sometimes choose in place of others, as when we choose a school for our child. The logic of consumer sovereignty clearly fails in these cases where the chooser is not the consumer. Parents may choose a school for their child with particular assumptions in mind – that the child will leave school at 16, or that education is just about securing a well-paid job. These assumptions may serve the parents' interests more than the child's happiness.

Even if the chooser *is* the consumer or user, their choices may affect others. Individual decisions to be vaccinated against infectious diseases, or to obtain further skills through post-compulsory education, benefit wider society as well as the individual concerned. It might be objected that individual choices often have such external effects: the problem is not specific to choices over public services. This is true, but it does not support the argument for increasing overall happiness by extending freedom of choice. On the contrary, when individual choices have external effects, governments regularly intervene to restrict or override consumer sovereignty. Smoking has harmful external effects on non-smokers, so cigarettes are heavily taxed; my decision to drive into central London increases the traffic level others must suffer, so I must pay a 'congestion charge' tax. And there is a distinctive type of external effect that is almost unique to the public services. Normally we consume goods or services only up to the point where the perceived benefit outweighs the price. But public services are often free, so there is no incentive for self-restraint. The resulting tendency to overuse free services imposes costs on others. When hypochondriacs rush to their doctor at the onset of a cold, this reduces the amount of time the doctor has to deal with more serious illnesses. And every teacher is sadly familiar with the pushy parent unreasonably demanding extra for their child at the expense of others.

The discussion so far raises two major doubts about putting more choice and control in the hands of service users. First, they are likely to fail to choose in their own best interests, because of the complexity and importance of the decisions involved. Second, service users consider only their own interests, rather than the overall happiness of all members of society. However, as Le Grand emphasizes, it does not follow that leaving control where it is, in the hands of doctors, teachers and other service providers, is preferable. Although ordinary members of the public may not make good decisions when choosing public services, perhaps service providers are worse. At first glance, this seems unlikely. Consider medical decisions as an example. Doctors have more information, training and experience; this and their degree of professional detachment allow them to make decisions calmly and unemotionally; they can choose in the patient's long-term interest, avoiding the temptation to focus just on the short term. Doctors are also far better placed to allocate resources to serve overall happiness, rather than the interests of a single patient. Le Grand has some reservations about this simplistic picture, but his main worry is not about the competence of service providers, but their motives. He argues that we cannot rely on service providers altruistically attending to the interests of service users, because providers, like everyone else, are mainly driven by self-interest. In short, doctors and teachers are species of *Homo economicus* too.

It is true that the motives of service providers are crucial. If providers simply look after their *own* interests, then the interests of users will not be met, unless for some reason they happen to coincide. So if doctors, teachers and managers act as *Homo economicus,* then the case for delegating power to them is dramatically weakened. The case for turning service user pawns into queens is correspondingly stronger. But is Le Grand right to regard service providers as fundamentally selfish?

As we have repeatedly seen, the claim that people are fundamentally selfish is an article of faith in economics, and Le Grand is no exception. In a section entitled 'What We Know', he states 'That all individuals are to a great extent knaves – that is, motivated in large part by material self-interest – is almost uncontroversial.'[11] This lack of controversy, almost, presumably explains why Le Grand sees no need to cite evidence. Still, it is a striking omission, since Le Grand's entire analysis – and most of the British public service reforms of recent years – rest on this assumption. As we shall see below, although Le Grand concedes that service providers may be partly altruistic, this possibility has little impact on the ultimate design of policy.

Chapter 2 discussed substantial evidence suggesting that people are often altruistic. While this evidence alone should be enough to overturn the *presumption* that public service employees are generally selfish, evidence from the public sector itself is especially welcome. Le Grand himself has documented much of this evidence, but as ever there is a problem of interpreting motives.[12] Economists are usually reluctant to rely solely on interview evidence, because talk is cheap. It's easy to say, for example, that you are motivated mainly by 'serving the community'. But sometimes motives can plausibly be inferred from actual behaviour. These examples provide evidence of altruism: residential care home providers in the not-for-profit sector charge less than ordinary private sector providers; both set prices lower than they could do.[13] In the US a study of case workers in job centres has been very influential, not least because of the credibility of the lead researcher, Nobel Prize-winning economist James Heckman.[14] The case workers receive performance-related pay: their pay increases as more of their clients find well-paid work. If the case workers were selfish, they would try to 'cream-skim' the most employable applicants, so as to maximize their *own* pay. In fact, Heckman found the reverse effect. Weaker applicants were more likely to be accepted, suggesting the case workers try to help the most disadvantaged.

To sum up, the argument for widening choice, and more generally turning pawns into queens, depends crucially on assuming public sector providers are substantially self-interested. However, even if that assumption is correct, the argument is not necessarily won, for two reasons. First, self-interested doctors may still on average make better decisions than their patients, leading to better services, simply because they know so much more. Self-interest erodes their huge knowledge advantage, but does not necessarily cancel it out altogether. Second, the quality of public services is not, contrary to appearances, the only relevant consideration in determining whether choice should be widened. The *distribution* of public services also matters. Even if, on average, we receive slightly better services, this might be outweighed by a significant increase in inequality of provision, especially if those enduring the worst services now receive poorer services still.

Problems with ensuring real choice

The debate over the impact on inequality of widening choice is complex and inconclusive. Economic theory makes no general predictions, and empirical evidence is difficult to assess, not least because of the multiple ways of measuring inequality. One fact, however, has overwhelming empirical support: even among public services that are completely free, the rich currently obtain better services than the poor. This is because they demand them: service outcomes depend strongly on who shouts loudest. And the loudest, pushiest, most insistent users tend to be the wealthiest and most highly educated, rather than those who may benefit the most. The question is whether the introduction of choice will do anything to change this logic. Le Grand concedes that for it to do so measures to widen choice must be accompanied by assisting the poor with the costs associated with exercising choice, such as transport costs to distant hospitals or schools. If we generously assume that full assistance would be provided in practice, Le Grand's conclusion is positive. He argues that the rich currently act as queens in any case, and introducing choice offers a chance for the poor pawns to catch up; but he provides no further evidence or explanation.[15] My view is that increasing choice simply increases the occasions on which the rich, the articulate, the confident and agitators in general ensure they obtain the best on offer.

A more powerful argument to support the idea that widening choice *increases* inequality arises when demand for services exceeds supply. It is the problem of 'cream-skimming': when a school is oversubscribed, the school will usually have some control over which children to admit. Choice by users is then subverted, becoming choice by providers. If schools are rewarded according to their exam results, they obviously have an incentive to select the most able children, who will typically come from wealthier families. So the children from more advantaged backgrounds are able to enter the most sought-after schools, while the poor must go elsewhere. The educational gap then widens further as the advantaged children benefit from being educated among other advantaged children. Economists call the process 'sorting'; sociologists call it 'stratification'; 'educational apartheid' better conveys its impact on children. Of course this process has been widespread for many years: house prices in the neighbourhood of good schools rise, excluding poorer families from these schools. The empirical question is whether the new parental choice mechanisms reduce inequality, compared to selection by house prices. The most detailed UK evidence suggests not. Once parental choice is constrained by capacity limits at the better schools, the result is greater inequality than is already in the system.[16]

Probably the most powerful evidence of cream-skimming is in US health care: US private insurers have very high administrative costs compared to Medicare (or the British National Health Service) because they spend so much on trying to screen out less healthy people who are likely to be more costly to treat.[17] In the British NHS, this cream-skimming was relatively limited in the past: doctors and hospitals treated patients largely on the basis of need. But the introduction of choice mechanisms and performance measures gives providers analogous incentives to those US insurers who avoid more severely ill patients. This tendency, combined with the rich exercising more choice (because they are better informed and find it easier to travel to a distant hospital), suggests that health outcomes will become more unequal. In particular, poorer people may on average end up waiting longer for treatment.[18] The behaviour of US health care insurers shows that spare capacity in the system – supply exceeding demand – is not enough to prevent cream-skimming. Yet it is a prerequisite for ensuring that choice is genuinely in the hands of users rather than providers. Economists who support widening choice emphasize that existing schools and hospitals must be free to expand and contract, new ones must be able to open, and poor ones to close. They recognize the political obstacles here, but sometimes ignore a deeper problem.

Their error arises from the default position of economic theory, in which education and health care are akin to ordinary goods like cars and coffee. And the supply of these ordinary goods *can* flexibly expand and contract to meet demand. Education and health care are very different. Apart from the obvious delays and constraints – training new doctors and teachers, planning and locating new buildings – there are more fundamental difficulties. It is not easy to replicate a good school, even if the resources and staff are available. There is no cookbook recipe for copying successful schools and hospitals elsewhere. Even if there are no problems of space and staffing, expanding an existing school may affect its character, and so its success. It is not just a matter of 'scaling up' education production. The most intractable problem is that users do not simply want a choice of school or hospital, but a choice of *good* school or hospital. Unfortunately, these are inevitably few in number, because 'good' is defined in relative terms, especially in education. As explained in Chapter 3, education is largely a positional good; no amount of expansion will increase the numbers who receive a *relatively* good education.

Setting these problems aside, there remains the obvious cost in resources of intentionally maintaining permanent spare capacity in the system. Spare capacity is inherently wasteful. Put another way, widening choice through spare capacity may bring benefits, but more might be achievable by spending the resources directly on service improvements.

Spare capacity is not the only cost that advocates of turning pawns into queens tend to overlook. First, there is plenty of populist talk about these new consumer queens receiving highly personalized services, tailored to meet their individual preferences. This sounds attractive, but it directly encourages Baumol's cost disease (Chapter 3). It is precisely the personalization of services which makes them especially labour-intensive – and therefore increasingly costly *relative* to the price of goods and services in general. Baumol's cost disease does not imply that personalization is too costly or unaffordable. But personalization strongly conflicts with attempts to increase efficiency in public service provision; ironically it is portrayed as part of a process of making services more efficient, when in fact it does the opposite, at least according to the usual efficiency measures. Second, the cost of choice to consumers can be substantial (Chapter 2), and I suggested above that complex, important choices about health care and education may be especially daunting. There is evidence that some health service users prefer not to be offered choice.[19] Although users can always decline the offer, even this 'choice not to choose' can be stressful, as explained in Chapter 2. If significant numbers of users do indeed decline to choose, then the (alleged) beneficial impact on the whole system of introducing choice will be correspondingly reduced. But the administrative costs of choice mechanisms would remain. This third type of cost should not be underestimated. As well as the obvious costs of providing information – maintaining and monitoring an elaborate system of school and hospital performance measures – there is the cost of employing a new class of public service worker, the choice adviser. These advisers are now in place throughout England to assist parents with school choice, and have also been introduced in parts of the NHS. It is difficult to deny that such advisers help pawns become queens, but might it not be better simply to spend the money on more doctors and teachers? And why not let the doctors and teachers provide the choice advice?

This brings us back to the question of motivation, both of public service workers *and* those attempting reform. Introducing choice advisers suggests the government believes doctors and teachers cannot be trusted to offer advice in the patient or child's best interests. But the perspective of many doctors and teachers is the opposite: it is the government which cannot be trusted, because the project of turning pawns into queens will not serve the public interest. This results in two further costs of the project. We began with a broadly utilitarian underlying rationale – increasing overall happiness. But the happiness of public service workers matters too, and this will suffer if their morale deteriorates and they no longer feel trusted. And poor morale means poorer service for users. Beyond these direct costs lurks a deeper problem, a basic clash of values between front-line staff and those who seek public service reform, aptly dubbed *kulturkampf* by one commentator.[20] We shall return to this cultural struggle later.

In the meantime, what are we to conclude? The conventional, narrow, economic assessment asks whether choice between public services can be made to mimic choice between washing powders, what the benefits are if it can, and how much it costs. A dull, equivocal conclusion is inescapable. The empirical evidence is inconclusive. Widening choice has advantages and disadvantages, and the balance of the two will vary from case to case. But the conventional assessment is crucially incomplete. In asking whether widening choice improves public services, the *kulturkampf* is ignored, and assumptions are made concerning what counts as a service improvement – and who decides. Policies aiming to widen choice cannot be assessed in isolation. Their success ultimately depends on the motives of public service workers, and these in turn are affected by other policies: introducing targets, incentives and audits may transform the values and motives of public service workers. This brings us to the task of assessing another aspect of commodification in the public services, namely the plethora of targets, incentives and audits.

The audit culture: Squeezing out virtue

Together, the combination of targets, incentives and audits has come in Britain to be known as the 'audit culture'.[21] (A more common epithet in the US might be 'top-down-command-and-control'.) The rise of this culture in the public sector is closely related to the project of widening choice. But unlike that project, the audit culture is now widely ridiculed. There are many cautionary tales: in the accident and emergency departments of British hospitals, there are targets for the time patients are kept waiting. In order to meet the target, some hospitals reclassified waiting trolleys as 'beds with wheels'; other hospitals instructed ambulances carrying patients to wait outside for a while in order to reduce the measured waiting time.[22] In essence, targets distort behaviour and lead to perverse, unintended consequences. In the US, although Medicare is regarded as less of a top-down-command-and-control system than the NHS, there are still perverse incentive structures. In general, Medicare involves fee-for-service payments to doctors; this means that bad doctors are paid more than good ones, because Medicare pays doctors to fix the mistakes they have previously made.

There is an optimistic view that these kinds of problems can be avoided by carefully chosen targets and incentive structures, but this view is not supported by most independent reviews of the audit culture.[23] On the contrary, Goodhart's Law (introduced in Chapter 5) is frequently mentioned: when a measure becomes a target, it ceases to be a good measure. Goodhart's Law suggests that distortions and unintended consequences are an *unavoidable* part of any target regime. Once people or their activities are being targeted, their behaviour inevitably changes, either unintentionally or because they actively seek to manipulate the measurements.

Targets set priorities; that is part of their purpose. Another kind of distortion, less widely discussed but at least as important, is the tendency of audit cultures to distort priorities, not just set them. Since targets must be measurable, and targets become priorities, then the inevitable effect is to prioritize the measurable. Objectives for which data is lacking, or more fundamentally objectives which are inherently non-quantitative, will be ignored in favour of those which can be measured. Yet qualitative objectives may be just as important. Merely because an objective is qualitative does not imply we cannot evaluate our success in meeting it, but the assessment will involve judgement rather than measurement. Probably the most general qualitative objective is good quality. External auditors cannot judge quality; only doctors can judge good doctoring, and so on. So external auditors will inevitably pick a quantitative proxy, distorting effort away from quality towards the auditable measure.

The distortion of priorities caused by the audit culture can be deeply damaging to the morale of affected workers. The problems arise particularly starkly in the context of performance-related pay (PRP). According to standard economic theory, it is straightforward to ensure workers try their hardest – simply offer a financial inducement for good performance. This seems to be the worldview on which much of the audit culture is based. Reality is very different. Most workers 'multitask', and if performance pay is attached only to some aspects of their job, it will lead to the relative neglect of the rest. PRP can also have adverse effects if employees work together in teams. It is then difficult or impossible to measure individual performance, but if the performance of the team as a whole is rewarded, this creates an incentive for team members to rely on the effort of their colleagues. Another problem is that a worker may serve many masters, each of whom has different views about which aspects of the job matter most. Taken together, the problems posed by Goodhart's Law, multitasking, team working, multiple masters, and the fundamental difficulty of defining and measuring a qualitative 'output' greatly limit the applicability of PRP schemes. More generally, these problems undermine any system of targets supported by financial carrots and sticks.

The problems with the audit culture are not specific to the public sector; they arise in the commercial world too. But a crucial part of the case against the audit culture in public services is that the problems become more severe in the public sector. For instance, team working is ubiquitous – it is almost impossible to identify and reward individual contributions to the output of educating a child or healing the sick. And PRP is more likely to demotivate employees because it will often be linked to the final outcomes we care about (such as eventual full recovery after an operation), not direct outputs (numbers who receive the operation). Although this linkage seems appropriate, it demotivates because final outcomes are highly likely to depend on factors beyond the employee's control.

Economists advocating the 'reform' programme have increasingly acknowledged these threats, and some of the more extreme ambitions of the audit culture have been abandoned. However, the same underlying economic analysis still dominates thinking, so this will be the focus in what follows. Besides, it is easy to overstate how far economists have recognized the weaknesses of the audit culture. Some of them still doubt the existence of a public service ethos; many more remain skeptical of relying on it. In any case, they argue that even if auditing in the public domain brings additional costs, its benefits are nevertheless sufficient to outweigh them. Where the burden of the audit culture is too great, markets are the preferred solution, not the public service ethos. Finally, many economists believe the distinctiveness of the public sector is exaggerated. For example, regarding the problems posed by team working:

> There appears to be no shortage of high-powered incentive rewards in merchant banking, yet it is not obvious that individual contributions to the profitability of a deal are any easier to identify than in the hospital setting.[24]

In reply to this defence of the audit culture, critics can begin by pointing out that just because it is common in sectors such as merchant banking, that does not imply it is necessarily beneficial even there, because of the problems outlined above. But more than that, critics of the audit culture must explain why the public sector is different. Why, for instance, is PRP more common in banks than hospitals? Is the difference caused by opposition from powerful public sector unions, or is there a more fundamental reason? Again, the analysis of Julian Le Grand, Tony Blair's chief adviser on these matters, deserves discussion – not just because of the influence it continues to have, but because it represents a sophisticated attempt by an economist to explore the limits of the audit culture in the public sector.

Squeezing out virtue

Le Grand essentially only discusses PRP. However, PRP reveals the audit culture's effect on employee motivation in particularly stark fashion. Besides, much more of the audit culture is encompassed by PRP than first appearances suggest. Once a target or audited output is linked to any kind of reward or penalty for the employees involved, then it effectively represents a form of PRP, even if not explicitly acknowledged as such.

Traditionally, economic analysis of the public services has caricatured its workers as either purely self-interested, or purely altruistic, both traits being fixed and uninfluenced by government policy. Clearly this is a gross simplification. Motives are not one-dimensional, and are influenced by the actions of others, including government.

Chapter 2 described how intrinsic motivation can be eroded or even destroyed completely by the introduction of explicit financial incentives. Whether the financial incentive is payment for giving blood, or compensation for accepting a hazardous waste storage site locally, or a fine for picking up your children late from nursery, the effect can be the opposite of that intended by those introducing the incentives. Similarly, PRP schemes can be counterproductive if their financial incentive effect is outweighed by a reduction in other motives, such as a decline in loyalty due to a feeling of being manipulated by the employer. Le Grand accepts this possibility but argues that the evidence is mixed. He reviews evidence concerning volunteers undertaking charitable or community activities. When payment was offered to the 'volunteers', they worked harder as the payment increased – but less hard than when offered no payment at all.[25]

On the other hand, caring activity by care workers was encouraged by the presence of payments, even though these workers were at least partly motivated by altruism.[26] Le Grand's explanation of this conflicting evidence is novel. He argues that relatively small monetary payments can encourage altruistic activity. However, people are partly motivated by making sacrifices, and this motive will be eliminated altogether if they receive payments which remove any sense of sacrifice. Of course if the payments are high enough, pure self-interest will take over. This is Le Grand's 'Theory of Public Service Motivation'. He concludes:

> The evidence concerning the relationship between financial rewards and the supply of public services suggests that there may be reward thresholds above and below which behaviour is rather different. Below the lower threshold, financial rewards may be viewed as reinforcing … supply, since they signify social approval of the sacrifice the individual is making in pursuing his or her activities. Extra payments above the threshold, however, erode the magnitude of the sacrifice that he or she is making, and thereby partly erode the motivation for the act. However, as payments increase further, another threshold is reached … and supply increases again.[27]

Le Grand's theory captures some important truths, but leaves some equally important questions unanswered. Its central claim is that sacrifice can be a motive in itself, with the opportunity to make a greater sacrifice acting as a stronger motive. However, sacrifice for sacrifice's sake seems irrational, a kind of hair-shirted narcissism. Nor does the theory explain why small payments reinforce sacrifices, while larger ones erode them. And it is striking that Le Grand largely sidelined his own theory when advising the Blair government on public service reform. The lesson of the theory is that governments should be wary of paying at a rate between the two thresholds, in the zone where extra payments erode altruistic motivation and thus may lead to a deterioration in service quality. But as Le Grand acknowledges, the theory is of limited value in reality because we do not know where the thresholds lie.[28] Nevertheless, the theory is a sophisticated improvement on attempts to reform public services on the basis that workers are all species of *Homo economicus*. Yet the theory's sophistication is misplaced. It introduces needless quantitative sophistication by reducing all motives to a single monetary dimension with multiple thresholds, but lacks the qualitative sophistication of context. Context matters. The response of a doctor or teacher to the introduction of monetary incentives will be shaped by many contextual factors; contrary to Le Grand's theory, the amount of money involved may sometimes be less important.

First, different descriptions of an incentive payment may elicit different reactions. It might be a reward, a bonus, compensation or merely expenses. There is also a huge difference between introducing incentive payments and asking if people want to keep them. This point alone may largely explain the conflicting evidence that Le Grand cites: payment was introduced for the volunteers, while the care workers were interviewed with the payments already in place. Clearly the framing of the incentive often matters at least as much as its monetary value. (Although, as discussed in Chapter 2, economists often regard people influenced by these framing effects as irrational.) Second, certain activities, such as care for the elderly or for those with mental health problems, tend to be undervalued or even unnoticed, compared to other forms of health care. Offering payment may have a beneficial effect on motivation by bringing recognition and respect to such activities. Third, payment may also lead to an increase in an activity because the worker feels they can now afford to do it. Carers may undertake more care work instead of other paid employment; hospital consultants may undertake more NHS work and less private practice. Motives here are not simplistically self-interested because in both cases the workers may suffer an overall pay cut.[29]

The problem with Le Grand's theory is akin to that of the cost–benefit view of emotions discussed in Chapter 2. According to that view, emotions are regarded as psychic costs and benefits, weighed up on the same scale as financial costs and benefits, so more of one should substitute for less of another. If cash payment is a substitute for reduced intrinsic motivation, then public service workers will continue doing the activity in question, providing the payment is large enough. But Le Grand's conclusion that financial incentives still work, providing they are large enough, is not consistent with the evidence presented in Chapter 2. Nor does Le Grand's theory, or the cost–benefit view, explain evidence showing that the damage caused by financial incentives lingers long *after* they have been removed. When payments for giving blood are abolished, blood donation does not return to the levels donated originally. Similarly, if financial incentives are removed, the behaviour and morale of workers is not immediately restored. Once trust is lost, it cannot quickly be rebuilt.

It is worth emphasizing why all this matters to those of us uninvolved with public services, except as end users. To understand how public service employees interpret the goals and assumptions of senior managers and politicians, we must examine the employees' distinctive values and motives. Without that understanding, any project to improve public services is doomed. More generally, to make progress with that project, we need to understand what is distinctive about public services, both their strengths and weaknesses. This may seem too obvious to mention, but recall the temptation of many economists to begin with the same one-size-fits-all theory, whether analysing the market for health care, housing or houseplants. The provision of public services is not just private market-based provision gone astray. Our understanding of public services needs to go beyond this simplistic starting point. Le Grand's approach is an improvement but shares the same essential weakness: it claims to offer a theory of public service motivation, yet there is nothing in it referring to what is distinctive about public services.

What is distinctive about public services?

Progress with this question is only possible if the pretence of economics as scientific analysis, free of context and ethical principles, is abandoned. Once that is done, we can readily distinguish the public domain from both the market world and private life.

> The private world of love and friendship, and the market world of interest and incentive, are not the only dimensions of human life in society. There is a public domain with its own values… In the public domain people act neither out of the kindness of their hearts, nor in response to incentives, monetary or otherwise, but because they have a sense of serving the community.[30]

Unlike in our private life, relationships in the public domain are typically between strangers, so we do not act 'out of the kindness of our hearts'. But as we have seen, on many occasions when dealing with strangers our actions extend beyond furthering our own self-interest. We give blood, we return wallets we find in the street, we give lifts to hitchhikers. In the public domain, self-interest is not all that matters because we recognize that we interact as equal citizens of a common society. Unlike in the market, values such as equality, fairness and need become relevant to determining how goods and services should be distributed. And unlike in private life, values such as loyalty and favouritism may be harmful, because they can lead to nepotism.[31]

This is clearly an idealistic, rose-tinted picture of the public domain, but so too is the usual portrayal of markets and private life: friends sometimes lie or are disloyal; markets are essentially about competition, but sellers sometimes collude to subvert it.[32] The point is that the public domain involves an independent, distinctive ideal, which shapes the motivations, relationships and values of participants in that domain, even if unconsciously. It is worth stressing that distinctive means just that; it does not necessarily mean superior. As a minimum, my argument requires just this idea: public service provision has a distinct status, a kind of importance not shared by the provision of ordinary market goods. Bluntly, we care about the provision of health care in a way that we do not about the provision of washing powder. This is why we fund it out of general taxation.

Several features of the public services follow from this idea alone. First, public service employees experience an additional intrinsic motivation, arising from the importance of what they do, an importance recognized by society as well as them. There is now reliable empirical evidence of this, for example from careful interview-based research studying doctors and nurses.[33] Second, since public services are important, we all have views on what should be provided and how it should be distributed. So the public services must be democratic and accountable. Third, these views draw on moral values, so our ultimate goals for the public domain are inherently qualitative – *good* education, or *fair* health care provision. Contrast these with a key goal in the private sector – profit, an inherently quantitative goal. Fourth, there will be conflicting goals for public service provision arising from intractable conflicts between the underlying values. For example, those who see widening choice as increasing freedom may nevertheless worry that it reduces equality.

Although some of these features appear outside the public services too, it is difficult to imagine any non-public organization in which they *all* occur. Put together, the presence of intrinsic motivation, the need for democracy and accountability, and conflicting, qualitative goals, have profound implications for what goes wrong with the audit culture, and how public services can be improved. The incompatibility of qualitative goals with audit cultures which prioritize the measurable was discussed in the previous section; the other features deserve further discussion.

Intrinsic motivation: The 'public service ethos'

In searching for a fundamental distinction between the motivations of workers in different organizations there is no better starting point than the different objectives of those organizations. Organizations with the ultimate objective, reason for being, of profit, will motivate people differently from organizations in the public domain which pursue other ultimate goals. This much is now widely agreed. There is a growing consensus among economists that audit and incentive schemes such as performance pay should be less intensively applied in the public sector, because of the distinctive motivations of its workers.[34] Compared to the private sector, the argument runs, public sector workers are more likely to be trying their best already, because they are specifically motivated to fulfil the goals of the organization, and there is often a cultural code of professionalism. So there is much less scope for incentive schemes to have any positive effect.

This is before we consider the possibility that explicit financial incentives can also be counterproductive by eroding intrinsic motivation. So when will incentive payments supplement the public service ethos, and when will they erode it? The contextual factors mentioned above in discussing Le Grand's theory will be relevant: how the incentive is described or framed, whether it brings recognition and respect, and the financial circumstances of the recipients. But most importantly, in reacting to explicit financial incentives, public service employees will think carefully about the goals and assumptions of the senior managers, bureaucrats or politicians who introduced them. There are two dangers. First, if the managers assume that employees' intrinsic motivation is inadequate on its own, this implicit criticism serves to undermine employee self-esteem, which in turn leads to a doubting and devaluing of their own intrinsic motivation. Second, if the goal of managers or politicians is perceived to be control, manipulating behaviour through the use of incentives, then intrinsic motivation will again be undermined: it is futile and unnecessary to have intrinsic motivation if you feel forced to do something regardless. Intrinsic motivation withers along with perceived autonomy. In extreme cases, if those being audited are forced to pursue goals with which they disagree on principle, and the control imposed by auditing is impossible to avoid, then the effect on their morale and motivation can be devastating. Organizations work best when their members agree with its objectives, or at least do not repudiate them. Put another way, the use of explicit financial incentives should be seen as a *symptom* of the failure to win commitment from public service employees to the goals set by managers or politicians, not a cure for this failure.[35] This raises the question of why public service employees have goals that conflict with those of their managers, or politicians, in the first place.

Conflicting goals

We all have views on what public services should be provided and how they should be distributed. Again, whether or not the ethical origins of these views are explicitly articulated, there will be principled disagreement about the nature of public service provision in a way that is unlikely for, say, the provision of washing powder. These fundamentally conflicting views about the goals of public services may arise at various levels. There may be disagreement between service providers and the government, between providers and the public, and between public and government. And among the providers, there may be disagreement between front-line workers and their managers. And disagreement between members of any of these groups.

Yet the public service reform debate often proceeds as if these disagreements never arise. Only unprincipled disagreement is acknowledged – any disagreement is attributed to a tussle between narrow vested interests. Here again, standard economic theory, simplistically interpreted, casts a long shadow. In this view, there can be no principled disagreement over how a public service should be run, because there is established best practice. Best practice is usually whatever maximizes economic welfare; this objective is put into practice via cost–benefit analysis.[36] Best practice is thus the practice with the greatest balance of monetary benefits over costs. The data which enter into cost–benefit analysis are supposed to be based on consumer preferences, because of consumer sovereignty – consumers are the best judge of their own happiness. It follows that if service providers or the government disagree with consumers (the public), then the providers or the government must be wrong. Such disagreements are not hard to explain, or so the argument goes; they arise because the providers and the government are both essentially self-interested, driven by their own concerns.

Yet examples of principled disagreement are not hard to find. In the US study of job centre case workers mentioned above, the case workers clearly disagreed with the priorities set by their managers: they wanted to help the most disadvantaged, rather than simply get as many people as possible into employment. At a more general level, there are principled disagreements about the role of education. Some UK politicians appear to have a much narrower role in mind than teachers, considering a successful education system to be measured largely in terms of its contribution to national economic performance. So students are strongly encouraged to study science subjects post-16 – even though the rhetoric of consumer choice suggests subject provision should follow students' preferences, not attempt to lead them. The principled disagreement here is potentially three-way, with students, teachers and government each having conflicting views about the role of education.

Principled disagreement over the goals of public service provision is a fundamental threat to the audit culture. It implies there may be multiple goals not just because of the practical complexity of the public service, but because of multiple underlying principles governing its provision. So the risk of problems arising from multiple goals – such as perverse effects and Goodhart's Law – is substantially increased. More importantly, principled disagreement calls into question the goals set by the audit culture in the first place. Both the front-line staff working in the service and the public as service users may reject the economists' definition of best practice, because they begin from very different first principles about the values and goals of the service. The key question is not 'more audit or less?' but something like 'which set of ethical principles should govern public service provision?'

So public service workers may seek to sidestep a government target not because it is in their self-interest to do so, but because they believe pursuing the target will lead to a deteriorating service. Service users agree: for example, most of the public would like to see resource priorities in the NHS determined more directly by doctors. We may elect the politicians, but we trust the doctors more. How does the audit culture tackle these problems of trust?

Trust and the *kulturkampf*

As we have seen, the default economic analysis which haunts discussion of public services begins by assuming that public services are just like ordinary goods and services delivered in commercial markets. In these markets, there are no problems of trust and accountability, at least in theory. As a consumer, I need not look beyond my nose. I need only be concerned with what I get for the money I pay. I enter into contracts with sellers, and if the product I buy is not as it should be, I can sue. In this market model, then, when I contract with another party, I do not need to rely on trusting them to keep their side of the bargain, because if they do not, I can use the law to enforce the contract. It is this market model which leads naive supporters of the audit culture in the public services implicitly to assume that trust can be dispensed with. But the reasoning bears scant relation to reality: it is impossible to draw up a contract which includes everything that matters, a problem first noticed by Aristotle. Humans do not have perfect foresight, so there will be details and circumstances which the bargaining parties have not even considered, let alone contracted for, but which become important once the contract is implemented. Even if something is explicitly specified in the contract, there will very often be room for different interpretations of the relevant clause. So the contracting parties must trust each other after all, each hoping that the others will honour the spirit of the contract as well as the letter. All this is familiar in the commercial world, and business people adopt many strategies to build the necessary trust, most obviously by entering into long-term relationships, where people are less tempted to break promises for fear of the business they might lose in future. Nevertheless, trust sometimes breaks down.

When the market model is applied in the public sector, problems of trust become much more severe. Due to the complex, essentially qualitative nature of public services themselves, there is a larger gap for trust to fill between the spirit and the letter of contracts. It is much harder to specify clear and comprehensive contracts or targets concerning relatively abstract objectives such as good health care or educational outcomes than concerning the provision of a specific physical product.

The public services are also there to serve *us*, not their regulators or the government. But it is the government and bureaucrats who devise and commission contracts, and receive the audits, not the public. Since we cannot devise, monitor and enforce contracts with public service providers directly, we must trust others to do so on our behalf. In practice, this means we must trust the government, the government must trust its own bureaucrats, the bureaucrats trust the auditors, the auditors trust the service managers, and the managers trust the front-line workers. At every stage, attempts to replace trust with contract are subject to all the difficulties just described; in some cases the attempt is inconceivable – the citizens cannot in any practical sense contract with their own government. It is not fanciful to describe the problem in this way. In the UK, the NHS is subject to a hierarchy of internal auditing, and the top level of internal audit is externally audited by the Department of Health. The department's audit is then audited by the Audit Commission, which is itself audited by a Select Committee of Parliament (the select committee relies on a private firm of auditors).

It is hard to overstate the indispensable role of trusting public service workers to exercise their judgement. Since the audit culture cannot manage without trust, it has simply transplanted it. Doctors and teachers may not be trusted, but those who audit them are. And if they are not, it can only be because we rely on the judgement of the auditors at the next level up. But we cannot pass the trust buck for ever. After all, why should we trust the economists who proposed bringing the market model to the public sector in the first place? If no one can be trusted, then the motives of these economists are suspect too; they may be concerned with publishing their research in prestigious academic journals, or securing lucrative consultancy work advising on 'Public-Private Partnerships'.[37] Such concerns would heavily influence the advice provided by purely self-interested economists. A world where no one can be trusted is a very lonely one. Trust is unavoidable.

Yet the audit culture works to undermine trust. Auditing signals that those being audited are not trusted, which in turn leads them to repay that lack of trust in kind. Here lies the heart of the *kulturkampf.* Public service workers embrace the values, goals, relationships and motivational assumptions of the public domain; those who seek to audit and incentivize them very often embrace the market model. The two sides do not trust each other with good reason – their cultures are incompatible.[38]

To sum up, there are unavoidable problems with auditing the public services, which arise directly from inherent features of the public domain. Taken together, the presence of intrinsic motivation, the need for democracy and accountability, and conflicting, qualitative goals capture much of what is often described as the public service ethos. The economics of public service reform obscures the difficult questions about what kind of public services best serve the public interest – ethical questions of need and fairness. Quantification attempts to add a veneer of scientific objectivity and trustworthiness, but in fact undermines trust.

What conclusions can be drawn? First, the ideology of the public service 'reformers' appears to be ultimately incompatible with the very idea of *public* services. For example, if increased choice is regarded as good in itself, then presumably it would be better if citizen-consumers could choose whether they want 'public services' at all – the alternative being lower taxes and having to organize private provision. This libertarian perspective is widespread in the US and US libertarians find it peculiar that greater choice is advocated without questioning public provision in general. Since the choice culture challenges the idea of universal public provision, it is hardly surprising that public service workers are uneasy. The *kulturkampf* between reformers and public service workers may itself be the greatest obstacle to future progress. At the very least, the fundamental ethical principles at stake must be clarified and openly debated.

Second, it is mistaken to view the use of audits and markets in the public services as an alternative to the old-fashioned ideal of trusting workers to follow a public service ethos. The market model is not a real alternative because markets *rely* on trust, especially in the public domain.

Third, we should not be overly concerned about loss of control over the public services if the audit culture is rolled back. Placing trust means recognizing that those in whom trust is placed have a degree of autonomy. It necessarily involves ceding some control. But although the public services would be subject to less detailed control, this does not mean they cannot be accountable. The new accountability promised by the audit culture has proved to be empty rhetoric because, as we have seen, it reduces accountability to a series of performance indicators chosen for ease of measurement and control rather than tracking real performance; and it makes public sector workers accountable to regulators and government, not the public, the service users. True accountability involves giving an account of your performance to those with the time and competence to assess it. They could be experts, lay people or a mixture of both, but in any case this kind of qualitative reporting process should be more intelligible than elaborate auditing to members of the public without specialist knowledge. With the essential proviso that recipients of these accounts of performance be genuinely independent of government, this should help restore democracy to the process of accountability.[39]

Finally, less reliance on financial carrots and sticks need not make it harder to motivate workers. On the contrary, by rolling back the audit culture, employees are allowed a degree of autonomy, which is essential to intrinsic motivation. Non-monetary rewards, such as titles, honours and awards, can have an important role because they are much less likely than financial incentives to undermine intrinsic motivation. They reward overall long-term effort or performance, and there is no contractual arrangement or other obligation on the employer to confer them, so if used sensitively, their purpose goes beyond any cynical motivation of performance. They can be conferred through a fair and consistent process which rewards the employee's devotion to duty – unlike PRP, which is often dependent on factors beyond the employee's control. And unlike money, the value of different titles, honours and other non-material forms of status is hard to compare, so these incentives are less vulnerable to the corroding effects of adaptation and rivalry.[40]

This chapter has used public services as a case study for examining problems of commodification. It is time to draw some more general lessons.

Commodification: Everything for sale[41]

I have largely focused on just one aspect of commodification, the process of quantification in terms of money. Some economists argue that putting monetary values on things does not in itself turn them into commodities, so we need not worry. For instance, they maintain that putting a price on life does not count as commodifying it, because that also requires the ability to buy and sell people as in slavery. But we can sidestep esoteric debates about the exact meaning of commodification; as we have seen, great damage is done by the introduction of monetary quantification in the first place. Chapter 6 showed how cost–benefit analysis distorts the values of life and nature by attempting to express them in monetary terms. There the examples were environmental, but the same approach has been applied in cultural policy too: the UK Government insisted that the 'cultural value' of Stonehenge be expressed in monetary terms when deciding what to do about a busy road nearby.[42] In this chapter, similar problems arise in an audit culture of ubiquitous monetary quantification. Economists such as Le Grand have overstated the difference between an audit culture and the effects of introducing markets and competition. In both cases most of the damage is done by the pricing activity alone.

It is the practice of valuing things in terms of money which in itself leads us astray. Almost all of us have an instinctive sense that some things should not be valued in terms of money. But what exactly are we objecting to? When we wrongly attach monetary values, are we just showing bad manners, committing some kind of socio-economic faux pas; or acting unwisely because of the undesirable consequences? More seriously, are we in some cases making a logical error (like trying to measure the temperature of a poem); or acting immorally; or doing something which is downright wicked?

These questions are hard to unravel. If we suppose for the moment that monetary valuation is merely a scientific process of measurement, many problems still arise, as we have seen in the last two chapters. As well as the practical difficulties, monetary measurement presupposes a common scale of value; but the thing being measured may have multiple dimensions or attributes, with different kinds of values not reducible to being measured along a common scale. Or the thing being measured may have inherently qualitative attributes, which cannot be measured on any quantitative scale. Apart from these problems of monetary measurement, deeper difficulties appear once we recognize that monetary valuation does not take place in a social vacuum; it is *not* a neutral scientific act of measurement.

The meaning of monetary valuation

As we saw in Chapter 6, economists who calculate the value of a 'statistical life' argue that they are not really valuing life in any fundamental or ethical sense. But when a government report values a specific reduction in the risk of death for 1000 people at say, $30 million, this is not an abstract measurement. It has profound ethical significance. It means the report recommends that, all other things being equal, policies which yield this reduced risk and cost less than $30 million should go ahead, but policies which cost more should not. Put more bluntly, the benefits from 'saving $30 million' and 'reduced risk of death for 1000 people' are treated as having equal value; they can be regarded as substitutes for one another. Yet this is not how most of us see the world.

Pricing nature

When people were asked to put a monetary value on some piece of the natural world, as part of a 'contingent valuation survey' (discussed in Chapter 6), this is what some of them said: [43]

'Putting a price on nature is immoral.'

'You can put a value on nature, but not a value in monetary terms. A value is what we teach our children.'

'If you feel passionately about something, it's difficult to put a monetary value on it … perhaps someone who doesn't feel impassioned [sic] about the [wetland] and its importance, perhaps they're the only people who could.'

'It's not ours to sell.'

'Do you mean to tell me that I've been raped and you think there is some amount of money that will make me think it never happened?'

The point of the tale about George Bernard Shaw at the head of this chapter is that once we put a price on something, no matter how high, its character changes and something of value is lost. [44] Consider our relationship to friends and those we love. Part of what it means to be a true friend is to refuse to put a price on the friendship. Once we contemplate that, something important about the friendship is lost. On the contrary, people often show the special significance of a relationship to them by expressly refusing to put a monetary value on it. When a mother refuses to sell one of her children to a neighbouring tribe, even though she is on the verge of starvation, we see the refusal, regardless of its merits, as an expression of love.

The same refusal to contemplate a monetary valuation extends beyond our close relationships. There are some good things which cannot be bought with money, or if they are lost, money is hopelessly inadequate compensation. Examples include good health and great works of art: we say there is 'no substitute' for good health; the painting by Rembrandt is 'irreplaceable'. Since the monetary valuation of something implies money is a substitute, a replacement or proper compensation, we reject it in these cases. More directly, we often express our understanding of the special significance of these good things simply by saying they are 'priceless'. Since money has purely instrumental value, attaching a price to something suggests that it is simply a means to another end. If there were a market for babies then a child could come to know its original price, and compare itself with the cost of ordinary goods like the family car – or other children. The child's sense of its uniqueness is undermined.

The corrosive effects of money arise just from discussing money in certain contexts, or undertaking a monetary valuation. Actual exchange or trade need not take place for damage to be done. Thus sexual love is not the same as prostitution without paying a fee. Money talk casts doubt on the motives and purposes of the people involved, regardless of whether money actually changes hands or direct harm is done. Returning to the example of a market in babies, suppose a couple conceive a child they intend to sell, but then have a lottery win and so decide to keep it. The motives of the parents remain suspect. Their primary purpose was to make money, treating the baby as a means to an end, a motive which seems callous and morally objectionable in itself.

CBA and the audit culture in the public sector should be seen against the background of this complex set of meanings of money. Often the key problem is the same simple yet fundamental one as that involved in pricing a friendship: the monetary valuation implies exchangeability or substitutability between money and the thing being valued, but most people reject this implication. Economists have responded to these concerns, but before turning to their views, there are two other general implications of monetary valuation which deserve spelling out.

First, monetary valuation gives the rich more say than the poor. Once goods, services and outcomes are measured in terms of money, they will come to be shaped much more by the views and wants of the rich than the rest of us. In CBA, the value of a rich person's life is greater, and their preferences have more impact, because they are willing to pay more for what they want. And the rich gain more from the monetary measurement of public services, because they are more able to take advantage of any choice of service. This effect is exacerbated by new incentives for service providers to cream off the 'best' consumers – health care for the healthiest, education for the relatively well-educated.

Second, monetary valuation implies new and controversial rights. Monetary valuation treats parts of the environment like pieces of property which can be bought and sold. But many of us reject the idea of ownership rights over the natural world; we merely have *use* rights, accompanied by duties of preservation. In the public services, monetary valuation effectively grants new, controversial rights to politicians or the regulators they have appointed. These rights concern the details of the service being provided, such as the treatment priorities in a hospital, or the reading scheme to be used by a primary school. Monetary valuation introduces strong incentives by rewarding what is measured and ignoring or down-playing everything else. Politicians or regulators give themselves the right to set these priorities. They do so in the name of consumer sovereignty, although most final consumers – the public – have little increased power and trust the front-line staff more than their political masters. The front-line staff see it not so much as a loss of control, but that politicians award themselves rights which *no one* ought to have. Professionalism and the public service ethos *obliges* front-line staff to do the best possible job subject to the constraints they face; they make daily judgements to achieve this; they cannot legitimately choose to do otherwise in response to the latest government incentive scheme.

In defence of monetary valuation?

Many economists are deeply skeptical of the idea that some things are 'priceless', or that attempting to put a monetary value on them will somehow corrode their value. On the contrary, they maintain that virtually everything has a price, that is, a sum of money a person would accept in return for giving up the valued thing. The economist draws a Shakespearean lesson from the tale about George Bernard Shaw: 'The lady doth protest too much, methinks.'[45] The lady has her price, and her protest is just an attempt to conceal it. Economists justify this seemingly cynical conclusion by arguing that in everyday life all of us *do* put a monetary value on so-called irreplaceable or incomparable good things, even if implicitly or unconsciously.[46] The sharpest example concerns the decisions we regularly make to incur an increased risk of our own death, for the sake of a saving in terms of time, effort or money. We cross the street to pick up a $50 banknote lying on the other side; we make a detour down a dangerous road to save $10 by using a shop there; we take a dangerous job with a bigger salary. But do these actions really show that we put a price on risk to our life?

There are many problems with this argument. To begin with, it is hard to infer, from observing someone's choices alone, how they understand the choice and the motives behind their decision. As discussed in Chapter 6, a person may take a dangerous job rather than a safe one for many reasons; we cannot infer a willingness to 'trade off' an increased risk of death in return for a high salary. But even in apparently simple cases, there are many possibilities other than trade-off thinking. When I cross the street to pick up the $50 note, I may believe that the probability of death is zero because I look before I cross the street. When I make a detour down a dangerous road, I may do so merely out of habit. Clearly, we do not consciously and explicitly put a price on risk to our life, but the point here is more than that; we do not implicitly put prices on risk to life either. That is, we do not even act as if we think in these trade-off terms, because we choose on different grounds altogether.

Suppose we set these objections aside and grant that *some* people in *some* contexts do implicitly put a monetary value on the increased risk of their own death. It does not follow that we are on a slippery slope towards everything having a price. At best, it might imply that these people, to be consistent, ought to be willing to put prices on other so-called priceless goods. It certainly does not mean that the rest of us, who refuse to measure the value of certain things in terms of money, are irrational, self-deluded or unwilling to face up to tough choices.

However, the taunt about refusing to confront tough choices brings us to another argument in favour of monetary valuation. Intelligent, rational decision making requires that we compare all the pros and cons of the options available. That is only possible, the argument runs, if they are expressed in a comparable way on a common scale, and money is the obvious unit of measurement. Conversely, economists argue, a refusal to use monetary valuation reflects an unwillingness to confront tough but unavoidable trade-offs. This view is made explicit in justifying CBA; in discussion of public services, it becomes the claim that all outputs must be monetized in order to ensure 'value for money'.

The argument appears simple and compelling, but it does not bear close scrutiny. We can choose rationally if we are able to make all-things-considered comparisons between the options in order to determine which is best. However, the ability to compare the options on a common scale of value would give us more information than this: it would allow us to say how much better the best option is, compared to its rivals. So comparing the options on a common scale gives us more information than we require to make rational choices. Thus a common scale of value is unnecessary; and so a common *monetary* scale is less necessary still. There is a more radical possibility too: contrary to what is widely believed, rational decision making may not even require us to make all-things-considered comparisons. But how can they be avoided?

The picture of measuring the pros and cons on a common scale (economists talk about the 'measuring rod of money') is such a comfortable one that it deceives us into thinking there is no other way to make decisions. It is a comfortable image because it suggests that hard choices can be turned into mechanical exercises in moral mathematics. Just feed the measurements into the decision-making machine, crank the handle and out pops the answer. Hard choices are made easy. Contrast this dream with how hard choices are really made. The following description will be familiar to all of us, perhaps when making choices concerning a career or someone we care about.

Hard choices

Different options each have different reasons in their favour. I must judge which reasons count most strongly in this particular choice, on the basis of listening to competing arguments. (Even if I am deciding in isolation, often it helps to air the arguments by going through them with a friend.) Since I can choose only one option, I must reject all the rest, and, in doing so, something valuable will have to be sacrificed, no matter what I finally decide. Partly because of this, I feel unease, discomfort, regret or anguish afterwards, even if I am sure I have made the right decision.

It is hardly what we would expect decision making to feel like if we could in fact make all-things-considered comparisons between the options and confidently pick the best one. Against this background we may start to take seriously our inability to compare. Once we do so, it seems unrealistic and unnecessary to insist on finding the best option. On reflection, the intuition that we should find the best option has shaky foundations, emerging from the vision of decision making as moral mathematics, a turn of the handle on the decision-making machine. In real life we rely on a much stronger intuition: never choose an option which is known to be worse than another available. This intuition is a much better first principle of decision making. It recognizes that our comparative powers are limited. For example, sometimes we do not know which of two options is best, all-things-considered, but we know that all the other options are worse. In these circumstances, we can equally comfortably – or more accurately, equally *un*comfortably – settle for either of them.[47] This may seem frustratingly incomplete, but it reflects the toughness of the choice rather than denying it.

And if private decisions, such as those concerning career choice, can be this tough, there is no reason to expect that public policy decisions will be any easier. There is no magic formula for public policy decision making, because there is rarely a right decision waiting to be found. For all the reasons discussed in this and the preceding chapter, some things cannot be measured in terms of money; attempts to do so will be misleading or harmful. This is not a nihilistic conclusion, nor does it rule out finding an alternative to CBA and similar exercises in moral mathematics. Regarding alternatives to CBA, there is no general answer. It depends on the decision in hand, why we turned to monetary valuation in the first place, and the problems which forced us to reject it. In some practical contexts, the solution may be far from revolutionary. It may be possible to rescue a form of CBA involving in-kind valuations rather than monetary ones.[48] The idea is that it is easier and more informative to measure the value of things by comparing them with what is similar, rather than comparing them with money. For example, if a local government authority is trying to decide whether to buy a local meadow and preserve it as a nature reserve, it would compare the benefits to the community against those accruing from alternative ways of spending the same budget – perhaps improvements to local school buildings or longer opening hours at the day-care centre for the elderly. In-kind valuation seems attractive but has obvious limitations, including the difficulty in many cases of finding 'similar' alternatives. What is 'similar' to the benefits to be gained from mitigating climate change?

One admirable motive behind some forms of moral mathematics is the desire to base policy not on expert judgement but on the views of ordinary people. If monetary valuations are obtained from surveys, they are supposed to reflect these views. From this perspective, CBA is highly democratic. But as explained in Chapter 6, people do not have coherent, well-developed preferences about the value of life, or more prosaically, about how much extra pay they should receive in order to tolerate a riskier job. More generally, people often lack considered, fully developed views on the difficult policy issues that are the subject of CBA; that is, they do not have views of the sort that can be readily summarized in reply to simple survey questions, let alone measured in terms of money. To give people the chance to think through, discuss, develop and explain their views on complex policy issues, a political forum is required. In recent years, several innovative kinds of political forum have been developed. Some of them are now being applied to real-world public policy making: in the UK, 'citizens juries' have attracted notable support from the Blair and Brown governments. Citizens' juries are loosely modelled on legal juries; a group of lay people hear evidence from expert witnesses for and against various policy options, and then discuss the issues with each other and the experts before making some kind of collective recommendation. These new political forums can be helpful, but there is no magic formula for a political process either. Citizens' juries face particular difficulties in ensuring that: (i) a jury of less than 20 people is seen as representative of the wider community; and (ii) a diverse range of voices, especially those usually marginalized from political processes, are heard on the jury.[49]

In other contexts, expert judgement may be favoured instead, but not judgement forced into the framework of monetary valuation. There are many possible alternative frameworks depending on the issue at stake – the precautionary principle was one approach mentioned in Chapter 6. But in the rush to embrace these new innovations in decision making, it is easy to overlook a more fundamental point. There may be no need for a new alternative to CBA at all.

CBA is not the decision-making procedure it might appear to be. Most economists recognize it as an aid to decision making, not a complete replacement. They accept that the recommendation which emerges out of CBA is just that, a recommendation, which must take its place alongside other contributions to the political process of policy making. Nevertheless, while they concede that politics is unavoidable in practice, many economists still consider it undesirable. Policy determined by CBA remains the ideal, and economists' advice takes this for granted; policy goals other than economic welfare, impacts not measured in terms of money, and various qualitative discussion-based procedures for informing the decision are all criticized, sidelined or simply ignored. Apart from the obvious ethical bias, the key problem with this perspective is that even as an ideal, CBA in isolation is impossible. Politics, in the form of political judgement, is an inevitable, ineliminable part of decision making, even in principle.

This puts the worry about alternatives to CBA in a new light: CBA cannot itself be a replacement for politics, merely a supplement. So alternatives to CBA, including discussion-based forums like citizens' juries, are worth the continuing experiment (even a fraction of the resources devoted to CBA would make a huge difference), but they are not essential. Only political judgement is indispensable, and very often we manage with this alone. Most political decisions are made without the aid of CBA. At the beginning of Chapter 6 I suggested that most of us would find it absurd if foreign policy decisions (invading Iraq, or so-called humanitarian military interventions in Africa) were made on the basis of a monetary valuation of the pros and cons. Equally, no one seriously suggests that monetary values could capture what is most at stake in policy decisions about abortion or capital punishment. So there clearly *are* limits to the use of monetary valuation, and given all the problems with extending monetary valuation to new areas, the burden of explaining why these extensions do not go beyond those limits should lie with the advocates of monetary valuation. In other words, if economists wish to extend monetary valuation into new, implausible areas, the burden of justifying the legitimacy of this extension should be on them.

Yet the only justification economists have offered is plainly inadequate. They argue that CBA is relevant whenever resource constraints are involved.[50] Yet clearly, resource constraints are *always* involved. There are always alternative ways to use resources, and choices always have resource implications. The conclusion that CBA should always be used, and used as the sole determinant of policy, is absurd. For example, policy on the use of capital punishment would be determined by comparing the direct financial costs to the state against the costs of imprisoning people for life sentences. A more sophisticated CBA would also attempt to estimate the cost to society of crime committed by lifers after early release, and the forgone earnings of innocent people who were mistakenly executed (both estimates weighted by their probabilities). Once we reject the idea of basing policy *solely* on these considerations, we are left with the claim that CBA should nevertheless always be used in an advisory role, because it is somehow relevant. This extreme conclusion that CBA should always be used is self-contradictory. Cost–benefit reasoning always rejects such absolute conclusions. Rather, CBA will sometimes fail a cost–benefit test itself – the relevance of monetary cost–benefit considerations to the issue in question will sometimes be too marginal to justify the expense of conducting a CBA. For most of us, capital punishment looks like one such case: concerns about killing the innocent, or the morality of the state executing its citizens, innocent or not, will so outweigh any cost–benefit considerations that conducting a CBA misses the point. It would be a waste of money.

Conclusion: Not everything has a price

It bears repeating that debates about the limits of CBA matter not just because of the influence of CBA on government policy making, but because of their relevance to wider debates about whether markets should be used to allocate certain goods and services. Some limits to the use of markets are uncontroversial and very familiar. We restrict the participation in markets of children and others who may not understand the full consequences of their actions. And we restrict markets in which extremely bad outcomes could occur, such as those involving trade in babies, body parts, hard drugs or military weapons. These are ethical limits to markets. In the last two chapters we have uncovered some more. They are limits to monetary valuation, so they apply not just to markets proper but whenever there are real resource implications from prices being attached. It is worth summarizing these limits in broad terms here.

Basic needs, citizenship and community

Some goods and services, such as education and health care, have a special importance. They are important because they are *needs:* the preconditions for the pursuit of any worthwhile life; there is almost universal consensus about their special role here. Society best shows it recognizes their importance by making them available equally to every citizen, and by providing them directly rather than distributing the cash to purchase them. Provision based on citizenship is by definition equal while market outcomes are inevitably unequal. Another argument reaches the same conclusion. What does it mean to be a member of a community? The answer must refer to what we have in common. So things which are kept out of markets, but instead made available equally to all, form a key part of what we have in common. By contrast, shifting goods such as education and health care into the marketplace, or stimulating market-like provision through financial incentives or the forced expression of 'consumer choice' undermines our sense of community. It erodes what we have in common and so weakens the ties that bind us.

Markets deny the expression of moral convictions

One important way in which people express their deeply held moral convictions is by refusing to compromise them in return for money. Again, simply introducing prices is often enough to challenge moral convictions, even if the thing concerned cannot actually be traded in markets. In Chapter 2 we saw how support among residents for the local siting of an unwanted nuclear waste facility fell by more than 50 per cent once monetary compensation was offered. The obvious explanation is that people object to being bribed. A key element in moral concepts like bribery, honour and loyalty is their expression through, or in opposition to, money. Similarly, people express their moral convictions through giving blood, or staying late at work because they believe the work is important. The introduction of financial incentives, with or without actual markets, denies the opportunity to express particular moral convictions; the denial is made worse because other ethical assumptions are implied instead.

Markets presuppose controversial ethical assumptions

We have seen the variety of small but controversial ethical assumptions which are built into the process of attaching prices, the first step towards markets. It is not a neutral scientific enterprise to attach monetary values to life, the natural world or the benefits from a new medical treatment. Rather, monetary valuation implies the thing being valued is not unique but exchangeable; it also suggests new motives and purposes for the people involved. The deepest ethical assumption often goes unnoticed, the assumption to think in terms of markets in the first place. For example, since climate change mitigation is seen as potentially conflicting with economic growth, it is assumed to be an 'economic' decision to be made using CBA. From another perspective, climate change fundamentally concerns our obligations to future generations; it is a political and ethical decision in which reasoned argument matters more than how much people are able or willing to pay to promote their view. Thinking in terms of markets also implies that there are implicit rights of ownership over something, otherwise it makes no sense to talk of prices, buying and selling. Yet many of us dispute these assumed rights of ownership, like the woman who responded to the monetary valuation survey by saying, 'It's not ours to sell.'

Problems with using markets are of course widely recognized in economics and public policy making. But the main problems which are recognized, such as firms exercising monopoly power, are those which can be seen as market 'imperfections' – a failure of the real market to match up to the theoretical ideal. The solution involves perfecting or extending the market; that is, the introduction of new markets or the regulation of existing ones. So a new market in carbon emissions is proposed to deal with environmental problems, and regulations are introduced to curb monopoly power. In short, these problems with markets are distinctive because the economists' solution for them involves more markets, not fewer.

It will be clear by now that most of the problems with markets discussed in this book are not like this. They arise when there is a conflict between our ethical principles and the ethical underpinnings of markets themselves, no matter how 'perfect' the market. So the problems cannot be solved by introducing new markets or refining existing ones. Instead we must resolve the conflict, either by abandoning our principles, or by rejecting market methods altogether.

Finally, two pragmatic objections need to be addressed before we can escape the obsession with measuring value in terms of money, and stop thinking of economics as good only for this task.

First, it is sometimes suggested that arguments against markets will only persuade those with leftish politics. However, there are many contemporary restrictions on free markets which find favour with the traditional Right.

Examples include immigration controls and planning law. More importantly, the idea that expanding the domain of markets represents a return to the heyday of 19th-century laissez-faire capitalism, before the dead hand of government began to interfere, is a grotesque misrepresentation of history. It was Victorian capitalists who first developed the idea of a public service ethos, because they recognized the need to separate politics, specifically the civil service, from business interests. Similarly, the commercialization of education is a very recent trend; private schools in the UK were mostly established as charities.[51]

Second, it is often claimed that only arguments couched in terms of money have any persuasive power in the world of *realpolitik*. Put bluntly, money talks. But this view effectively concedes that the domain of markets and monetary values has already expanded – when it is precisely this expansion which is still open to debate. Otherwise there would be no pragmatic case for talking money. For there are clearly many realms in which money does not talk: it is not the way to win arguments about the death penalty. And there is little sign that it is persuading people or governments to take significant action on climate change. Money talk is especially unpersuasive when, as in climate change discussions, it rests on dubious numbers. The point is not that things are adequately valued only if the monetary values are large enough. In cases such as climate change, money talk is unpersuasive because meaningful monetary values do not exist.

Much of this book can be seen as arguing against the 'money talks' perspective. For that perspective is rooted in the belief that arguments about money, in the world of economic ideas and economic processes, can be separated from arguments about ethics. And that belief is false. Economics is inherently ethical.

Chapter Eight

Conclusion

George Stigler, Chicago economist and Nobel Laureate, was asked why there are no Nobel prizes awarded in subjects such as sociology, psychology and history. He replied: 'Don't worry. They already have a prize in literature.'[1]

Economics as taught 'in America's graduate schools … bears testimony to a triumph of ideology over science'. (Joseph Stiglitz, Nobel Laureate economist[2])

…The ideas of economists and political philosophers, both when they are right and when they are wrong, are more powerful than is commonly understood. Indeed, the world is ruled by little else. Practical men, who believe themselves to be quite exempt from any intellectual influences, are usually the slaves of some defunct economist. Madmen in authority, who hear voices in the air, are usually distilling their frenzy from some academic scribbler of a few years back. (John Maynard Keynes, *The General Theory*)

What economists don't admit

Economics shapes our lives in countless ways. Each chapter of this book has illustrated this in a practical context. In the process we have uncovered some common themes in the way orthodox economists think. Considered in isolation they might seem only of academic interest, but as previous chapters and Keynes' remarks suggest, they should interest all of us. Three themes are worthy of special mention.

Economic imperialism

Economic imperialism is the trend for orthodox economics to invade other ways of thinking and attempt to colonize them, replacing them with economic concepts, values and tools of analysis. It features an arrogant unwillingness to listen to or learn from others. Although it is an intellectual invasion rather than a physical one, the consequences are real. They include the spread of markets into new areas of life, inappropriately assuming that people are selfish, and the excessive use of quantification, especially in terms of money, to frame decision making.

Often there is nothing wrong with markets, self-interest and monetary quantification: economic analysis and economists' policy advice remains extremely valuable in the right context. Orthodox economics is not universally flawed, but it has overreached itself into spheres where it becomes misleading. One way of bringing its limitations into sharp contrast is to consider those parts of real life where orthodox economics works well. Examples include the auctions of government debt and mobile phone radio frequencies, the new markets trading in carbon emissions allowances, and some specialized financial markets. In these fields, economic theory has been applied fairly directly to yield useful insights and policy recommendations, without generating difficult ethical dilemmas. Indeed, the influence of economics goes further: in some cases, economists have not just given advice, but devised the entire framework in which economic activity takes place. The mobile phone spectrum auctions and specially designed carbon trading markets only exist because economists invented them. So it is hardly surprising that economics works well in these contexts.[3] They are self-contained closed systems in which the decision makers involved have the time, ability and financial incentives to act like *Homo economicus.* When businesses and governments buy and sell carbon credits or mobile phone spectra, they have a great deal to gain or lose from the transaction and so devote considerable efforts to making the right decisions. They can call on expert advisers, often economists themselves. The decisions to be made, while complex, are made amenable to standard economic analysis because everyone knows the rules of the game, and everyone knows that everyone knows... and so on. The branch of economics called *game theory* is ideal in these circumstances. And everyone knows that everyone is trying to act like *Homo economicus* in pursuing a clear objective, such as maximizing profit or financial return, which makes predicting the behaviour of rival buyers and sellers much easier. This is not to belittle the achievement here: economists have solved practical problems put to them, and probably contributed to the greater good in doing so. And there are some other significant successes,[4] but they all illustrate that economic theory works only in very special circumstances. Devising specific institutional arrangements – auctions or specially designed markets – is one example of a more general trick popular in economics.

Bending the world to fit the theory

The old joke bears repeating: when confronted with something which works in reality, the economist asks 'That's all very well in practice, but how does it work in theory?' So if reality fails to fit economic theory, the answer is to change reality. One approach, exemplified by bespoke pollution trading markets, is to devise legal frameworks, social structures, economic incentives and whatever else is necessary to create realities which fit with economic theory. Alternatively, economists simply assume that people think and act in the way that economic theory says they do. This assumption is more powerful than it sounds, because it can be self-fulfilling: under the influence of economists' ways of thinking, people can come to behave in line with economic theory. The clearest example here is the repeated assumption of self-interested behaviour in economic analysis. As we saw in Chapter 2, this can lead people to become more self-interested, for various distinct reasons: the financial incentives that are introduced following the advice of economists; the economists' claim that to act unselfishly would be irrational; the repeated message that most people are self-interested, leading me to withdraw trust, cooperation or altruism towards others, because I expect them to act selfishly towards me. The self-fulfilling nature of some economic analysis is one instance of a more general phenomenon: economics can be 'performative'.[5] That is, the act of doing or performing it, of studying the world using the ideas and tools of economics, may change the world being studied. In other words, merely using economic theory can help to bend the world to fit that theory. When economic analysis is self-fulfilling, economists are tempted to be smug. But other performative aspects of economics are not so reassuring. Chapter 7 provided two examples. According to Goodhart's Law, attempting to measure something, for the purpose of controlling or targeting it, tends to change it, undermining the meaning or purpose of the measurement. And financial incentives for public service workers can backfire, leading them to behave in the opposite way to that expected by economic analysis.

Traditional science observes the world from the outside; it does not alter the phenomena it seeks to study. So when economics is performative it is certainly not a 'science' as the term is usually understood. And it is unavoidably ethical in a fundamental sense: when the use of economics to study the world changes the world being studied, we should ask whether these changes are desirable, just as we would when assessing an economic policy. The scope of economists' value judgements stretches beyond the obvious, the realm of economic policy making, to include all performative economic analysis, because in both cases these judgements affect the world.

When we come to ask economists *why* they bend how they see the world to fit the theory, the standard answer is that they are simply trying to describe people's behaviour in such a way as to be able to study it, using their powerful analytical tools. Put differently, economists plead guilty to assuming people think and behave in unrealistic ways, but argue that otherwise the mathematics underpinning economic analysis becomes unmanageable. However, the possibility of performative economics suggests another answer: the strategy can be self-fulfilling. So for instance assuming that people behave like *Homo economicus* makes them more likely actually to do so. This explanation raises a further question.

The ethics of economists

Do economists *want* the world to look more like their theory? We have seen much evidence suggesting that they do: economic theories may be presented as simplified stories about how we behave and think, but they lead a double life as parables about how we *ought* to behave and think. This is why many economists use value-laden words in an odd way; for instance, labelling behaviour 'irrational' merely because it does not fit their description of reality. The boundary between 'fact' and 'value judgement' becomes hard to distinguish, because descriptive 'facts' turn out to be based on value judgements drawn from theory.[6] There are many examples. When measuring happiness, many common perceptions of ordinary people, such as Peak-End evaluation, are ignored or overruled (Chapter 5). Bayesian economics assumes people use probabilities when thinking about uncertainty, because the theory says they would be irrational otherwise (Chapter 6). Similarly, because rational people are supposed to make decisions by comparing the alternatives against each other on a common scale, and money is supposed to be one such neutral, practical scale, economists assume we do in fact make decisions in this way. Economists insist we act *as if* we put money values on lives, loves and friendships, no matter how strongly we deny it. And economists favour objective measures of risk, based on the risk's objective probability, over the subjective measures that people use, taking account of the perceived danger, whether it can be avoided, how feared it is, and so on.

A repeated pattern of inconsistency emerges here: economists are constantly jumping back and forth between insisting on consumer sovereignty and sidelining it. It is a tension between economics as 'democracy', a kind of social engineering to give people what they want, and economics as 'science', with objectively correct answers. On the one hand, economists argue we should respect people's preferences in their raw form, warts and all, because people are the best judge of their own interests. On the other, economists repeatedly adjust, refine or simply ignore raw preferences – and analogous raw data reporting views about happiness – arguing that people are irrational or mistaken in these cases. Often it is far from clear what principle of rationality is at stake, and even when the principle is made explicit, the appeal to it seems arbitrary. The point here is *not* that we should fall back on raw preferences because the consumer sovereignty story is accurate. On the contrary, in many cases it is legitimate to dismiss raw preferences as irrational; besides, applied economics can barely begin if it relies on the emaciated foundations provided by orthodox economic theory alone. In practice, economists must almost always make some judgements about the content of people's preferences, not just their structure, in order to derive policy recommendations. The problem is that orthodox economic theory lacks the intellectual resources to do so.

There is little sign yet of these resources being imported into economics. Instead there are increasingly elaborate attempts to sidestep the problem, for instance by insinuating that economic theory describes a superior form of rationality, without bothering to develop an ethical argument to justify this claim. A recent example comes from neuroeconomics. Much attention has been given to the growing evidence that *Homo economicus* tendencies can be traced to a specific region of the brain, the prefrontal cortex, a much newer region in evolutionary terms than brain regions associated with more emotional behaviour.[7] The message seems to be that *Homo economicus* thinking is superior, because it is more advanced in evolutionary terms. But by the same faulty logic, reading and writing are superior to various physical activities such as sex; and men are superior to women.[8]

Another response is to claim that economists only argue about facts, not values, hinting that ethical debate has no place in economics proper, or that it is futile, because all economists agree.[9] But clearly economists *do* argue about values, such as the discount rate discussed in Chapter 6, which reflects the priority to be given to future costs and benefits relative to current ones. It is inevitably an ethical judgement. Economists overlook their own value judgements for various reasons, ranging from simple embarrassment about the presence of ethics in a so-called science, to frustration that outsiders do not understand basic economics. There is a widespread but implicit belief that non-economists are stupid. The economist Bryan Caplan is more explicit, devoting a book to discussing how non-economists repeatedly suffer from 'antimarket bias, antiforeign bias, make-work bias, and pessimistic bias'.[10] That is, compared to economists, non-economists 'do not understand the "invisible hand" of the market ... underestimate the benefits of interaction with foreigners ... equate prosperity not with production, but with employment'. Lastly they are 'overly prone to think that economic conditions are bad and getting worse'.[11] It is true that Caplan produces strong evidence to show that ordinary people think differently about economics to those with PhDs in the subject (surprise, surprise). But remarkably, nowhere in the book does he seriously consider the possibility that ordinary people may have good reasons – such as different ethical starting points – for reaching different conclusions to economists.[12] The public need not be foolish, irrational or ignorant.

So when communicating with outsiders, economists exaggerate or simplify their arguments to focus attention on them, often neglecting to mention the value judgements on which the arguments rest. Although the reasons for this neglect need not be Machiavellian, some economists do appear to have manipulative motives. They worry that any public mention to non-economists of the assumptions or limitations behind conventional economic wisdom would give 'ammunition to the barbarians'.[13] Or as Caplan puts it, 'professional humility is dangerous'.[14] In other words: open the black box, and veto economics ceases to act as a veto anymore. Caplan argues that initially undergraduates should be kept in the dark too, advising fellow academics not to mention the assumptions or limitations behind textbook economics, and to tell their students 'I'm right, the people outside this classroom are wrong, and you don't want to be like *them,* do you?'[15] He concludes that 'democracies fall short because voters get the foolish policies they ask for'.[16] But rather than dismissal, seeking a compromise between democracy and science would seem to be a better way forward.

Libertarian paternalism is one currently fashionable attempt at this compromise.[17] In practice, it means trying to steer a person's decision making in the right direction, rather than restricting free choices directly or banning some choices altogether. For example, in deciding whether to enter a pension scheme, libertarian paternalists argue that we should have to 'opt out' rather than 'opt in', so that mere inertia does not prevent us from making choices which bring important long-term benefits. Libertarian paternalists often use this example as an ideal illustration of their philosophy in practice, and see it as influencing government policy. But if this is a leading achievement of libertarian paternalism, it is tempting to conclude that it tells us little we did not already know. Libertarian paternalism is good as far as it goes, but that is not very far. By trying to reconcile the irreconcilable – that is, combine libertarianism with paternalism – economists and policy makers end up with a minimalist ethics, which answers few practical questions. The ethical heavy lifting, deciding *when* to interfere to influence individual decisions, and *when* to ban some choices altogether (such as driving a car without a seat belt), is done elsewhere. And the minimalist strategy does not ensure that the ethics is uncontroversial or explicit. Libertarian paternalists borrow various assumptions from economics, such as consequentialism (outcomes are judged solely by their consequences), and the claim that consequences can be quantified in terms of money. They almost always take these assumptions for granted, rather than defending them explicitly.

Much of the tension between economics as 'democracy' and economics as 'science' is more apparent than real. A compromise is unnecessary once two features of democracy and science are noted. Economics cannot be a science, at least as traditionally understood, because it has an inevitable ethical dimension. And ethical debate, especially about whether some people's preferences should be partially or wholly ignored, must be recognized as central to democracy – democracy is not just about adding up predetermined preferences in elections.

Answering some objections

Throughout this book, I have tried to discuss the more important criticisms of my arguments where space permitted. But there are some more general objections, and I respond to three of them here.

Critics of economics are hostile to science

Science gives secure, reliable answers (often called 'the truth') to some questions. We should be grateful and revere the truth. However, just because the answers are reliable, it does not follow that the questions are important or in pressing need of an answer. Many economists seem to have ignored this point and picked questions which can be addressed using the formal mathematical methods now fashionable in economics. These economists are akin to the drunkard we met earlier – the one who searched for his wallet under the street light, not because he lost it there, but because that was where he could see. Research methods should be determined by the needs of the topic rather than the conventional boundaries of an academic discipline. Economists should give much greater priority to studying contemporary real-world problems, regardless of whether formal mathematical tools are applicable.

It is no part of this book to denigrate science or quantification. Rather, I argue that some forms of quantification, especially in terms of money, are inappropriate in some contexts. Too many attempts to quantify in economics run ahead of conceptual clarity and understanding. It is foolish to try to measure something unless exactly what is being measured is clear, and why it matters. As we have seen, many economic debates which appear to be empirical, concerning the correct numerical value of some measurement, or how best to interpret some data, turn out to be disagreements about the value judgements which determine how a concept is defined and why it is important. At a deeper level, these disagreements lead to arguments about the stories (economists call them 'models') and theories used in structuring an economic analysis. My position is straightforward: different problems may require radically different tools, stories and theoretical frameworks. In other words, horses for courses.[18] 'Radically different' means that the theories may even contradict each other. This kind of intellectual diversity is the mark of any mature science such as physics – quantum mechanics and general relativity are fundamentally incompatible – and reflects a pragmatic response to the complexity of the phenomena being studied.

Since most orthodox economists now define economics in terms of a common method and theoretical framework, intellectual diversity is ruled out. Dissenting voices are banished *by definition*.[19] Even economists with a blue-blooded orthodox economics background are instantly cold-shouldered, or worse, the moment they adopt unorthodox research methods. Truman Bewley, an eminent Yale economic theorist, had been puzzling for years over the question, 'Why don't wages fall in a recession?' He stunned the profession by adopting a research method almost never used by economists in this field: interviewing business people to ask them why.[20] Bewley encountered great hostility from fellow economists. When asked whether he was training young economists at Yale to use interviews as a research method, he replied, 'No, that would ruin their careers.'[21]

These attitudes characterize intolerant dogma, not science. At least ideally, true science exhibits openness towards alternative theories and modes of analysis. In economics, more openness and tolerance is urgently needed in academic research and even more so in economics education and the policy-making world. This desirable tolerance in the practice of scientific research should not be confused with a postmodernist 'anything goes' attitude towards the truth. It does not imply settling for lazy incoherence, or deny the possibility of finding the truth, but implores openness and humility in searching for it.

Since orthodox economics adopts formal mathematical methods, it is supposed to be 'rigorous', while subjects like history and sociology are implicitly accused of lacking rigour. But rigour means 'the quality of being extremely thorough, exhaustive or accurate';[22] if anything, the in-depth case studies practised in history and sociology qualify better than the one-size-fits-all models of economics. At the very least, economics has no monopoly on rigour. Or as one wise economist put it, 'Mathematics brought rigor to Economics. Unfortunately, it also brought mortis.'[23] A related issue is the worry that if economics relaxes its insistence on mathematical methods, it will become simply a branch of history or sociology studying 'economic' phenomena. But there is a vast methodological space between the methods of historians and sociologists and those of formal mathematical economics. It consists of analysis which, although more abstract than much history and sociology, nevertheless resists the futile search for universal explanations, employing rich, context-specific descriptions instead. 'Abstract' here means that economic analysis is like a map, a simplification of reality, rather than a fictional story making idealized assumptions about the world, which everyone knows are false.[24]

Governments are not to be trusted

Some readers may suspect that I assume governments are always benign. It is true that I have devoted very little attention to whether governments can be trusted to *try* to develop good policies, or if instead politicians and bureaucrats are more interested in lining their own pockets. However, I have not explored other aspects of policy development either; no assumption of benign government is intended. Nevertheless, previous chapters suggest two lessons which bear on this issue. First, the traditional check on the self-interest of politicians and bureaucrats is democracy. It may be flawed, but it is all we have. One purpose of this book is to encourage these democratic checks by exposing the economics behind conventional political arguments to wider scrutiny. In particular, although some of the details of economic analysis are inevitably beyond the grasp of non-economists, the ethical judgements and assumptions behind economic policy recommendations can be grasped by most people. Making them explicit and bringing them into public debate should help to give us more understanding of, and so power over, the policies chosen in our name.

Second, there turns out to be a contradiction at the heart of the rationale for being suspicious of government. It should be no surprise by now that this rationale is the *Homo economicus* doctrine. The argument goes as follows. Since everyone is selfish, that includes politicians and bureaucrats. In a subdiscipline now often called 'political economics',[25] economists assume that politicians and bureaucrats will put their own private self-interest first, pursuing policies which directly or indirectly ensure re-election or greater wealth or status for themselves or their cronies. This leads these economists to a general skepticism about the possibility of beneficial government involvement in economy and society, and so a tendency to favour laissez-faire. Leave people alone to get on with their lives, because there is too much danger that state intervention will do more harm than good.

Now for the contradiction: applied consistently, this analysis undermines itself. The story so far forgets the economists themselves: we must assume that they are relentlessly selfish too. Economists cannot be trusted to provide unbiased advice, because they will be encouraging governments to adopt policies which favour them privately (such as tax cuts for the tax bracket in which the economist happens to fall). By the same logic, nor can we trust the academic economists proposing policies on the basis of a *Homo economicus* view of human behaviour, since they have a vested interest. These economists are guaranteed a helping of fame and fortune if their policy recommendations are adopted, regardless of whether the policies ultimately work. And the more distinctive and radical the policy, the more it is directly associated with the economists, and the more they stand to gain. And some of the recommendations of economists most closely associated with *Homo economicus* are very radical indeed.[26] So embracing the *Homo economicus* worldview involves a paradox, what philosophers call a 'performative contradiction'. To make it the basis of government policy requires that we trust a particular group of economists. But the *Homo economicus* doctrine itself suggests we should not trust them.

I am not suggesting that economists cannot be trusted. But a strict application of the *Homo economicus* doctrine leads us into a nihilistic world where nothing can be known for sure because no one can be trusted. Once we grant an exception to economists and decide to trust them, then we should be consistent and trust the politicians and bureaucrats (and everyone else) too. Of course we know that politicians are sometimes led astray by the prospect of private gain – but there is also evidence of academic scientists being similarly influenced.[27] There is no reason to believe academic economists are any different. In the real world, the *Homo economicus* doctrine is redundant. Our trust in someone is not blind and can be withdrawn, but life is hopeless if we are unwilling to grant it in the first place.

Economics has already changed for the better

Many economists accept some of the criticisms I have expressed about orthodox economics. But they turn this concession to their advantage, arguing that the criticisms apply to a version of economics which few economists now believe. In other words, my criticisms are outdated, redundant. Perhaps the strongest evidence in their favour lies in the recent explosive growth of behavioural economics. Behavioural economics tries to study how people actually behave, and takes seriously much of the psychological research into choice discussed in Chapter 2. It is true that the rise of behavioural economics has led to many of the old certainties – like assuming all economic actors are self-interested – being questioned. However, behavioural economics and other new developments in economics fall far short of rendering my arguments obsolete, for several reasons. First, although it represents a quiet revolution in economic thinking, the revolution is still in its early stages and relatively little has yet changed. Many economists have not changed their thinking at all and the arguments in this book may be met with derision or incomprehension. Critics of orthodox economics are rarely given a fair hearing. Canadian economist Bill Rees, who pioneered the influential 'ecological footprint' concept, was told by a senior colleague that his career would be 'nasty, brutish and short' if he persisted with his research into ecological limits to growth.[28] Another economist recently concluded: 'There is too much ideology... Economics is often a triumph of theory over fact... What I've learned is that anyone who says anything even obliquely that sounds hostile to free trade is treated as an apostate.'[29] These comments are striking because they come from Alan Blinder, Princeton economist and former vice chairman of the US Federal Reserve, hardly a hotbed of radicalism.

Second, even where behavioural economics has been enthusiastically adopted, it is easy to overstate the implications. As it stands, behavioural economics does not involve a radical critique of orthodox economics, more an attempt to incorporate some lessons from psychology into the orthodoxy. It is definitely not a merger of economics and psychology, but an attempted takeover of some psychological concepts which seeks to disrupt orthodox economics as little as possible. For instance, some psychologists have gone beyond rejecting the realism of *Homo economicus* to question whether it is a good model for how we ought to behave, but economists largely ignore this. And many self-proclaimed behavioural economists still regard phenomena such as altruism and framing effects[30] as *exceptions* to the general rule that people behave as orthodox economic theory predicts. Finally, few economists are willing to give up the idea of a single, grand overarching model of human behaviour, as befits their notion of what a science should look like. The model is 'optimization': people always act as if they are optimizing – maximizing or minimizing something. Much behavioural economics still rests on optimization and therefore cannot accommodate some of the most important insights from psychology and decision theory.[31] Psychology, the experimental science, has long since abandoned this one-size-fits-all framework as futile and settled for a series of overlapping (and inevitably somewhat incompatible) models and mechanisms.

Third, a little economics is a dangerous thing: the economics that most people know is limited solely to the orthodox version, whether propagated through undergraduate courses or *Freakonomics*. While new perspectives like behavioural economics are discussed in optional specialist courses, these are not taken by the majority of students who are not specializing in economics but nevertheless go on to (mis)use economics in government, business and the media. Behavioural economics is certain to remain at the margins rather than the core of the curriculum while economists maintain that it just deals with exceptional cases and define economics in terms of the mathematical methods required to study *Homo economicus*.

Fourth, there are large areas of economics research which are highly respected and regarded as 'cutting-edge', yet they remain as absurdly unrealistic as they ever were. Game theory is one example. It may be ideal for analysing the behaviour of 'players' in auctions or structured carbon trading markets, but because it assumes these players all act like *Homo economicus,* it makes some staggering assumptions. Game theory's universal assumption that everyone knows the rules of the game means much more than it seems: it means that everyone instantly knows all possible strategies which could logically be deduced from these rules. An analysis of chess in the spirit of game theory would assume that both the players are, at the very least, as good as top grandmasters.[32]

Fifth, unreconstructed unrealistic economics is not in decline but continues to spring up in new areas to which it is ill-suited, as though to confirm the charge of economic imperialism: political economics, for example, is a rapidly growing field.

Beyond these limitations, there is a crucial respect in which developments such as behavioural economics do not address the critique in this book. These developments have sought to help economics evolve a more realistic description of the world. But I have been mainly concerned not with this description itself but the basis for the policy recommend-ations which economists make. Recall David Hume's dictum – 'you cannot get an "ought" from an "is"'. To go from description to recommendation economists must add ethical judgements. These judgements have been the focus of this book, and behavioural economics has almost nothing to say about them. Almost, because insofar as these judgements depend on insights about individual economic behaviour, then behavioural economics may have an impact. Consider the discount rate again. As we saw in Chapter 6, economists choose an appropriate discount rate based on facts about interest rates, rates of 'time preference' (how impatient we are), and so on. Behavioural economics may influence this choice by providing insights about how impatient we really are. But this contribution does not affect my main argument: what is often presented as economic 'fact' – such as the relative balance of costs and benefits concerning a policy to reduce climate change – depends on various hidden, complex and controversial ethical judgements, including the choice of discount rate. And economists often speak of 'deriving' the discount rate, as though it were a neutral mathematical process of deduction, rather than one invoking various assumptions, not least the ethical judgement that individual impatience in private decision making is relevant to determining society's priorities.

Summing up, behavioural economics and other innovations in a similar spirit are not the answer, because large areas of economics research, and most economics teaching, looks set to continue to ignore them; economists' policy advice inevitably involves making judgements, not just establishing facts; besides, many apparent economic facts turn out to be judgements on closer inspection, and this tendency is enhanced by economists' temptation to assume people behave as economic theory says they *ought* to behave.

Finally, it is worth noting that although orthodox economics has not yet recognized the proper place of ethics, there are of course a number of great economists who have done so. In modern times, perhaps the leading example is Amartya Sen's *On Ethics and Economics,* in which he states, 'economics, as it has emerged, can be made more productive by paying greater and more explicit attention to the ethical considerations that shape human behaviour and judgement'.[33]

Beyond affluenza: There *is* an alternative

So how should we respond to the problems of 'affluenza' which opened this book? The defining mantra of veto economics is: 'there is no alternative'. So it is argued that there is no alternative to the kind of frantic economic lives we now lead and the problems of affluenza which accompany them. This is a book of ideas rather than detailed policies, so the remarks here are sketchy, but it is worth drawing together some strands of just one possible alternative which has emerged in preceding chapters. To begin with, Chapter 3 showed how economic growth comes in many forms, and a number of very different but realistic outcomes for economy and society are available, if we are serious about pursuing them.

There are many choices to make, but the most obvious one is between using the fruits of economic growth for more things, or less demanding work. In Britain, there is little doubt that work has become more demanding, even though basic contractual working hours for many have fallen.[34] Formal overtime and informal 'staying late' has increased, as well as longer commutes, more business travel and 'optional' weekend meetings. Nor is it just a matter of people spending longer away from home. Work itself has become more intense, less secure, and so more stressful. Truly 'free' time disappears as new technologies dissolve the boundary between work and non-work. And with the disappearance of standard working hours, workers struggle to share free time with the rest of their family, especially when all adults in the household are working. But none of this is inevitable. In Chapter 1, I noted that back in 1930 Keynes correctly predicted average economic growth in the UK through to the early 21st century. He went on to argue that this continuing economic growth means that radical changes in our way of life are both within our grasp and necessary for happiness.[35] He suggested that a 15-hour working week will become normal; this is not far-fetched, but achievable within 50 years while maintaining current real incomes using a plausible assumption of labour productivity growth at 2 per cent per annum. A ten-hour reduction in the working week is feasible within just ten years.[36]

It is often objected that if we use economic growth to work less rather than consume more, unemployment will rise. But there is no reason why this need be so. Part of the confusion arises because in this scenario measured growth would underestimate true, underlying economic growth.

Growth as currently measured in government statistics would fail fully to reflect underlying economic growth as economists understand it, since the statistics do not properly capture productivity gains turned into working time reductions. The argument runs that if measured growth is too low or negative, this means that less output is being produced, which implies that fewer working hours are needed to produce it. As economists put it, the *demand for labour* falls, so unemployment rises. But in our scenario, since people are already working less overall, the *supply of labour* will also fall, to offset the fall in demand. There is no reason why unemployment should rise.

Turning now to how a change in the nature of economic growth may be brought about, some of the proposals made by happiness economists look promising, even if we reject their commitment to quantifying happiness. The proposals aim to counterbalance the powerful psychological forces of adaptation and rivalry, both of which encourage us to use the fruits of growth to chase higher income, although it makes us no happier. To begin with, there is an obvious role for education to discourage futile status competition and explain how some truly valuable positional goods are, by their very positional nature, in intrinsically limited supply. Education can also be used positively to nurture a broader understanding of what it means to live a good life, rather than simply accumulating material wealth. To contemporary ears, this proposal may sound naive, but it has a distinguished ancestry in economics, stretching from Smith to Keynes to Galbraith. Besides, it has a realistic, practical side: education to give people the skills to play sport and musical instruments, to be creative, appreciate art and culture, and stimulate scientific curiosity. Of course these activities already form part of any enlightened modern education, but they have been increasingly sidelined in favour of the misguided and ineffective pursuit of education-as-job-training. Finally, we need not fear stagnation if people stop pursuing higher income so fervently. As noted in Chapter 7, status will always be a great motivator, and non-material forms of status, such as titles, honours and awards, can play an important role.

However, to make significant progress towards an alternative form of economic growth, more radical policies will be required. For instance, Richard Layard suggests restricting advertising because of the sterile positional competition over material goods that it encourages. Existing tax allowances for advertising could be cut, and advertising to children could be banned, as in Sweden. Layard also proposes discouraging performance-related pay because it promotes excessive rivalry and status competition between workers. This provides a further reason for limiting the use of performance-related pay, in addition to the erosion of trust argument in Chapter 7. But the main radical proposal, on which there is widespread agreement among happiness economists, is very simple. Tax should be increased to discourage the vicious circle of spending on material goods, and encourage us to devote more time to things which make us happier. The happiness economists disagree about whether higher tax should apply to all income (income tax) or just that part of income we spend (in the US sales tax; in Europe VAT), although the broad impacts are similar. As individuals we can independently choose to change our own priorities away from material excess, but I emphasized in Chapter 3 that much of our concern with relative income is not mere envy but a rational response to a world where so many important things are positional goods. So there is an essential role for government to lead and encourage a *coordinated* switch away from pure status goods.

Traditionally, economists worry that higher income taxes have a harmful distortionary effect on economic activity. But as argued in Chapter 4, some tax increases have little efficiency cost, because they counterbalance distortions already present, namely adaptation and rivalry. In economic terms, rivalry is like pollution (my gains in relative position have the side effect of harming yours) and adaptation is like addiction (I continue to chase higher income even though it does not make me happier). The economic case for taxing them is analogous to that for taxing pollution and addiction. There is an efficiency gain, not an efficiency loss. And once we step back and put the ethical economics of tax and spend in a wider context, Chapter 4 provides a further argument for why there may be no efficiency loss: a tax increase need not discourage work if people regard the public services it makes possible as a kind of payment in kind.

The argument that selective increases in taxation counterbalance the unhappy effects of adaptation and rivalry comes as a relief, and just in time, because the pressure on public expenditure is relentless. Baumol's cost disease (Chapter 3) showed that labour-intensive 'personalized' services are bound to become much more costly over time, relative to other goods and services, because they do not benefit from the huge productivity gains in other sectors, especially manufacturing. Both health care and education are perfect examples of services which are inevitably labour-intensive, partly because the idea of good quality in these sectors is so closely associated with personalized, labour-intensive treatment or teaching. If health care and education are to remain publicly funded, then taxes must rise. Before concluding that this is politically unacceptable, it cannot be overemphasized that health care, education and other personalized services will soon cost more, *regardless* of whether they are publicly or privately provided. We cannot avoid a bigger bill; higher taxation is simply one way to pay it. Baumol's cost disease implies taxation must rise merely to maintain the status quo. But most economists agree that there is a long-term trend in rich societies for demand for key public services to rise. This is hardly surprising. As we live longer, we need more health care. We work longer, and all adults in the household have a job, so more childcare is required. We seek additional educational qualifications in order to gain access to skilled jobs. The leisure pursuits made possible by rising affluence (such as travel, sport or arts and cultural visits) lead to demands for better transport infrastructure. And so on. However, Baumol's cost disease does not mean public services are unaffordable: true, they are becoming relatively more expensive than most other goods and services, but this is because many other goods and services have become so much cheaper. Public services like health care and education are still cheaper than in the past in an important, absolute sense – in terms of the hours of work required to pay for them. That is, they are cheaper, measured in terms of average earnings. Tax revenue from new sources – environmental taxes, or taxes to counterbalance adaptation and rivalry – can pay for rising demand. So an alternative future is available. It is not vetoed by economics. Instead, economics is central to mapping the possibilities and showing what is at stake.

Rediscovering ethical economics

In many ways, this has been a timid book. It starts from the language, framework and preoccupations of orthodox economics, because that is the only game in town. But it is a rigid language, an emaciated framework, and its preoccupations are overwhelmingly inward-looking. It is tempting to conclude that what is required is the complete rejection of orthodox economics, to be replaced with a new economics backed by a new ethical framework. But this heroic conclusion is not the only possibility. Simply by developing and building on themes within existing economics, we can reach radical conclusions and open up new worlds not admitted by veto economics. We need not overthrow orthodox economics entirely. My arguments attempt to synthesize and build on the work of many others.

The first step to rediscovering ethical economics is to show ethics is indispensable to economics and to uncover the hidden ethical assumptions behind contemporary worldviews. The second step is to ask how our economic lives might be different if we adopt different ethical starting points. To begin with, they demand that we reclaim language from orthodox economics. Words like 'efficient' and 'rational' must be recognized as denoting ethical judgements. Loaded language like 'tax burden' could be balanced by replacing 'public expenditure' with 'public benefits'. My aim above all has been to go beyond this language and equip you with an understanding of the ethics underpinning contemporary economic arguments. What you do with that understanding is up to you.

Notes

Chapter 1

1   'Perhaps' because (i) the total sales of some economics classics may be greater, simply because they have been around for so long; and (ii) *Freakonomics* may not count as an economics book.

2   I borrow this apt term from Paul Krugman, an influential American economist.

3   Coyle (2002), p226.

4   See especially Kasser (2002), James (2007).

5   Technical note. In the language of economics, I have argued that Pareto improvements are not necessarily good things because inequality may increase. A standard objection to this argument is that, when relative position matters, then absolute gains for all do not imply everyone is better off, if inequality has increased. So there is no Pareto improvement after all. My reply to this objection: this refinement of Pareto efficiency is rarely taught or mentioned in textbooks, and hardly ever discussed by applied economists. They talk of absolute gains for everyone as bringing about Pareto improvements, and Pareto improvements are almost universally regarded as unambiguously good. There is an understandable reason for this omission: everyone gaining in absolute terms is rare enough, without demanding that inequality does not rise too. Interpreting Pareto improvements as incorporating this extra condition would render them almost extinct – and much harder to measure. So in practice, the solution is not to refine the meaning of Pareto improvement, but to abandon the idea that it always represents a change to be welcomed.

6   Smith (1976 [1759]), p183.

7   Keynes (1931), p371.

8   On current trends, income per head in 2030 looks set to be right in the middle of the range predicted by Keynes in 1930. See Samuel Brittain, *Financial Times*, 3 January 2002.

9   See for example the UK Government's 2003 White Paper, *The Future of Air Transport* (available at www.dft.gov.uk/about/strategy/whitepapers/air/); MacLean and Jennings (2006).

10   Nobel Prize-winning economist, Milton Friedman, in Friedman (1953), p5.

Chapter 2

1   Easterly (2001), pxii.

2   Stigler (1981).

3   Tullock (1976). Economist Gordon Tullock was co-author with Nobel Laureate James Buchanan in much of his prize-winning work.

4   James (2007).

5   Johnson and Goldstein (2003).

6   Based on an example in Kahneman and Tversky (2000), p12.

7   See Nisbet and Ross (1980), cited in Schwartz (2004), p59.

8   Schwartz (2004), p54.

9   See Kahneman and Thaler (2006) and Loewenstein and Schkade (1999).

10   Nisbett and Kanouse (1968).

11   Unpublished research cited in Kahneman and Thaler (2006), p224.

12   DellaVigna and Malmendier (2006).

13   This thought experiment was conducted by Hsee (2000). My own experience confirms it.

14   Redelmeier and Kahneman (1996).

15   Offer (2006) provides a rich historical survey.

16   See for example his article in *The Guardian*, 15 May 2007.

17   There are many other psychological phenomena that challenge the economic view of choice, in addition to those just discussed. For surveys see Frey and Benz (2004) and Rabin (2002).

18   As argued influentially in Hahn and Hollis (1979), Ch 1.

19   This approach to consumer theory was first proposed by Lancaster (1966).

20   Interview with Sir John Krebs, then Director of the Food Standards Agency, *Prospect*, April 2005.

21   Becker and Murphy (1988). We will soon meet Gary Becker's striking ideas again.

22   Ralph Waldo Emerson, 'Wealth' in *The Conduct of Life* (1860), Boston, Ticknor and Fields.

23   Karl Marx (1847) *Wage Labour and Capital*, Ch 6.

24   Frederick and Loewenstein (1999), Barber (2007).

25   Brickman et al (1978). See also Frederick and Loewenstein (1999), p312, who cite a large number of studies reaching the same conclusions.

26   Loewenstein and Schkade (1999), p90.

27   Schkade and Kahneman (1998).

28   Frank (1999), Ch 6; Frederick and Loewenstein (1999) Clark, et al (2008).

29   Van Praag and Frijters (1999).

30   Frank (1999), Ch 6.

31   Frederick and Loewenstein (1999), pp314–317.

32   See deBotton (2004) and Marmot (2004).

33   For balanced discussion of various aspects of this debate see Anand (1993a), Schmid (2004), Hargreaves-Heap et al (1992) and Hausman and McPherson (2006).

34   Note for economists: it might be objected that behavioural economics is beginning to influence the entire profession. But this conclusion seems premature; for example, orthodox game theory remains highly influential, but it uses a model of choice untouched by behavioural economics. In any case there remains a huge gap between the view of choice implicit in most behavioural economics, and that espoused by psychologists, a point emphasized by Kahneman in the conclusion to his Nobel lecture: Kahneman (2003), p1469.

35   Morgan et al (2006) and Varian (2003) are examples. In some universities, economics students can learn about the psychological critique in specialist courses, but these are almost always optional. And these specialist courses are rarely offered to the much larger group taking economics as just one part of a broader degree in business, social science or

public policy. The result is that the default view is all that is studied by the vast majority of students who do not go on to become academic economists, but use economics more informally – and influentially – in government, business and the media.

36 Milgrom and Roberts (1992).

37 Becker (1996).

38 Kay (2004), p186.

39 An early study was Hornstein et al (1968). In recent experiments conducted for the Reader's Digest, the lowest rate of return was 57 per cent (in Asian countries), rising to more than 70 per cent in Scandinavia.

40 See Rowthorn (1996) for discussion and full Hayek references.

41 My analysis here follows Hausman and McPherson (2006), p80.

42 The game was originated by Güth et al (1982). See Fehr (2000) and Fehr and Fischbacher (2003) for authoritative surveys of the ultimatum game and related research.

43 Elster (1999), Ch 4; Nussbaum (2001).

44 Based on Elster (1999), p303.

45 The two economists were Uri Gneezy and Aldo Rustichini. See Gneezy and Rustichini (2000). It is impossible to tell from their paper whether they expected the fine to work or not, although throughout they view behaviour from the perspective of orthodox economics. For instance, they understand the restraining role of social norms in strictly ball-and-chain terms (Gneezy and Rustichini [2000], p13, note 12).

46 Gneezy and Rustichini also mention the social norm 'once a commodity, always a commodity' as another possible explanation of the parents' behaviour. (After the fine is removed, the opportunity to collect children late is seen as a commodity available for free, and hence heavily demanded.) But they do not acknowledge the great difficulty in reconciling this norm with orthodox economics.

47 Levitt and Dubner (2005), p13.

48 Levitt and Dubner (2005), p20.

49 Levitt and Dubner (2005), p21.

50 Titmuss (1970).

51 This interpretation draws on Singer (1973). Arrow (1972) is a Nobel Laureate economist's famous critique of Titmuss.

52 See Upton (1973) and Schwartz (1990).

53 Deci et al (1999) survey 128 psychological studies and reach this conclusion. Frey and Meier (2005) does the same for 16 economic studies.

54 Frey et al (1996), Frey and Oberholzer-Gee (1997).

55 Bewley (1995).

56 The most influential research has been Marwell and Ames (1981), Frank et al (1993) and Frank et al (1996). Against this, Frey and Meier (2005) concluded that learning economics does *not* make students more selfish; they are already more selfish than average when they begin their undergraduate degree. But Frey did not allow for differing degrees of previous exposure to economics; besides, this 'selection effect' is hardly reassuring. Put crudely, it suggests that selfish people who want to go through life exploiting every opportunity, regardless of the cost to others, gain the training to pursue their ambition.

57 Economists should not be surprised by this debasement of their doctrine. Some have even encouraged it, as shown by the epigraphs to this chapter.

58 Frey (1997).

59   Hausman and McPherson (2006), p61; I draw on their discussion in what follows.

60   Becker (1993), p391.

61   Extreme versions of Ayer's emotivism might be one example. See Ayer (1936).

62   Hausman and McPherson (2006), p74.

63   See especially Goodin (1986) and Griffin (1986).

64   The issues raised in this paragraph are controversial ones. See Goodin (1986), Griffin (1986), Nagel (1986) and Scanlon (1975) for some of the more important contributions to an ongoing philosophical debate. I return to these issues in Chapter 5.

65   Conlisk (1996) provides an introduction to the regress problem.

66   The psychological research reported in the next few paragraphs is described in more detail in Schwartz (2004). His excellent book has strongly influenced my discussion of these problems.

67   Tversky and Shafir (1992).

68   Redelmeier and Shafir (1995).

69   Cited in Schwartz (2004), p142.

70   Schwartz (2004), Ch 10.

71   Schwartz (2004), p213.

72   Hesse-Biber (1997).

73   Levett (2003), Ch 5.

74   As well as the psychological evidence that our sovereign choices can make us miserable (e.g. self-control problems, addictive and competitive shopping, selfish behaviour erodes the trust and esteem of others), there is direct evidence that people who act more like *Homo economicus* are more likely to suffer from depression. See Schwartz et al (2002).

75   Damasio (1994), pp193–194.

Chapter 3

1   Jevons (1911), p14.

2   Pigou (1951), p292.

3   The argument is in the spirit of Pigou's retort to Jevons (previous note) – ordinary life could not proceed without interpersonal comparisons. If we need to look into other people's minds to discover how happy they are, then it seems we need to do so to understand what they say, too. The most influential analysis here is Donald Davidson's, who argues that we manage to understand each other by adopting a 'principle of charity': we assume that other people, like us, are trying to talk sense and understand them accordingly. The problem of interpersonal comparability of utility is resolved in a similar way. See Davidson (1986).

4   There is a strong consensus on this conclusion. For three very different analyses that all endorse this view, see Hamilton (2004), Layard (2005) and Clark et al (2008).

5   Blanchflower and Oswald (2004), Easterlin (2005).

6   Layard (2005), annex 3.1, available at http://cep.lse.ac.uk/layard/annex.pdf

7   Easterlin (2001).

8   Frey and Stutzer (2002).

9   Layard (2005).

10   US General Social Survey.

11   European Eurobarometer Survey.

12 Diener et al (1995).

13 Layard (2005), pp51–52.

14 Marmot (2004).

15 Mental illness is very difficult to measure over time, because of problems of definition, and changes in perception and diagnosis. But there is persuasive evidence that depression and mental illness rates have been rising steeply in Diener and Seligman (2004) and Layard (2005), Annex 'Mental Health' available at http://cep.lse.ac.uk/layard/annex.pdf. See also Hamilton (2004).

16 Hamilton (2004).

17 At the time of writing, a working paper by Stevenson and Wolfers (2008) uses new data analysis to argue that growth *is* associated with rising happiness. It has received much attention, not just among academics, but in mainstream media, including two articles in *The Financial Times*. (It is hard to believe that a paper arguing that money does *not* buy happiness would have received so much attention in the business press.) It is much too early to reject the emerging consensus (the three empirical conclusions) on the basis of one unpublished paper. In Chapter 5, I question the international comparisons on which Stevenson and Wolfers rely. In any case, they acknowledge that the US is an exception to their results, still showing declining happiness despite long periods of growth. And they emphasize that they have no evidence of whether growth causes increased happiness. In fact, part of any correlation between growth and happiness is likely to be due to happiness causing growth, not the other way round: there is robust evidence that happier people tend to have higher future incomes (Dolan et al [2008], p97). As I argue below and in Chapter 5, even if we ignore the direct evidence of happiness economics, the combination of psychological evidence, philosophical reflection and economic arguments concerning the inadequacy of GDP as a measure of well-being together form a strong presumption against growth leading to increased happiness.

18 For all the evidence mentioned in this paragraph see Frank (1997, 1999, 2004), who cites many different studies, but see especially Koslowsky et al (1995).

19 Frank (2004), p75.

20 Frank (1999), Ch 6.

21 For the evidence, see Frank (1999), Ch 6.

22 See the studies cited below, and also Stutzer (2003), Easterlin (2001).

23 Clark and Oswald (1996).

24 Clark (1996), quoted in Layard (2005), p45.

25 Neumark and Postlewaite (1998).

26 Slonick and Hemenway (1998).

27 Alpizar et al (2005).

28 Many happiness economists appear implicitly to assume status explains the concern with relative consumption; they often do not enquire into the reasons for this concern, but when they do so, refer to status, and rarely if ever to positional goods. And some recent interpretations – Brekke et al (2003) – of Hirsch's seminal work mention only the pure status-seeking type of positional good, ignoring the other forms social scarcity. For a critique of these interpretations see Lintott (2005).

29 Barber (2007), Chs 5 and 6.

30 Harrod told Tibor Scitovsky. See Scitovsky's foreword to Hirsch (1995). Scitovsky was responsible for introducing Hirsch to Harrod's obscure paper and encouraging him to develop it.

31   Adapted from Figure 1, Hirsch (1995), p21.

32   Hirsch (1995), p22.

33   Hirsch (1995), p6.

34   Dolan et al (2008), p98.

35   Baumol (1967).

36   Former US Senator Daniel Patrick Moynihan is a notable exception among politicians; see Moynihan (1993).

37   For some clear data on rising education and health costs, and a good introduction to Baumol's cost disease, see Baumol (2001). More recent data and discussion of US health care costs is in Krugman and Wells (2006).

38   Cox (2006) offers a provocative discussion.

39   For diverse evidence and research methods that all support this conclusion, see ten Raa and Schettkat (2001).

40   Baumol (1967).

41   See Baumol (2001), Krugman and Wells (2006).

42   Economic growth requires increased output per hour worked, or more hours worked, either through longer working hours, or more workers. Assuming a stable population and constant working hours, there is an essential connection between growth and labour productivity. As Paul Krugman puts it: 'Productivity isn't everything, but in the long run it is almost everything' (Krugman [1997], p11). Note that an expanding population may ensure growth without productivity improvements, but it will also increase the demand for public services.

43   Moller (2001). Technical note: more precisely, whether the services sector takes a growing share of output depends on the price elasticity of demand for its products, their income elasticity, and the ratio of productivity in the services sector to economy-wide productivity. Intuitively if, say, demand grows strongly with income but is insensitive to price increases (and service productivity lags behind), then the net effect of economic growth will be a rise in demand for the service, despite a higher price. There is much evidence that this outcome (high income elasticity and low price elasticity) holds for education and health in the US. See for instance Ryan (1992).

44   Triplett and Bosworth (2003, 2005).

45   For recent evidence from US health care for this 'two service sectors' argument, see Frogner (2008).

46   See for example Krugman and Wells (2006).

47   Baumol (2001), p24.

48   This ignores so-called 'fiscal drag' arising from tax-free allowances and higher-rate tax thresholds remaining unchanged in the face of rising incomes, so that a larger proportion of income is in fact taken in tax (another way of seeing this is to realize that the value of the tax-free allowance falls in real terms). I ignore this possibility because it raises relatively little additional revenue, and is in any case best understood as a hidden increase in tax rates.

49   Baumol (1993), p22.

50   Baumol (1993), p25.

Chapter 4

1   For example, in both the UK and US, marginal income tax rates have fallen in recent years.

2   This section draws heavily on Murphy and Nagel (2002).

3   Traditional public finance economics focuses on various principles of 'vertical equity' in the distribution of tax burdens, all of which take the ownership principle for granted. For example, the ability-to-pay principle of 'equal sacrifice' holds that fair taxation is that which extracts an equal sacrifice, measured from a baseline of pre-tax incomes. These principles of vertical equity make two faulty assumptions: they assume the pre-tax baseline is morally significant; and they examine the distribution of tax burdens in isolation, ignoring the benefits of government, paid for by taxation. The flaws in these assumptions will be explained below.

4   Murphy and Nagel (2002), p8.

5   For a philosophical discussion of whether ownership of pre-tax income is really 'impossible' or just 'impossible in practice', see Sterba (2004).

6   Nozick (1974), pxi.

7   Epstein (1985) may be a contemporary exception.

8   See Holmes and Sunstein (1999) for detailed discussion.

9   Murphy and Nagel (2002), p75.

10 Locke, *Second Treatise of Government*, 1690. A modern edition is Locke (1988).

11 Of course Locke's argument is much more sophisticated than the compressed version above, and has been subject to many different interpretations. A modern restatement is in Nozick (1974); see Kymlicka (2002) for an introduction to the debates.

12 Murphy and Nagel (2002), p33.

13 Blum and Kalven (1952), p517, quoted in Murphy and Nagel (2002), p25.

14 Blum and Kalven (1952), p517, quoted in Murphy and Nagel (2002), p25.

15 Fabian Society (2000), p45.

16 For a balanced survey of such arguments, see Slemrod and Bakija (2008), Ch 4.

17 See Slemrod (1995) for further details.

18 Showalter and Thurston (1997).

19 An introduction to the empirical research is in Stiglitz (2000), Ch 19; Heckman (1993) offers a survey.

20 Historically, tax changes were more likely to affect work incentives for women because of the effect of childcare and related costs. If after-tax income fell by say, 5 per cent because of a tax increase, the percentage change in true net income (after allowing for childcare costs) would be greater: the same absolute fall, but expressed as a percentage of the smaller net income figure. Effectively, the tax change is magnified. There are other 'second-earner' factors too. However, there is now less evidence of women-specific factors than in the past.

21 There may be other undesirable economic effects of tax increases beyond the scope of the discussion here, including various forms of tax avoidance, and reduced take-up of education and training. For a recent survey see Meghir and Phillips (2009).

22 That is, little impact assuming developed economy incomes and tax changes of the magnitudes common in recent years.

23 The substitution effect measures the extent of the distortion: the extent to which one activity is substituted for another – i.e. pre-tax behaviour is distorted – in response to an

income tax increase. If Peter carries on working as hard after the tax increase, this implies that the income effect fully offsets the substitution effect, not that the substitution effect is small. Both effects could be large, yet the amount of work undertaken is unchanged, because they cancel each other out. See Stiglitz (2000), Ch 19.

24   The metaphor originated with Okun (1975).

25   See Stiglitz (2000), Chs 19, 20.

26   This is true even of some versions of libertarianism.

27   This step in more detail: I emphasized that the distortionary effects of income taxation are defined against the baseline impact of a poll tax, which imposes no distortion because there is nothing people can do to reduce their liability to it. We saw that income taxes have a substitution effect; poll taxes do not, because they do not affect the relative prices of different economic activities. In contrast, the income effect is common to all taxes, since they all reduce our income. So the difference between the two types of tax is the substitution effect. But since the poll tax is the baseline, this difference measures the distortion caused by income tax. That is, inefficiency is measured by the magnitude of the substitution effect.

28   Stiglitz (2000), p562.

29   Proposals for a citizens' income usually involve the abolition of all standard exemptions from income tax. Suppose there is a citizens' income of $16,000, combined with a basic rate of tax of 40 per cent. Someone earning only $24,000 would pay the full 40 per cent in tax ($9600) but receive the $16,000 grant, leaving them better off overall by $6400. Someone earning $60,000 would pay $24,000 in tax, less $16,000: a net tax bill of $8000.

30   For more details see Stiglitz (2000), Ch 20, or, much more advanced, Atkinson and Stiglitz (1980).

31   Raventos (2007) makes a powerful case for a citizens' income.

32   Layard (2005), Ch 10. See also Hirsch (1995) and Frank (1999).

33   This section owes a great deal to Serena Olsaretti's detailed recent analysis of whether market rates of pay are deserved, presented in Olsaretti (2004), although parts of my argument are very different.

34   High-to-medium income male, Banbury, Conservative: Fabian Society (2000), p53.

35   Rawls (1999), p89.

36   A major modern statement of the contribution argument is Feinberg (1970); a sophisticated recent development is Lamont (1997).

37   In theory at least, free market employers do not discriminate: if Ann and Bill perform the job equally well, they will be paid the same.

38   Technical note. This claim might seem stronger than we need. It might seem that 'people deserve to be paid more if they contribute more' would suffice. However, this latter premise could justify only the pattern of pay inequality we see, *not* its extent. And it is the stronger claim in the text that is invoked by philosophers defending pay inequality on the basis of desert, including Miller (1999) and Riley (1989).

39   This seems to be Rawls' view. Feldman (1995) disagrees, offering the example of the mother who deserves our sympathy, because her child has just died, although she is not responsible for the death. But this is a different form of desert, not about whether we deserve credit or reward, which is the only kind of desert that justifies higher pay. Our sympathy might lead us to say that the mother deserves to be given time off or a reduced workload because of her bereavement. It would be very odd to say she deserved to be paid more.

40 See Dick (1975) for further discussion of the difficulties.
41 See Wolff (2003) and Moriarty (2005).
42 Rawls (1999), p89.
43 Sher (2003) shows how hard it is to define effort in a way that leaves it entirely within our control.
44 Frey (1997).
45 Fehr and Gachter (2000).
46 That is, cognitive dissonance is reduced once it is recognized that tax brings benefits as well as being unavoidable.
47 Torgler (2007).

Chapter 5

1 John Adams, second President of the United States. In Adams (1850–1856), p193.
2 Kahneman (1999), p22.
3 Kahneman (1999), p3.
4 See Frey and Stutzer (2007) for further details and full references.
5 Davidson et al (2000), Davidson (2000, 2004). Throughout, for the sake of simplicity in summarizing the neuroscience, I only describe results for right-handed people.
6 Coghill et al (2003).
7 Inglehart (1990).
8 Shao (1993).
9 Uttal (2001).
10 Uttal (2001).
11 See Farah (1994), Adolphs (2003) and Tingley (2006).
12 Veenhoven (2000).
13 This paragraph and the next two draw heavily on Wierzbicka (2004). See also her excellent book, Wierzbicka (1999).
14 Sokol (1997), cited in Wierzbicka (2004), p43.
15 The evidence on brain activity does not help either. Suppose that people in, say, East European nations have on average relatively dominant right sides (to use my terminology above), while Americans are relatively dominant on the left side. (I know of no research that demonstrates this, but suppose it is true.) These differences may be due to socialization in more or less cheerful societies over a period of time, rather than intrinsic differences in happiness.
16 Bentham (1789), quoted in Warnock (1962), p34.
17 Kahneman (1999), pp4–5.
18 Schwarz and Strack (1999) provide a detailed discussion.
19 Schwarz et al (1987)
20 Strack et al (1988).
21 Redelmeier and Kahneman (1996).
22 Kahneman (1999), p20.
23 Strack et al (1990).
24 Stone et al (1999), Kahneman et al (2004).
25 Annas (2004), pp45–46.
26 Kahneman (1999), p21.

27   Kahneman (1999), p15.

28   Kahneman (1999), p21.

29   Even if we grant that happiness is purely an empirical question of psychology, non-evaluative empirical investigation cannot alone *define* happiness. As the psychological literature shows, the candidate theories range from life satisfaction to affective state theories, via hedonism. They are too many and diverse for empirical research alone to pick one out. Empirical investigators need to know where to look before they can uncover any psychological facts. For example, the neuroscience discussed above assumes not just that 'feeling happy' is a localized brain process, but that happiness should be defined in terms of such momentary feelings. See Haybron (2000).

30   See for instance Frank (1997), p1833; Frey and Stutzer (2007); Kahneman et al (1999), preface; Layard (2005), pp232–236.

31   Two philosophical clarifications: (i) following Bentham, the happiness experts treat good (bad) feelings and pleasures (pains) interchangeably; (ii) it is unclear whether the happiness experts require a good feeling or pleasure to be desired for it to count as promoting happiness. The following discussion ignores the issues raised by (i) and (ii); nothing in my argument depends on them. But see Crisp (2007).

32   Nozick (1974), pp42–43.

33   Layard (2005), p114.

34   Hamilton and Rush (2006). I am grateful to Clive Hamilton for making me aware of this survey.

35   Layard (2005), pp112–113.

36   Haybron (2000), p208.

37   Nussbaum (2004), p68.

38   In a recent defence of the version of happiness espoused by the happiness experts, Crisp (2007) argues that Mill's higher pleasures can be reconciled with that approach: there is just one kind of feeling that matters (enjoyable experience). But even if this is true, since Crisp recognizes that Mill's higher pleasures can be 'discontinuously more valuable' (p633) than other pleasures, the incomparability problem remains.

39   Layard (2005), p260, emphasis added.

40   Layard (2005), p123.

41   Layard (2005), p23.

42   Layard (2005), p122.

43   Biswas-Diener et al (2004), p24. Layard and Kahneman also reach to these correlations in attempting to widen the appeal of targeting self-reported happiness (e.g. Layard [2005], p23), even though Layard in particular insists it is the ultimate goal.

44   Parfit (1984), Appendix I.

45   Ryff and Keyes (1995), Ryan and Deci (2001), Keyes et al (2002).

46   See the debate between Diener et al (1998) and Ryff and Singer (1998). My objection to the PWB approach is more basic: I believe it escapes few of the criticisms I make of standard happiness psychology. In short, PWB is anti-democratic in the way it leaves little role for politics; its focus on quantification leads to numerical measures of happiness not readily open to assessment by non-specialists; and it is too personal, focusing on the good life for an individual, rather than public ethics (see below). Finally, there is some evidence that PWB indexes of happiness are well correlated with self-reported happiness – this reinforces my view that PWB is much less of a real alternative to self-reported happiness than it might first appear.

47 Nussbaum (2004), pp65–66.

48 For a clear concise analysis that reaches this conclusion, see Parfit (1984), Appendix I.

49 See in particular Goodin (1995), Chs 1 and 4.

50 There is increasing anthropological support for this claim – see in particular Brown (1991).

51 For a detailed attempt to specify a comprehensive list of capabilities and what they involve, see Nussbaum (2000).

52 There are of course some more theoretical arguments in favour of hybrid theories. Here are two. First, adaptation is a problem with the Greatest Happiness principle. The classic example comes from Sen's work on underdeveloped countries: the very poor in those countries are so accustomed to poverty and oppression that their self-reported happiness may not be especially low; providing relatively small increases in income to such people might bring large improvements in their self-reported happiness. This might exhaust our responsibilities to such people under the Greatest Happiness principle, even though they remain cripplingly poor. Layard's response to this argument is that adaptation to wealth is even more powerful, which is why transfers from rich to poor will typically increase the sum of happiness. So the Greatest Happiness principle 'is inherently pro-poor' (Layard [2005], p120). But this provides a counterbalancing effect; it does not address the essential problem. Adaptation implies that someone born rich who has recently suffered an unexpected financial loss, taking them down to an average income, should be taxed less than someone who has always received an average income, because the former person will not have adapted to their new circumstances and so will miss money more. This confounds our intuition. The hybrid theories escape these problems because our basic needs (or our perfect preferences) for income are quite similar, so the very poor warrant increased resources even while they are accustomed to their circumstances. Second, there is the problem of 'interpersonal comparability' mentioned in Chapter 3. Happiness economics assumes, roughly, that a two-point improvement in my happiness index is equivalent to a two-point improvement in yours, so that even if a policy involves both winners and losers, we can calculate the overall effect on happiness. But many philosophers have long argued we cannot perform these interpersonal comparisons without getting inside another's head, experiencing feelings as others do – and this is impossible. If interpersonal comparability is a problem, then it is not one the hybrid theories face. The focus on perfect preferences or basic interests switches attention away from people's heads towards the properties of goods. See Goodin (1991), pp245–246.

53 Layard (2005), pp122–123.

54 This paragraph is heavily influenced by Goodin (1995).

55 Again, Layard is more explicit than other happiness economists and psychologists, but since they cite him approvingly, it is fair to assume they do not substantially disagree. An exception is Frey and Stutzer (2007), who reject the goal of maximizing national happiness. I agree with some of their reasons – such as the exclusion of politics and Goodhart's Law (see below) – but disagree with their suggested alternative, which appears to be 'the best possible fulfilment of individual preferences' (p16). Nor is it clear why they endorse the use of happiness data to influence the reform of constitutional and political institutions, but not to determine public policy itself.

56 Dolan et al (2008), p107.

57 Oswald (2005).

58 And should they ignore the happiness of non-humans as well? There is growing evidence

that it is meaningful to talk of the happiness of non-humans, especially the higher apes, and some philosophers see few reasons for giving it less significance. See for example Cavalieri and Singer (1995).

59   Goodhart (1975).
60   And the more exacting the measurement, and the shorter the timescale over which measurement takes place, the greater the energy of the disturbance and the greater the unpredictability of the outcome.
61   Andrew Oswald, *Financial Times*, 17 March 2005.
62   Layard (2005), p180.
63   Di Tella et al (2001).
64   Layard (2005), p152.

Chapter 6

1   Lomborg (2004).
2   Quoted in Hausman and McPherson (1996), p9.
3   Pearce et al (2003), pp136–137.
4   Ackerman and Heinzerling (2004), p73.
5   Terry Barker, in oral evidence to the House of Lords Economic Affairs Committee, 22 February 2005; House of Lords (2005), II, 78–86.
6   House of Lords (2005), I, §101, 102, 105, 168–170.
7   House of Lords (2005), I, §111, 116, 171–174.
8   Stern (2007), p163.
9   Stern (2007), pxv.
10   See especially Stern (2007), pp35–37, 50–54, 59–60.
11   House of Lords (2005) I, §39–41, 153–154.
12   Stern (2007), pp37–39.
13   In 2000 prices. *Federal Register*, 22 January 2001 (66): 7012.
14   Dorman (1996), especially Ch 3.
15   As demonstrated by Sunstein (2005), p135.
16   Two examples of Viscusi's work. First, smokers die young, which according to Viscusi, saves the state money because of lower health care costs. Viscusi (1995) concluded that if 'taken at face value', then 'cigarette smoking should be subsidized rather than taxed' (quoted in Ackerman and Heinzerling [2004], p72). Second, Viscusi (1998) argued that since people spend about 10 per cent of extra income on risk reduction, if income falls, less will be spent on risk reduction. Viscusi concluded that environmental regulations that cost $50 million in national income will lead to a $5 million fall in risk reduction expenditure, which he then interpreted as 'one lost life' on the basis of his other work.
17   See Ackerman and Heinzerling (2004). Dorman (1996) develops a detailed critique of the wage differentials approach.
18   Broome (1978).
19   Posner (2004), pp165–170, discussed approvingly by Sunstein (2005), pp160–161. Neither Posner nor Sunstein seem to realize that this example reveals a general flaw with valuing life in terms of risk, not just one applying to small probabilities of catastrophe.
20   Paul Slovic, perhaps the leading psychologist in the field, has summarized his research in Slovic (2000).

21   Breyer (1993).
22   Ackerman and Heinzerling (2004), p128.
23   Classically, by Mishan (1977). More recently, by Sunstein (2005).
24   HM Treasury (2003), Annex 2, p63. This is the figure in 2000 prices, and apparently includes gross lost output, medical and ambulance costs.
25   For example, this is a recurrent theme among many of the contributions to Adler and Posner (2001) and Layard and Glaister (1994).
26   Sunstein (2005), p131.
27   Metz et al (2001), p483. Available at www.grida.no/climate/ipcc_tar/wg3/302.htm. The $1 million value of life is in 1999 prices.
28   Griffin (1977), p54.
29   Costanza et al (1997).
30   Pearce (2007) includes a succinct critique.
31   For a balanced account see Houghton (2004), especially Ch 9.
32   Shrader-Frechette (1985), p48.
33   See for example, Shrader-Frechette (1985), Hahn (1996), Pearce (2000), and in the context of climate change alone, Metz et al (2001), p460.
34   This example is taken from Ackerman and Heinzerling (2004), p137.
35   Some Bayesians take a different 'objective' view of probability, but the 'subjective' view described here dominates orthodox economics.
36   Anand (1993b) and Hargreaves-Heap et al (1992) introduce the Paradox, and the general debate about Bayesianism.
37   Stern (2007), p39.
38   The most well-known philosophical critiques are those of Rawls (1971) and Parfit (1984).
39   Price (1993), p100 offers a good summary of their views.
40   Ramsey (1928).
41   There are tentative signs of a shift in the consensus. The *Stern Review* rejects the argument for pure time preference based on impatience. However, it still assumes a small degree of pure time preference, arguing that there is a non-trivial probability that the human race may not recognizably survive into the distant future, because of catastrophes such as a meteorite impact or devastating nuclear war. The Review assumes pure time preference equivalent to the human race facing an almost 1 in 10 chance of extinction within 100 years, which seems implausibly large if this is really the only justification. See Stern (2007), pp35–36, 53.
42   This is a simplification. If it is believed that (a) some forms of life saving are worth less (such as saving the lives of the very old, or those with a low remaining life expectancy); and (b) we can in practice systematically prioritize those lives that are more worth saving, then additional lives saved in the future will on average be worth progressively less. But both (a) and (b) are controversial. There are other complications too. See Broome (1999), pp61–63.
43   For UK practice, see HM Treasury (2003). A good discussion of US practice is found in Ackerman and Heinzerling (2004), Ch 8. The *Stern Review* is an important recent exception; it explicitly recommends lower discount rates for goods such as non-renewable resources, and acknowledges that in some cases the appropriate rate might even be negative. See Stern (2007), pp35–37, 57–60.
44   This version of the argument that future generations are disenfranchised draws heavily on Broome (1999), Ch 4.

45   Weitzman (1998), p202.

46   Weitzman (2001).

47   HM Treasury (2003). A report for the Office of the Deputy Prime Minister explicitly recommended declining discount rates as a response to the philosophical objections: OXERA (2002), p13. The *Stern Review* shares this conclusion, although for different reasons. See Stern (2007), pp35–37, 56–57.

48   Pearce et al (2003) provide an introduction to the field.

49   Li and Löfgren (2000).

50   For example, many versions of the argument assume that our future on earth is infinite, not finite. Most physicists would regard this as a mistake. For detailed discussion and critique of these sacrifice arguments see Broome (1992).

51   Cowan and Parfit (1992) and Parfit (1984), Appendix F, untangle the confusions clearly.

52   Frederick et al (2002).

53   To gain a sense of the level of detail required in CBA, and hence the ad hoc assumptions that are made, consider the valuation of time associated with transport projects. The UK Department of Transport assumes, among other things, that time spent sitting in a traffic jam is less unpleasant (i.e. less costly) than time spent walking or waiting at a bus stop. Obviously the effect is to favour cars over other modes of travel. See HM Treasury (2003), Annex 2.

54   Sunstein (2005), Ch 1 is a recent critique.

55   There is support for this version of the precautionary principle from lawyers (Sunstein, 2005), philosophers, (Rawls, 1971), economists, both critical (Ackerman and Heinzerling, 2004) and more mainstream (Woodward and Bishop, 1997), and sociologists, geographers, policy scientists and others (O'Riordan and Cameron, 2002).

56   See also Sen (2001) and Richardson (2001).

57   For a comprehensive, persuasive critique see Nord (1999).

58   This remark is widely attributed to Keynes, although in Keynes' lifetime it was attributed by Gerald Shove to one Wildon Carr. See Shove (1942). I thank Geoff Harcourt for this information.

59   In response to objections to discounting, David Pearce asserts 'not discounting is formally equivalent to discounting at a particular number which happens to be zero per cent' (Pearce et al [2003], p124). 'Formally equivalent' means that the two are treated interchangeably.

60   Office of Management and Budget (attached to the White House), 1990–1991, quoted in Ackerman and Heinzerling (2004), p189.

Chapter 7

1   £100 was still a lot of money at the time. This famous exchange involving Shaw may nevertheless be apocryphal. There appears to be no agreed source.

2   This example is found in Andre (1995).

3   Schwartz (2004), p32.

4   Public Administration Select Committee Inquiry 'Choice, Voice and Public Services' (2004–2005): Memorandum 'The Case for User Choice in Public Services,' p5.

5   British Medical Journal online survey, quoted in Coulter (2002), pxi.

6   For example, concerning the choice of hospital by patients, one authoritative summary

of recent research states: 'Evidence from UK pilot schemes in which there was direct choice indicates that choice was widely taken up and exercised by all types of patient. But the scheme was precisely targeted and individuals given financial compensation for travel. Evidence from the Nordic countries and France suggests that without this financial compensation, richer individuals are more likely to exercise choice' (Burgess et al [2005]), p10).

7   'Choice emerges as both a means of introducing the right incentives for improving services for users, and as a desirable outcome in and of itself: that is, it is both intrinsically and instrumentally valuable.' Public Administration Select Committee Inquiry 'Choice, Voice And Public Services' (2004–2005): Memorandum 'The Case For User Choice In Public Services', p3.

8   Le Grand (1990) first introduced the language, but his most detailed analysis is Le Grand (2003), with some more recent evidence added in Le Grand (2007).

9   Thaler and Sunstein (2008), Ch 10.

10 Reported in Krugman and Wells (2006).

11 Le Grand (2003), p30.

12 Le Grand (2003), pp31–35.

13 Forder (2000).

14 Heckman et al (1996).

15 This step in his argument turns out to be nothing more than simple assertion, even in a paper devoted solely to discussing the impact of widening choice on equality: see Le Grand (2006), p704.

16 Burgess et al (2005).

17 In 2003, administrative costs used less than 2 per cent of the Medicare budget, but consumed 13 per cent of private health care insurers' resources; see Krugman and Wells (2006).

18 Burgess et al (2005).

19 Coulter (2002); Schwartz (2004), pp29–33.

20 Marquand (2004).

21 See Power (1997) for an early influential analysis.

22 See Social Market Foundation (2005) for these and similar tales.

23 See for example, an authoritative recent study of the effect of the audit culture on the British NHS: Bevan and Hood (2006).

24 Grout and Stevens (2003), p224.

25 Frey and Goette (1999).

26 See Leat and Gay (1987) and Leat (1990), discussed in Le Grand (2003), pp43–45. The caring activities included care of the elderly, child-minding, and foster parenting. Evidence of altruism came from both interviews and the fact that workers did not demand or expect extra pay for extra work.

27 Le Grand (2003), p67.

28 Le Grand (2003), p67.

29 Le Grand hints at some of the issues in this paragraph, but does not directly discuss their influence.

30 Dahrendorf (1995), p39, quoted in Marquand (2004), p28.

31 See Marquand (2004) for an excellent development of these themes.

32 I take these examples from Marquand (2004), p28.

33 Hodgson (2008) cites Janssen et al (1999) and Benson and Dundis (2003).

34 See for example Dixit (2002).

35 Besley (2003), p243.

36 Sometimes there is mention of equity and distributional considerations, but these are rarely acted upon because of the difficulty of incorporating distributional weights into cost–benefit analysis, as discussed in Chapter 6.

37 I am not aware of research on this kind of self-interested bias among academic economists; but there is some evidence of it among academic scientists: e.g. Resnik (2007).

38 It might seem that there are analogous 'wars' in the private sector too. But when a firm contracts with its supplier, their goals do not conflict. Each firm seeks to maximize profit, which is not incompatible with the other firm doing so. Firms' goals *would* conflict if they contracted with their direct competitors in the same market, which is why they almost never do so. Cartels are an exception – precisely because in that case the interests of the competitors coincide.

39 My discussion here owes much to O'Neill (2002).

40 Brennan and Pettit (2005) have pioneered some of the economics of non-material forms of status, while Frey and Benz (2005) explicitly discuss the public sector.

41 The discussion in this section is influenced by a wide range of philosophical sources, but especially Andre (1995), Hsieh (2007), O'Neill (2007) and O'Neill et al (2008).

42 See for instance www.dft.gov.uk/pgr/roads/network/strategic/programme/decisionletters/stonehenge2/

43 Responses like these are discussed in Schkade and Payne (1994), Vadnjal and O'Connor (1994), Clark et al (2000) and Svedsater (2003).

44 See especially O'Neill (2007), Part I, for further discussion of the points made in this and the next paragraph.

45 *Hamlet* (III, ii, 239).

46 See for instance Frank (2001) and many other economists discussed in Aldred (2006). Most applied economics on valuing life rests on this logic.

47 Sometimes there are secondary considerations, additional less important factors, which may help us make a final choice between two otherwise 'tied' options.

48 See for example Mansfield et al (2002).

49 For up-to-date discussion of new types of political forum, and their problems, see http://deliberativedemocracy.anu.edu.au

50 This seems to be the standard view among economists, although there is strikingly little discussion in the literature. There is a brief outline of the resource constraints argument in Beckerman and Pasek (2001).

51 This point is made eloquently by Crouch (2003).

Chapter 8

1 Quoted by Robert Kuttner in *Atlantic Monthly*, 1985. Ironically, it is arguable that there is no Nobel Prize in economics either. The Swedish central bank established a prize in economics in 1968, and provides the prize money, rather than it emerging out of the will of Alfred Nobel in 1901, as with the science and peace prizes. The Nobel prize website makes a clear distinction between these and the 'prize in Economics' that has the different full title: 'The Sveriges Riksbank Prize in Economic Sciences in Memory of

Alfred Nobel'. Descendants of Alfred Nobel have criticized use of the label 'Nobel prize in Economics'. See Gingras (2007).

2　Quoted in Fullbrook (2007), p2.

3　Although even here it is easy to overstate the direct applicability of economic theory. For example, in discussing auctions of radio spectrum, which he helped design, Paul Klemperer warns that even sophisticated government and business decision makers struggle to understand some aspects of auction theory. Auction design that overemphasizes auction theory at the expense of messy political realities has gone badly wrong in practice. See Klemperer (2006).

4　Although some economists seem dismissive, I would propose social choice theory. This shows, among other things, the desirable ethical principles that different voting rules (first-past-the-post, proportional representation etc.) satisfy; and the combinations of desirable ethical principles that *no* voting rule satisfies (including rules we may not yet have invented). But again, social choice theory inhabits a kind of closed system. For a *relatively* accessible introduction to the beautiful world of social choice theory, see Sen (1999).

5　Mackenzie et al (2007). The idea of performativity originated in linguistic philosophy with Austin (1962).

6　Just one example of the weakness of a simplistic fact/value distinction; in this book I have used this distinction uncritically for no reason other than the need for brevity. See Putnam (2002).

7　Cohen (2005).

8　Men are more likely than women to use the kind of cognitive reasoning associated with the prefrontal cortex.

9　Dasgupta (2005).

10　Caplan (2007), p30.

11　Caplan (2007), p10.

12　To take Caplan's favourite example, free trade: although orthodox economists favour free trade in most circumstances, there are often good reasons to limit it, especially in developing countries, as other influential economists recognize. See Stiglitz (2002) and Chang (2007). So popular opposition to particular forms of globalization need not be based on ignorance. More generally, ordinary people may reach different conclusions from economists simply because they give greater weight to equality and less to 'welfare maximization'.

13　Dani Rodrik, an economist at the Kennedy School of Government at Harvard, quoted in *New York Times* article by Patricia Cohen, 11 July 2007. Rodrik does not himself share the worry.

14　Caplan (2007), p204.

15　Caplan (2007), p201.

16　Caplan (2007), p22.

17　See Thaler and Sunstein (2008) for an introduction.

18　I borrow this phrase from the influential heterodox Cambridge economist, Geoff Harcourt.

19　I could cite countless examples, but two recent ones from popularizing books aimed at non-economists: (i) Coyle (2007) defines economics in terms of its formal methods. This leads her to assert, pointlessly but revealingly, that John Kenneth Galbraith would not count as an economist in modern terms (p231); and (ii) Senior Cambridge economist Partha Dasgupta (2007) repeatedly uses 'modern economics' to refer to orthodox economics, implying either that contemporary economists do nothing else, or that if they do, they are hopelessly old-fashioned.

20   Bewley (1995). He was only able to find four previous studies since 1945 involving economists interviewing business people about wages.

21   Quoted in Bergmann (2007), p4.

22   *Oxford English Dictionary.*

23   Attributed to Kenneth Boulding.

24   For excellent discussion of the distinction between abstraction and idealization, see Runde (1996).

25   Many economists call it 'political economy', appropriating an old name for economics, one that now stands for a more interdisciplinary approach. This appropriation must either be an act of hubris to demonstrate their dismissal of that approach, or an act reflecting pure ignorance.

26   For instance, in the work of Gary Becker mentioned in Chapter 2. Also see Lazear (2000), a self-congratulatory hymn to the achievements of economic imperialism.

27   Resnik (2007).

28   Reported in 'Thought Control in Economics' by Tom Green, *Adbusters* 78, July–August 2008.

29   Reported in *New York Times* article by Patricia Cohen, 11 July 2007.

30   Framing effects (Chapter 2) arise when choice is influenced by how alternatives are described or framed, even though there may be no objective differences.

31   For example, the work on bounded rationality by two Nobel Laureates: Simon (1983) and Selten (2001).

32   Hopefully the word 'spirit' will ensure game theorists realize my example is not literal but suggestive. Although no game theorist would be foolish enough to attempt to analyse chess, the reason for that does not undermine my point that common knowledge is a much more powerful assumption than is often understood.

33   Sen (1987), p9.

34   Bunting (2005) offers an overview; Green (2006) is a more academic study.

35   Keynes (1931).

36   This illustrative example is taken from Hamilton (2004), p218. The figures assume a current working week of 40 hours.

References

Ackerman, F. and L. Heinzerling (2004) *Priceless*. New York, New Press

Adams, C. (ed) (1850–1856) *The Works of John Adams*, volume IV. Little, Brown and Co, Boston, MA, p193

Adler, M. and E. Posner (eds) (2001) *Cost–Benefit Analysis: Legal, Economic and Philosophical Perspectives*. Chicago, Chicago University Press

Adolphs, R. (2003) 'Cognitive neuroscience of human social behavior.' *Nature Neuroscience* 4: 165–178

Aldred, J. (2006) 'Incommensurability and monetary valuation.' *Land Economics* 82(2): 141–161

Alpizar, F., F. Carlsson and O. Johansson-Stenman (2005) 'How much do we care about absolute versus relative income and consumption?' *Journal of Economic Behavior and Organization* 56: 405–421

Anand, P. (1993a) *Foundations of Rational Choice under Risk*. Oxford, Clarendon

Anand, P. (1993b) 'The philosophy of intransitive preference.' *Economic Journal* 103: 337–346

Andre, J. (1995) 'Blocked exchanges' in *Pluralism, Justice and Equality*. D. Miller and M. Walzer (eds) Oxford, OUP

Andrews, F. and S. Withey (1976) *Social Indicators of Well-being*. New York, Plenum

Annas, J. (2004) 'Happiness as achievement.' *Daedalus* Spring: 44–51

Arrow, K. (1972) 'Gifts and exchanges.' *Philosophy and Public Affairs* 1(4): 343–362

Atkinson, A. and J. Stiglitz (1980) *Lectures on Public Economics*. London, McGraw-Hill

Austin, J. (1962) *How to Do Things with Words*. Oxford, Clarendon

Ayer, A. J. (1936) *Language, Truth and Logic*. London, Gollancz

Barber, B. (2007) *Consumed*. New York, Norton

Baumol, W. (1967) 'Macroeconomics of unbalanced growth.' *American Economic Review* 57(3): 415–426

Baumol, W. (1993) 'health care, education and the cost disease.' *Public Choice* 77: 17–28

Baumol, W. (2001) 'Paradox of the services' in *The Growth of Service Industries*. T. ten Raa and R. Schettkat (eds) Cheltenham, Edward Elgar

Becker, G. (1993) 'The economic way of looking at behaviour.' *Journal of Political Economy* 101(3): 385–409

Becker, G. (1996) *Accounting for Tastes*. Cambridge, Harvard University Press

Becker, G. and K. Murphy (1988) 'A theory of rational addiction.' *Journal of Political Economy* 96: 675–700

Beckerman, W. and J. Pasek (2001) *Justice, Posterity and the Environment*. Oxford, OUP

Benson, S. and S. Dundis (2003) 'Understanding and motivating health care employees.' *Journal of Nursing Management* 11(5): 315–320

Bentham, J. (1789) *An Introduction to The Principles of Morals and Legislation*. New York, Hafner Press

Bergmann, B. (2007) 'Needed: A new empiricism.' *The Economists' Voice*. Available at www.bepress.com/ev/

Besley, T. (2003) 'Incentives, choice, and accountability in the provision of public services.' *Oxford Review of Economic Policy* 19(2): 235–249

Bevan, G. and C. Hood (2006) 'What's measured is what matters: Targets and gaming in the English public healthcare system.' *Public Administration* 84(3): 517–538

Bewley, T. (1995) 'A depressed labor market as explained by participants.' *American Economic Review* 85: 250–254

Biswas-Diener, R., E. Diener and M. Tamir (2004) 'The psychology of subjective well-being.' *Daedalus* Spring: 18–25

Blanchard, O. (2008) *Macroeconomics*. London, Pearson Education

Blanchflower, D. and A. Oswald (2004) 'Well-being over time in Britain and the USA.' *Journal of Public Economics*, 88: 1359–1386

Blum, W. and H. Kalven (1952) 'The uneasy case for progressive taxation.' *University of Chicago Law Review* 19: 417–520

Brekke, K., R. Howarth and K. Nyborg (2003) 'Status-seeking and material affluence: Evaluating the Hirsch hypothesis.' *Ecological Economics* 45: 29–39

Brennan, G. and P. Pettit (2005) *The Economy of Esteem*. Oxford, OUP

Breyer, S. (1993) *Breaking the Vicious Circle*. Cambridge, Harvard University Press

Brickman, P., D. Coates and R. Janoff-Bulman (1978) 'Lottery winners and accident victims: Is happiness relative?' *Journal of Personality and Social Psychology* 37: 917–927

Broome, J. (1978) 'Trying to value a life.' *Journal of Public Economics* 9: 91–100

Broome, J. (1992) *Counting the Cost of Global Warming*. Cambridge, White Horse Press

Broome, J. (1999) *Ethics out of Economics*. Cambridge, CUP

Brown, D. (1991) *Human Universals*. New York, McGraw-Hill

Bunting, M. (2005) *Willing Slaves*. London, HarperPerennial

Burgess, S., C. Propper and D. Wilson (2005) *Choice*. Bristol, Centre for Market and Public Organisation

Caplan, B. (2007) *The Myth of the Rational Voter*. Princeton, Princeton University Press

Cavalieri, P. and P. Singer (eds) (1995) *The Great Ape Project*. New York, St Martin's Press

Chang, H.-J. (2007) *Bad Samaritans*. London, Bloomsbury

Clark, A. (1996) 'L'utilité est-elle relative?' *Economie et Provision* 121: 151–164

Clark, A. and A. Oswald (1996) 'Satisfaction and comparison income.' *Journal of Public Economics* 61(3): 359–381

Clark, A., P. Frijters and M. Shields (2008) 'Relative income, happiness and utility'. *Journal of Economic Literature*, 46(1): 95–144

Clark, J., J. Burgess and C. Harrison (2000) '"I struggled with this money business": Respondents' perspectives on contingent valuation.' *Ecological Economics* 33(1): 45–62

Coghill, R., J. McHaffie and Y.-F. Yen (2003) 'Neural correlates of interindividual differences in the subjective experience of pain.' *Proceedings of the National Academy of Sciences* 100: 8538–8542

Cohen, J. (2005) 'The vulcanization of the brain.' *Journal of Economic Perspectives* 19(4): 3–24

Conlisk, J. (1996) 'Why bounded rationality?' *Journal of Economic Literature* 34: 669–700

Costanza, R., R. D'Arge and 11 others (1997) 'The value of the world's ecosystem services and natural capital.' *Nature* 387: 253–260

Coulter, A. (2002) *The Autonomous Patient*. London, Nuffield Trust

Cowan, T. and D. Parfit (1992) 'Against the social discount rate' in *Philsophy, Politics and*

Society: Future Generations. P. Laslett and J. Fishkin (eds) New Haven, Yale University Press

Cox, R. (2006) *The Servant Problem.* London, I.B. Tauris

Coyle, D. (2002) *Sex, Drugs and Economics.* New York, Texere

Coyle, D. (2007) *The Soulful Science.* Princeton, Princeton University Press

Crisp, R. (2007) 'Hedonism reconsidered.' *Philosophy and Phenomenological Research* 73(3): 619–645

Crouch, C. (2003) *Commercialisation or Citizenship.* London, Fabian Society

Dahrendorf, R. (1995) Report on Wealth Creation in a Free Society. London (private printing)

Damasio, A. (1994) *Descartes' Error.* New York, Putnam

Dasgupta, P. (2005) 'What do economists analyze and why: Values or facts?' *Economics and Philosophy* 21(2): 221–278

Dasgupta, P. (2007) *Economics: A very Short Introduction.* Oxford, OUP

Davidson, D. (1986) 'Judging interpersonal interests' in *Foundations of Social Choice Theory.* J. Elster and A. Hylland (eds) Cambridge, CUP

Davidson, R. (2000) 'Affective style, psychopathology and resilience.' *American Psychologist* 55: 1196–1214

Davidson, R. (2004) 'Well-being and affective style: Neural substrates and biobehavioural correlates.' *Philosophical Transactions of the Royal Society* 359: 1395–1411

Davidson, R., D. Jackson and N. Kalin (2000) 'Emotion, plasticity, context and regulation.' *Psychological Bulletin* 126: 890–906

deBotton, A. (2004) *Status Anxiety.* London, Penguin

Deci, E., R. Koestner and R. Ryan (1999) 'A meta-analytic review of experiments examining the effect of extrinsic rewards on intrinsic motivation.' *Psychological Bulletin* 125(3): 627–668

DellaVigna, S. and U. Malmendier (2006) 'Paying not to go to the gym.' *American Economic Review* 96: 694–719

Di Tella, R., R. MacCulloch and A. Oswald (2001) 'Preferences over inflation and unemployment.' *American Economic Review* 91(1): 335–341

Dick, J. (1975) 'How to justify a distribution of earnings.' *Philosophy and Public Affairs* 4: 248–272

Diener, E. and M. Seligman (2004) 'Beyond money: Towards an economy of well-being.' *Psychological Science in the Public Interest* 5(1): 1–31

Diener, E., M. Diener and C. Diener (1995) 'Factors predicting the subjective well-being of nations.' *Journal of Personality and Social Psychology* 69: 851–864

Diener, E., J. Sapyta and E. Suh (1998) 'Subjective well-being is essential to well-being.' *Psychological Inquiry* 9: 33–37

Dixit, A. (2002) 'Incentives and organizations in the public sector.' *Journal of Human Resources* 37: 696–727

Dolan, P., T. Peasgood and M. White (2008) 'Do we really know what makes us happy?' *Journal of Economic Psychology* 29: 94–122

Dorman, P. (1996) *Markets and Mortality.* Cambridge, CUP

Easterlin, R. (2001) 'Income and happiness.' *Economic Journal* 111: 465–484

Easterlin, R. (2005) 'Feeding the illusion of growth and happiness', *Social Indicators Research,* 74(3): 429–443

Easterly, W. (2001) *The Elusive Quest for Growth.* London, MIT Press

Elster, J. (1999) *Alchemies of the Mind.* Cambridge, CUP

Epstein, R. (1985) *Takings*. Cambridge, Harvard University Press

Fabian Society (2000) *Paying for Progress*. London, Fabian Society

Farah, M. (1994) 'Neuropsychological inference with an interactive brain: A critique of the "locality" assumption.' *Behavioral and Brain Sciences* 17: 43–104

Fehr, E. (2000) 'Fairness and retaliation.' *Journal of Economic Perspectives* 14(3): 159–181

Fehr, E. and U. Fischbacher (2003) 'The nature of human altruism.' *Nature* 425: 785–791

Fehr, E. and S. Gachter (2000) 'Cooperation and punishment in public goods experiments.' *American Economic Review* 90(4): 980–994

Feinberg, J. (1970) 'Justice and personal desert' in *Doing and Deserving*. J. Feinberg (ed) Princeton, Princeton University Press

Feldman, F. (1995) 'Desert: Reconsideration of some received wisdom.' *Mind* 104: 63–77

Forder, J. (2000) 'Mental health: Market power and governance.' *Journal of Health Economics* 19: 877–905

Frank, R. (1997) 'The frame of reference as a public good.' *Economic Journal* 107: 1832–1847

Frank, R. (1999) *Luxury Fever*. New York, Free Press

Frank, R. (2001) 'Why is cost–benefit analysis so controversial?' in *Cost-Benefit Analysis: Legal, Economic and Philosophical Perspectives*. M. Adler and E. Posner (eds) Chicago, Chicago University Press

Frank, R. (2004) 'How not to buy happiness.' *Daedalus* Spring: 69–79

Frank, R., T. Gilovich and D. Regan (1993) 'Does studying economics inhibit cooperation?' *Journal of Economic Perspectives* 7(2): 159–171

Frank, R., T. Gilovich and D. Regan (1996) 'Do economists make bad citizens?' *Journal of Economic Perspectives* 10(1): 187–192

Frederick, S. and G. Loewenstein (1999) 'Hedonic adaptation' in *Well-Being: The Foundations of Hedonic Psychology*. D. Kahneman, E. Diener and N. Schwarz (eds) New York, Russell Sage

Frederick, S., G. Loewenstein and T. O'Donoghue (2002) 'Time discounting and time preference.' *Journal of Economic Literature* 40: 351–401

Frey, B. (1997) 'A constitution for knaves crowds out civic virtues.' *Economic Journal* 107: 1043–1053

Frey, B. and M. Benz (2004) 'From imperialism to inspiration: A survey of economics and psychology' in *The Elgar Companion to Economics and Philosophy*. J. Davis, A. Marciano and J. Runde (eds) Cheltenham, Edward Elgar

Frey, B. and M. Benz (2005) 'Can private learn from public governance?' *Economic Journal* 115: 377–396

Frey, B. and L. Goette (1999) 'Does pay motivate volunteers?' University of Zurich, Institute for Empirical Research in Economics

Frey, B. and S. Meier (2005) 'Two concerns about rational choice: Indoctrination and imperialism.' *European Journal of Law and Economics* 19(2): 165–171

Frey, B. and F. Oberholzer-Gee (1997) 'The cost of price incentives: An empirical analysis of motivation crowding out.' *American Economic Review* 87(4): 746–755

Frey, B. and A. Stutzer (2002) *Happiness and Economics*. Princeton, Princeton University Press

Frey, B. and A. Stutzer (2007) 'Should national happiness be maximised?' University of Zurich, Institute for Empirical Research in Economics

Frey, B., F. Oberholzer-Gee and R. Eichenburger (1996) 'The Old Lady visits your backyard: A tale of morals and markets.' *Journal of Political Economy* 104(6): 1297–1313

Friedman, M. (1953) *Essays in Positive Economics*. Chicago, University of Chicago Press

Frogner, B. (2008) 'Baumol's Cost Disease Afflicts Healthcare', conference of American Society of Health Economists, Duke University, North Carolina, June

Fullbrook, E. (ed) (2007) *Real World Economics*. London, Anthem Press

Gingras, Y. (2007) 'Beautiful mind, non-existent prize' in *Real World Economics*. E. Fullbrook (ed) London, Anthem Press

Gneezy, U. and A. Rustichini (2000) 'A fine is a price.' *Journal of Legal Studies* 29(1): 1–18

Goodhart, C. (1975) *Money, Information and Uncertainty*. London, Macmillan

Goodin, R. (1986) 'Laundering preferences' in *Foundations of Social Choice Theory*. J. Elster and A. Hylland (eds) Cambridge, CUP

Goodin, R. (1991) 'Utility and the good' in *A Companion to Ethics*. P. Singer (ed) Oxford, Blackwell

Goodin, R. (1995) *Utilitarianism as a Public Philosophy*. Cambridge, CUP

Green, F. (2006) *Demanding Work*. Princeton, Princeton University Press

Griffin, J. (1977) 'Are there incommensurable values?' *Philosophy and Public Affairs* 7: 39–59

Griffin, J. (1986) *Well-Being*. Oxford, Clarendon

Grout, P. and M. Stevens (2003) 'The assessment: Financing and managing public services.' *Oxford Review of Economic Policy* 19(2): 215–234

Güth, W., R. Schmittberger and B. Schwarze (1982) 'An experimental analysis of ultimatum bargaining.' *Journal of Economic Behavior and Organization* 3(3): 367–388

Hahn, F. and M. Hollis (1979) *Philosophy and Economic Theory*. Oxford, OUP

Hahn, R.(ed) (1996) *Risks, Costs and Lives Saved*. Oxford, OUP

Hamilton, C. (2004) *Growth Fetish*. London, Pluto Press

Hamilton, C. and E. Rush (2006) 'The attitudes of Australians to happiness and social well-being.' Canberra, The Australia Institute

Hargreaves-Heap, S., M. Hollis, B. Lyons, R. Sugden and A. Weale (1992) *The Theory of Choice*. Oxford, Blackwell

Hausman, D. and M. McPherson (1996) *Economic Analysis and Moral Philosophy*. Cambridge, CUP

Hausman, D. and M. McPherson (2006) *Economic Analysis, Moral Philosophy and Public Policy*. Cambridge, CUP

Haybron, D. (2000) 'Two philosophical problems in the study of happiness.' *Journal of Happiness Studies* 1(2): 207–225

Heckman, J. (1993) 'What has been learned about labor supply in the past twenty years?' *American Economic Review Papers and Proceedings* 83(2): 116–121

Heckman, J., J. Smith and C. Taber (1996) 'What do bureaucrats do?' New York, NBER Working Paper 5535

Hesse-Biber, S. (1997) *Am I Thin Enough Yet?* Oxford, OUP

Hirsch, F. (1995) *Social Limits to Growth* (revised edn) London, Routledge

HM Treasury (2003) *The Green Book: Appraisal and Evaluation in Central Government*. London, HM Treasury

Hodgson, G. (2008) 'An institutional and evolutionary perspective on health economics.' *Cambridge Journal of Economics* 32(2): 235-256.

Holmes, S. and C. Sunstein (1999) *The Cost of Rights: Why Liberty Depends on Taxes*. New York, Norton

Hornstein, H., E. Fisch and M. Holmes (1968) 'Influence of a model's feelings about his behavior and his relevance as a comparison other on observers' helping behavior.' *Journal of Personality and Social Psychology* 10: 220–226

Houghton, J. (2004) *Global Warming: The Complete Briefing* (3rd edn) Cambridge, CUP

House of Lords (2005) The Economics of Climate Change, House of Lords Economic Affairs Committee

Hsee, C. (2000) 'Attribute evaluability and its implications for joint-separate evaluation reversals and beyond' in *Choices, Values and Frames*. D. Kahneman and A. Tversky (eds) Cambridge, CUP

Hsieh, N. (2007) 'Is incomparability a problem for anyone?' *Economics and Philosophy* 231(1): 65–80

Inglehart, R. (1990) *Culture Shift in Advanced Industrial Society*. Princeton, Princeton University Press

Inglehart, R. and H.-D. Klingemann (2000) 'Genes, culture, democracy and happiness' in *Culture and Subjective Well-being*. E. Diener and E. Suh (eds) Cambridge, MIT Press

James, O. (2007) *Affluenza*. London, Vermilion

Janssen, P., J. de Jonge and A. Bakker (1999) 'Specific determinants of intrinsic work motivation, burn-out and turn-over intentions.' *Journal of Advanced Nursing* 29(6): 1360–1369

Jevons, W. (1911) *The Theory of Political Economy*. London, Macmillan

Johnson, J. and D. Goldstein (2003) 'Do defaults save lives?' Columbia University, Centre for Decision Sciences

Kahneman, D. (1999) 'Objective happiness' in *Well-Being: The Foundations of Hedonic Psychology*. D. Kahneman, E. Diener and N. Schwarz (eds) New York, Russell Sage

Kahneman, D. (2003) 'Maps of bounded rationality.' *American Economic Review*, 93(5), 1449–1475

Kahneman, D. and R. Thaler (2006) 'Utility maximisation and experienced utility.' *Journal of Economic Perspectives* 20(1): 221–234

Kahneman, D. and A. Tversky (eds) (2000) *Choices, Values and Frames*. Cambridge, CUP

Kahneman, D., E. Diener and N. Schwarz (eds) (1999) *Well-Being: The Foundations of Hedonic Psychology*. New York, Russell Sage

Kahneman, D., A. Kreuger, D. Schkade, N. Schwarz and A. Stone (2004) 'A survey method for characterizing daily life experience.' *Science* 306: 1776–1780

Kasser, T. (2002) *The High Price of Materialism*. Cambridge, MIT Press

Kay, J. (2004) *The Truth about Markets*. London, Penguin

Keyes, C., D. Shmotkin and C. Ryff (2002) 'Optimizing well-being: The empirical encounter of two traditions.' *Journal of Personality and Social Psychology* 82: 1007–1022

Keynes, J. M. (1931) *Essays in Persuasion*. London, Macmillan

Keynes, J. M. (1936) *The General Theory of Employment, Interest and Money*. London, Macmillan

Klemperer, P. (2006) 'Using and abusing economic theory' in *Applying the Dismal Science*. I. MacLean and C. Jennings (eds) London, Palgrave Macmillan

Koslowsky, M., A. Kluger and M. Reich (1995) *Commuting Stress*. New York, Plenum

Krugman, P. (1997) *The Age of Diminished Expectations*. Cambridge, MIT Press

Krugman, P. and R. Wells (2006) 'The health care crisis and what to do about it.' *New York Review of Books*: 23 March

Kymlicka, W. (2002) *Contemporary Political Philosophy*. Oxford, OUP

Lamont, J. (1997) 'Incentive income, deserved income, and economic rents.' *Journal of Political Philosophy* 5: 26–45

Lancaster, K. (1966) 'A new approach to consumer theory.' *Journal of Political Economy* 74: 132–157

Layard, R. (2005) *Happiness: Lessons from a New Science.* London, Penguin

Layard, R. and S. Glaister (eds) (1994) *Cost–Benefit Analysis.* Cambridge, CUP

Lazear, E. (2000) 'Economic imperialism.' *Quarterly Journal of Economics* 115(1): 99–144

Le Grand, J. (1990) 'Equity versus efficiency: The elusive trade-off.' *Ethics* 100: 554–568

Le Grand, J. (2003) *Motivation, Agency, and Public Policy.* Oxford, OUP

Le Grand, J. (2006) 'Equality and choice in public services.' *Social Research* 73(2): 695–710

Le Grand, J. (2007) *The Other Invisible Hand.* Princeton, Princeton University Press

Leat, D. (1990) *For Love and Money.* York, Joseph Rowntree Foundation

Leat, D. and P. Gay (1987) *Paying for Care.* London, Policy Studies Institute

Levett, R. (2003) *A Better Choice of Choice.* London, Fabian Society

Levitt, S. and S. Dubner (2005) *Freakonomics.* London, Allen Lane

Li, C. and K. Löfgren (2000) 'Renewable resources and economic sustainability.' *Journal of Environmental Economics and Management* 40: 236–250

Lintott, J. (2005) 'Evaluating the "Hirsch Hypothesis": A comment.' *Ecological Economics* 52: 1–3

Locke, J. (1988) *Two Treatises of Government.* Cambridge, CUP

Loewenstein, G. and D. Schkade (1999) 'Wouldn't it be nice? Predicting future feelings' in *Well-Being: The Foundations of Hedonic Psychology.* D. Kahneman, E. Diener and N. Schwarz (eds) New York, Russell Sage

Lomborg, B. (ed) (2004) *Global Crises, Global Solutions [The Copenhagen Consensus 2004].* Cambridge, CUP

Mackenzie, D., F. Muniesa and L. Siu (eds) (2007) *Do Economists Make Markets? On the Performativity of Economics.* Princeton, Princeton University Press

MacLean, I. and C. Jennings (eds) (2006) *Applying the Dismal Science.* London, Palgrave Macmillan

Mansfield, C., G. Van Houtven and J. Huber (2002) 'Compensating for public harms: Why public goods are preferred to money.' *Land Economics* 78(3): 368–389

Marmot, M. (2004) *Status Syndrome.* London, Bloomsbury

Marquand, D. (2004) *Decline of the Public.* Cambridge, Polity

Marwell, G. and R. Ames (1981) 'Economists freeride. Does anyone else?' *Journal of Public Economics* 15: 295–310

Meghir, C. and Phillips, D. (2009) 'Labour supply and taxes' in *Dimensions of Tax Design [Mirrlees Review].* J. Mirrlees (ed) Oxford, OUP

Metz, B., O. Davidson, R. Swart and J. Pan (eds) (2001) *Climate Change 2001: Mitigation.* Cambridge, CUP

Milgrom, P. and J. Roberts (1992) *Economics, Organization and Management.* Englewood Cliffs, Prentice Hall

Miller, D. (1999) *Principles of Social Justice.* Cambridge, Harvard University Press

Mishan, E. (1977) *Cost–Benefit Analysis.* London, Macmillan

Moller, J. (2001) 'Income and price elasticities in different sectors of the economy' in *The Growth of Service Industries.* T. ten Raa and R. Schettkat (eds) Cheltenham, Edward Elgar

Morgan, W., M. Katz and H. Rosen (2006) *Microeconomics.* Maidenhead, McGraw-Hill

Moriarty, J. (2005) 'The epistemological argument against desert.' *Utilitas* 17(2): 205–221

Moynihan, D. (1993) 'Baumol's Disease.' Kennedy School of Government, Harvard, Taubman Center for State and Local Government

Murphy, L. and T. Nagel (2002) *The Myth of Ownership*. Oxford, OUP

Nagel, T. (1986) *The View from Nowhere*. Oxford, OUP

Neumark, D. and A. Postlewaite (1998) 'Relative income concerns and the rise in married women's employment.' *Journal of Public Economics* 70(1): 157–183

Nisbet, R. and L. Ross (1980) *Human Inference*. Englewood Cliffs, Prentice Hall

Nisbett, R. and D. Kanouse (1968) 'Obesity, hunger, and supermarket shopping behavior.' *Proceedings of the Annual Convention of the American Psychological Association* 3: 683–684

Nord, E. (1999) *Cost–Value Analysis in Health Care: Making Sense out of QALYs*. Cambridge, CUP

Nozick, R. (1974) *Anarchy, State and Utopia*. Oxford, Blackwell

Nussbaum, M. (2000) *Women and Human Development*. Cambridge, CUP

Nussbaum, M. (2001) *Upheavals of Thought*. Cambridge, CUP

Nussbaum, M. (2004) 'Mill between Aristotle and Bentham.' *Daedalus* Spring: 60–68

O'Neill, J. (2007) *Markets, Deliberation and Environment*. London, Routledge

O'Neill, J., A. Holland and A. Light (2008) *Environmental Values*. London, Routledge

O'Neill, O. (2002) *A Question of Trust*. Cambridge, CUP

O'Riordan, T. and J. Cameron (eds) (2002) *Interpreting the Precautionary Principle*. London, Cameron May

Offer, A. (2006) *The Challenge of Affluence*. Oxford, OUP

Okun, A. (1975) *Equality and Efficiency: The Big Trade-Off*. Washington, DC, Brookings Institution

Olsaretti, S. (2004) *Liberty, Desert and the Market*. Cambridge, CUP

Oswald, A. (2005) 'Does happiness adapt? A longitudinal study of disability with implications for economists and judges.' Coventry, Warwick University working paper

OXERA (2002) *A Social Time Preference Rate for Use in Long-Term Discounting*. London, Office of the Deputy Prime Minister

Parfit, D. (1984) *Reasons and Persons*. Oxford, Clarendon

Pearce, D. (2000) 'Cost–benefit analysis and environmental policy' in *Environmental Policy*. D. Helm (ed) Oxford, OUP

Pearce, D. (2007) 'Do we really care about biodiversity?' in *Biodiversity Economics*. A. Kontoleon, U. Pascual and T. Swanson (eds) Cambridge, CUP

Pearce, D., B. Groom, C. Hepburn and P. Koundouri (2003) 'Valuing the future.' *World Economics* 4(2): 121–141

Pigou, A. (1951) 'Some aspects of economic welfare.' *American Economic Review* 41: 287–302

Posner, R. (2004) *Catastrophe*. Oxford, OUP

Power, M. (1997) *The Audit Society*. Oxford, OUP

Price, C. (1993) *Time, Discounting and Value*. Oxford, Blackwell

Putnam, H. (2002) *The Collapse of the Fact/Value Dichotomy*. Cambridge, Harvard University Press

Rabin, M. (2002) 'A perspective on psychology and economics.' *European Economic Review* 46: 657–685

Ramsey, F. (1928) 'A mathematical theory of saving.' *Economic Journal* 38: 543–559

Raventos, D. (2007) *Basic Income,* London, Pluto Press

Rawls, J. (1971) *A Theory of Justice*. Oxford, Clarendon

Rawls, J. (1999) *A Theory of Justice*. Oxford, OUP

Redelmeier, D. and D. Kahneman (1996) 'Patients' memories of painful medical treatments.' *Pain* 116: 3–8

Redelmeier, D. and E. Shafir (1995) 'Medical decision-making in situations that offer multiple alternatives.' *Journal of the American Medical Association* 273: 302–305

Resnik, D. (2007) *The Price of Truth*. Oxford, OUP

Richardson, H. (2001) 'The stupidity of the cost–benefit standard' in *Cost–Benefit Analysis: Legal, Economic and Philosophical Perspectives*. M. Adler and E. Posner (eds) Chicago, Chicago University Press

Riley, J. (1989) 'Justice under capitalism' in *Markets and Justice*. J. Chapman and J. Pennock (eds) New York, New York University Press

Rowthorn, R. (1996) 'Ethics and economics: An economist's view' in *Economics and Ethics?* P. Groenewegen (ed) London, Routledge

Runde, J. (1996) 'Abstraction, idealisation and economic theory' in *Markets, Unemployment and Economic Theory: Essays in Honour of Geoff Harcourt*. P. Arestis, G. Palma and M. Sawyer (eds) London, Routledge

Ryan, P. (1992) 'Unbalanced growth and fiscal restriction.' *Structural Change and Economic Dynamics* 3(2): 261–288

Ryan, R. and E. Deci (2001) 'On happiness and human potentials.' *Annual Review of Psychology* 52: 141–166

Ryff, C. and C. Keyes (1995) 'The structure of psychological well-being revisited.' *Journal of Personality and Social Psychology* 69: 719–727

Ryff, C. and B. Singer (1998) 'The contours of positive human health.' *Psychological Inquiry* 9: 1–28

Scanlon, T. (1975) 'Preference and urgency.' *Journal of Philosophy* 72(22): 655–670

Schkade, D. and D. Kahneman (1998) 'Does living in California make people happy?' *Psychological Science* 9(5): 340–346

Schkade, D. and J. Payne (1994) 'How people respond to contingent valuation questions: A verbal protocol analysis of willingness to pay for an environmental good.' *Journal of Environmental Economics and Management* 26: 88–109

Schmid, A. (2004) *Conflict and Cooperation*. Oxford, Blackwell

Schwartz, B. (1990) 'The creation and destruction of value.' *The American Psychologist* 45: 7–15

Schwartz, B. (2004) *The Paradox of Choice*. New York, Harper Collins

Schwartz, B., A. Ward, J. Monterosso, S. Lyubomirsky, K. White and D. R. Lehman (2002) 'Maximising versus satisficing.' *Journal of Personality and Social Psychology* 83: 1178–1197

Schwarz, N. and F. Strack (1999) 'Reports of subjective well-being' in *Well-Being: The Foundations of Hedonic Psychology*. D. Kahneman, E. Diener and N. Schwarz (eds) New York, Russell Sage

Schwarz, N., F. Strack, D. Kommer and D. Wagner (1987) 'Soccer, rooms, and the quality of your life.' *European Journal of Social Psychology* 17: 69–79

Selten, R. (2001) 'What is bounded rationality?' in *Bounded Rationality*. G. Gigerenzer and R. Selten. Cambridge, MIT Press

Sen, A. (1987) *On Ethics and Economics*. Cambridge, CUP

Sen, A. (1999) 'The possibility of social choice.' *American Economic Review* 89(3): 349–378

Sen, A. (2001) 'The discipline of cost–benefit analysis' in *Cost-Benefit Analysis: Legal, Economic and Philosophical Perspectives*. M. Adler and E. Posner (eds) Chicago, Chicago University Press

Shao, L. (1993) 'Multilanguage comparability of life satisfaction and happiness measures in mainland Chinese and American students.' Chicago, University of Illinois', report

Sher, G. (2003) 'Effort and imagination' in *Desert and Justice*. S. Olsaretti (ed) Oxford, Clarendon

Shove, G. (1942) 'The place of Marshall's Principles in the development of economic theory.' *Economic Journal* 52: 294–329

Showalter, M. and N. Thurston (1997) 'Taxes and labor supply of high-income physicians.' *Journal of Public Economics* 66: 73–97

Shrader-Frechette, K. (1985) *Science Policy, Ethics and Economic Methodology*. Dordrecht, Reidel

Simon, H. (1983) *Models of Bounded Rationality*. Cambridge, MIT Press

Singer, P. (1973) 'Altruism and commerce: A defence of Titmuss against Arrow.' *Philosophy and Public Affairs* 2: 313–320

Slemrod, J. (1995) 'What do cross-country studies teach about government involvement, prosperity and economic growth?' *Brookings Papers on Economic Activity* 2: 373–431

Slemrod, J. and J. Bakija (2008) *Taxing Ourselves* (4th edn). Cambridge, MIT Press

Slonick, S. and D. Hemenway (1998) 'Is more always better? A survey on positional concerns.' *Journal of Economic Behaviour and Organization* 37: 373–383

Slovic, P. (2000) *The Perception of Risk*. London, Earthscan

Smith, A. (1976 [1759]) *The Theory of Moral Sentiments*. Oxford, OUP

Social Market Foundation (2005) *To the Point: A Blueprint for Good Targets*. London, Social Market Foundation

Sokol, L. (1997) *Shortcuts to Poland*. Warsaw, Wydawnictwo IPS

Sterba, J. (2004) 'Murphy and Nagel: The myth of ownership (review).' *Ethics* 115: 628–631

Stern, N. (2007) *The Economics of Climate Change: The Stern Review*. Cambridge, CUP

Stevenson, B. and J. Wolfers (2008) 'Economic growth and subjective well-being.' Philadelphia, Wharton School, University of Pennsylvania. Available at http://bpp.wharton.upenn.edu/betseys/papers/Happiness.pdf

Stigler, G. (1981) 'Economics or ethics?' in *Tanner Lectures on Human Values*. S. McMurrin (ed) Cambridge, CUP

Stiglitz, J. (2000) *Economics of the Public Sector*. New York, Norton

Stiglitz, J. (2002) *Globalization and its Discontents*. New York, Norton

Stone, A., S. Shiffman and M. DeVries (1999) 'Ecological momentary assessment' in *Well-Being: The Foundations of Hedonic Psychology*. D. Kahneman, E. Diener and N. Schwarz (eds) New York, Russell Sage

Strack, F., L. Martin and N. Schwarz (1988) 'Priming and communication: Social determinants of information use in judgements of life satisfaction.' *European Journal of Social Psychology* 18: 429–442

Strack, F., N. Schwarz, B. Chassein, D. Kern and D. Wagner (1990) 'The salience of comparison standards and the activation of social norms.' *British Journal of Social Psychology* 29: 303–314

Stutzer, A. (2003) 'The role of income aspirations in individual happiness.' *Journal of Economic Behavior and Organization* 54: 89–109

Sunstein, C. (2005) *Laws of Fear*. Cambridge, CUP

Svedsater, H. (2003) 'Economic valuation of the environment: How citizens make sense of contingent valuation questions.' *Land Economics* 79(1): 122–135

ten Raa, T. and R. Schettkat (eds) (2001) *The Growth of Service Industries*. Cheltenham, Edward Elgar

Thaler, R. and C. Sunstein (2008) *Nudge*. New Haven, Yale University Press

Tingley, D. (2006) 'Neurological imaging as evidence in political science.' *Social Science Information* 45(1): 5–33

Titmuss, R. (1970) *The Gift Relationship.* London, Allen and Unwin

Torgler, B. (2007) *Tax Compliance and Tax Morale.* Cheltenham, Edward Elgar

Triplett, J. and B. Bosworth (2003) 'Productivity measurement issues in services industries.' Federal Reserve Bank of New York, Economic Policy Review

Triplett, J. and B. Bosworth (2005) 'Baumol's disease has been cured' in *The New Economy.* D. Jansen (ed) Chicago, University of Chicago Press

Tullock, G. (1976) *The Vote Motive.* London, Institute for Economic Affairs

Tversky, A. and E. Shafir (1992) 'Choice under conflict.' *Psychological Science* 3: 358–361

Upton, W. (1973) 'Altruism, attribution and intrinsic motivation in the recruitment of blood donors.' PhD dissertation, Cornell University

Uttal, W. (2001) *The New Phrenology.* Cambridge, MIT Press

Vadnjal, D. and M. O'Connor (1994) 'What is the value of Rangitoto Island?' *Environmental Values* 3: 369–380

van Praag, B. and P. Frijters (1999) 'The measurement of welfare and well-being: The Leyden approach' in *Well-Being: The Foundations of Hedonic Psychology.* D. Kahneman, E. Diener and N. Schwarz (eds) New York, Russell Sage

Varian, H. (2003) *Intermediate Microeconomics.* New York, Norton

Veenhoven, R. (2000) 'Freedom and happiness' in *Culture and Subjective Well-being.* E. Diener and E. Suh (eds) Cambridge, MIT Press

Viscusi, W. K. (1995) 'Cigarette taxation and the social consequences of smoking.' in *Tax Policy and the Economy* 9. J. Poterba (ed) Cambridge, MIT Press

Viscusi, W. K. (1998) *Rational Risk Policy.* Oxford, Clarendon

Warnock, M. (1962) *Utilitarianism.* London, Collins

Weitzman, M. (1998) 'Why the far distant future should be discounted at its lowest possible rate.' *Journal of Environmental Economics and Management* 36: 201–208

Weitzman, M. (2001) 'Gamma discounting.' *American Economic Review* 91(1): 261–271

Wierzbicka, A. (1999) *Emotions Across Languages and Cultures.* Cambridge, CUP

Wierzbicka, A. (2004) '"Happiness" in cross-linguistic and cross-cultural perspective.' *Daedalus* Spring: 34–43

Wolff, J. (2003) 'The dilemma of desert' in *Desert and Justice.* S. Olsaretti (ed) Oxford, Clarendon

Woodward, R. and R. Bishop (1997) 'How to decide when experts disagree.' *Land Economics* 73: 492–507

Index